Book
Center
3.50

D0883839

THE LETTERS OF ARCHIE BUTT

© Harris & Ewing

An old Negro said of Archie Butt when he passed him on the way to the White House in this dress uniform, "Dere goes de man what's de highest wid de mighty an' de lowest wid de lowly of any man in dis city"

THE LETTERS OF ARCHIE BUTT

Personal Aide to President Roosevelt

EDITED, WITH A BIOGRAPHICAL SKETCH
OF THE AUTHOR, BY

LAWRENCE F. ABBOTT

Archibald Willingham Butt.

GARDEN CITY NEW YORK
DOUBLEDAY, PAGE & COMPANY
1924

PRINTED IN THE UNITED STATES
AT
THE COUNTRY LIFE PRESS, GARDEN CITY, N. Y.

First Edition

LIST OF ILLUSTRATIONS

INTRODUCTION

A DISTINGUISHED Frenchman, I think it was Paul Sabatier, has somewhere said that "man is incurably religious." May it not also be said that man is an incurable gossip? We like to hear and read of the little private sayings and doings of great men and women as well as of their heroic deeds and historic achievements. Indeed, gossip in the sense of familiar chit-chat, if it be not mischievous, malevolent or unfriendly, is a most useful handmaiden of history. One can often obtain a juster estimate of great men and their influence from anecdotal literature than from the dignified and sometimes dry-as-dust chronicles of professional historians. It is the gossipy attitude toward the little events of daily life that makes the Autobiography of Benjamin Franklin, the Letters of Pliny the Younger, the Epistles of Erasmus, not only so readable, but so enlightening to the student of customs and manners.

The work of a newspaper reporter is not given high rank by literary critics, but in his stories of the actual incidents and personalities of life the reporter creates a literature which people read with more eagerness, and sometimes, I think, with more benefit, than laboured historical treatises. Herodotus is an immortal historian partly, if not largely, because he reports anecdotes about great men who have made history. His historical characters are thus not shadowy mythological figures but men of flesh and blood. Luther was a metaphysician, and few there are who read him now. His great contemporary Erasmus, on the other hand, was, among many other things, an accomplished reporter, and his Epistles and Colloquies are as readable and illuminating to-day as Walter Page's Letters.

Ralph Waldo Emerson is the typical highbrow to the uninitiated; his metaphysics are—to use his own simile—"an acquired taste like that for tomatoes and olives"; but when he lent his genius to reporting no one could be more true to personal detail. His interview with the poet Wordsworth, "a plain, elderly, white-haired man, not prepossessing, and disfigured with green goggles"; or with Coleridge, "a short, thick old man, with bright blue eyes and a fine complexion, leaning on his cane" and taking "snuff freely which presently soiled his cravat and neat black suit"; or with Carlyle, "tall and gaunt, with a cliff-like brow, self-possessed and holding his extraordinary powers of conversation in easy command; clinging to his northern accent with evident relish; full of lively anecdote and with a streaming humour which floated everything he looked upon"—any one of these interviews would to-day give Emerson a welcome on the staff of the most exacting metropolitan newspaper, not merely because of the subjects he chose to write about, but because of his method, because of his frank, intimate, personal, picturesque descriptions.

Archie Butt wrote of Washington and Washingtonians of his time in the spirit of Herodotus and Erasmus and Emerson—noble and dignified representatives of ancient, mediæval, and modern literature.

With this feeling about reportorial literature, when invited both by the publishers and by the family of the author to supervise these letters for publication in book form, I accepted the task for two reasons. First, they reveal from a unique point of view and bring into new relief the features of a man who is bound to be one of the outstanding figures of world history. After a somewhat intimate relationship with Theodore Roosevelt during the last ten years of his life, and after reading most of the estimates and personal recollections of him that have appeared in print since his death, I supposed that I had a fairly full comprehension of his magnetic personality and the extraordinary variety of his mind and spirit. But I found the letters of Archie Butt of unusual interest because they are a fresh and original disclosure of the character and qualities of the President he served, the man he lived with, and the friend he loved.

The truth is that Theodore Roosevelt was more kinds of a man than biographical literature has heretofore attempted to embody in one person. No one of his associates, no one of his interpreters, quite saw every side of him. It seems to me that these letters, as well as being read in the present with lively enjoyment, will be of distinct importance to the future historian, for they are the unstudied, spontaneous daily report of the little doings and casual sayings of a great man whose great deeds may be safely left to take care of themselves. In this respect they have a Pepysian flavour. Major Butt, however, had a far finer quality of spirit than the kindly, garrulous, industrious but somewhat little-minded Clerk of the Acts, whose Diary is one of the prizes of history. Moreover, Archie Butt was through and through a gentleman, which by no stretch of the imagination can be said of good old Samuel Pepys.

In the second place, these letters deserve publication not merely because of their subject, but because they are real contributions to epistolary literature. They disclose, between the lines, a most interesting and attractive personality in the writer. He was not one of those backbiters, described by the old Hebrew poet, "whose teeth are spears and arrows and their tongue a sharp sword." His pictures of public men and society people in the Capital are vivid but amiable and appreciative. He is gossipy without being trifling; personal without being impertinent; truthful without being bitter; and indulges in humour without infringing upon good taste. His letters are highly entertaining and amusing, as all kindly gossip should be; but they are much more than that. From them may be derived a more accurate impression of the social and political life of the United States than is usually given by the writers of academic essays. And they may quite possibly be drawn upon fifty or a hundred years from now as useful material in interpretations of the political currents of the United States in the first quarter of the 20th Century.

Archibald Willingham Butt—known to his intimates and friends from his boyhood to the day of his death by the affectionate nickname of "Archie"—was born in Augusta, Georgia, on September 26, 1865, just at the close of the Civil War. The Butt family was of distinguished old Colonial stock, and his paternal ancestors had established themselves in Georgia in very early days, although his mother had some Massachusetts blood in her veins. Like the first families of Virginia, the old Georgian families have a keen and abiding appreciation of the motto, *Noblesse oblige.* While there is nothing of pompous self-satisfaction or family snobbery in any of Archie Butt's voluminous letters there will be found some jocose allusions in conversations between him and President Roosevelt to "Georgia gentlemen" which indicate that he was not forgetful of his duty to maintain those standards of chivalry and courtesy that have always been a source of pride to Southerners of the ancient régime.

Indeed, Roosevelt himself did not scruple to express more than once his pleasure and satisfaction in the fact that his mother was a Bulloch of Georgia, and in his Autobiography he mentions, as if it were a just claim to distinction, that his maternal great-great-grandfather was the first Revolutionary "President" of that state:

My mother's people were predominantly of Scotch, but also of Huguenot and English, descent. She was a Georgian, her people having come to Georgia from South Carolina before the Revolution. The original Bulloch was a lad from near Glasgow, who came hither a couple of centuries ago, just as hundreds of thousands of needy, enterprising Scotchmen have gone to the four quarters of the globe in the intervening two hundred years. My mother's great-grandfather, Archibald Bulloch, was the first Revolutionary "President" of Georgia. My grandfather, her father, spent the winters in Savannah and the summers at Roswell, in the Georgia uplands near Atlanta, finally making Roswell his permanent home. He used to travel thither with his family and their belongings in his own carriage, followed by a baggage wagon. I never saw Roswell until I was President, but my mother told me so much about the place that when I did see it I felt as if I already knew every nook and corner of it, and as if it were haunted by the ghosts of all the men and women who had lived there. I do not mean merely my own family, I mean the slaves. My mother and her sister, my aunt, used to tell us children all kinds of stories about the slaves. One of the most fascinating referred to a very old darky called Bear Bob, because in the early days of the settlement he had been partially scalped by a black bear. Then there was Mom' Grace, who was for a time my mother's nurse, and whom I had supposed to be dead, but who greeted me when I did come to Roswell, very respectable, and apparently with years of life before her. The two chief personages of the drama that used to be repeated to us were Daddy Luke, the Negro overseer, and his wife, Mom' Charlotte. I never saw either Daddy Luke or Mom' Charlotte, but I inherited the care of them when my mother died. After the close of the war they resolutely refused to be emancipated or leave the place. The only demand they made upon us was enough money annually to get a new "critter," that is, a mule. With a certain lack of ingenuity the mule was reported each Christmas as having passed away, or at least as having become so infirm as to necessitate a successor—a solemn fiction which neither deceived nor was intended to deceive, but which furnished a gauge for the size of the Christmas gift.

My maternal grandfather's house was on the line of Sherman's march to the sea, and pretty much everything in it that was portable was taken by the boys in blue, including most of the books in the library. When I was President the facts about my ancestry were published, and a former soldier in Sherman's army sent me back one of the books with my grandfather's name in it. It was a little copy of the poems of "Mr. Gray"—an 18th-century edition printed in Glasgow.

Archie Butt's father and uncles served in the Confederate Army and Navy, and the entire family in all its branches made such sacrifices for the "lost cause" that at the age of fourteen, upon the death of his father, it was necessary for Archie to go to work in order to aid in the support of his mother and sister.

It is a commonplace of biography to say that men who have achieved any kind of distinction in life acknowledge a great debt to the influence of their mothers. This is certainly true in Archie Butt's case. His sister-in-law, Mrs. Lewis F. Butt, the "Dear Clara" of many of the letters in this volume, tells me that his mother "was a woman of unusual strength of character; she was deeply religious, had high ideals and lived up to them; she drew an unswerving line between right and wrong and was absolutely intolerant of the latter throughout her life; her sons seem always to have recognized her authority, and in their later life (during the period when I have known them) I have never seen higher respect or tenderer love than that exhibited by them for the mother who sacrificed so much for them in her early life." This statement is borne out by the letters which Archie Butt wrote almost daily to his mother from Washington, beginning when he became Presidential Aide in April, 1908, and continuing until her death in October of the same year. The reader will be struck, I think, as I have been, by the number of these letters which begin with the phrase "Dearest Mother" or "My darling Mother." Mrs. Butt was determined that her sons should have a good education, in spite of her lack of resources, and when the opportunity came (through the good offices of the rector of her church) to place them in the University of the South, at Sewanee in Tennessee, she moved there herself and paid some, if not all, of the expenses of their education by taking a position as librarian of the institution. Indeed her home was in an apartment in the library building, and here in the atmosphere of books Archie spent some of his undergraduate days.

Believing as I do that college associations and the college spirit have a profound if unconscious influence upon the sentiments and ideals of every undergraduate, I determined to try to discover for myself what there is in the atmosphere of the University of the South which apparently had such a formative effect on Archie Butt's character. Accordingly, in the midst of writing this introduction, I paid a visit to Sewanee. It is not an easy place for a Northerner to get to. The University is situated in a beautiful woodland on the Cumberland Plateau two thousand feet above sea level, about fifty miles northwest of Chattanooga. It can be reached only by a laboriously puffing train, climbing steep grades and rounding curves of short radius, or by an automobile crossing the divide on the admirable Dixie Highway. Its founders evidently meant that its students should not be diverted from their books and lectures by easy access to city life.

Sewanee has a romantic history. A group of Episcopal clergymen of the South, mostly Bishops, conceived the idea of the University and selected its site. Among them Leonidas Polk, Bishop of Louisiana, was the leader. Bishop Polk was educated at West Point, but resigned from the United States Army to enter the Church. The cornerstone of the first building of the institution was laid with appropriate ceremonies by Bishop Polk in October, 1860. Six months later, when the Civil War broke out, Bishop Polk took up arms again in defence of the seceded States of the South, became General Polk of the Confederate Army, and was killed by a cannon ball at the Battle of Pine Mountain. During the war the Cumberland Plateau was ravaged by the contending armies. The meagre buildings of the University were destroyed and even the cherished cornerstone was broken into bits and carried away piecemeal by Northern soldiers in accordance with the deplorable American habit which leads tourists to chip off and put in their pockets bits of monuments—as souvenirs of their successful banditry, I suppose. When peace came after four years of fighting, the founders of the University renewed their efforts with unabated courage, and the institution was reopened with a small group of students and a proportionately small number of devoted teachers. Some of the latter were ex-Confederate officers. General E. Kirby Smith, the well-known Confederate cavalry leader, who had been assistant professor of mathematics at West Point before the war, became professor of mathematics. His son, Dr. Kirby Smith, is now the medical director of the well-appointed hospital which the University maintains for the benefit of the entire surrounding community. General Josiah Gorgas, Chief of Ordnance of the Confederate Army, also a West Point graduate, was professor of engineering and was the second Vice-Chancellor of the University. His son William was educated at Sewanee, achieved an international reputation, and received honours from universities and scientific societies all over the world. I refer, of course, to the great sanitarian Surgeon-General William C. Gorgas, whose hygienic skill made the building of the Panama Canal possible, or at least saved it from the disastrous attacks of the fever which defeated De Lesseps and his courageous but disappointed band of engineers.

The University of the South is small, enrolling scarcely three hundred and fifty students, I believe. But it has an influence totally disproportionate to its size, especially in the field of letters and liberal culture. Not a few of its graduates have made their mark on national affairs. Among them, of course, the name of General Gorgas is preëminent, but it is also interesting to find on the list the names of Admiral Grayson, who was the devoted friend and personal physician of President Wilson; of Bishop William T. Manning of New York; and of the Rev. William M. Guthrie, the Rector of St. Mark's Church, New York City, who thinks that Greek dancing should be made a part of the services of the Episcopal Church, and has thereby fallen into some difficulty with his ecclesiastical superior and former college mate, Bishop Manning. I was amused to learn, by the way, at Sewanee, that when the Bishop and the recalcitrant rector were undergraduates together they often used to be on opposite sides of controversial questions, and their intellectual "scrapping" was joyously encouraged by all undergraduate beholders.

The founders from the first had a conception of this University as a place where the students should come in contact, as Matthew Arnold advised, with the best that has been thought and said in the world, and should do this in surroundings of natural and architectural beauty. The place has an atmosphere which is all its own and which its alumni and friends refer to as "the Sewanee spirit." This is partly produced, perhaps, by the situation of the University. It stands by itself on a mountain top; it commands a view of one of the most beautiful valleys of the South; its grounds are laid out on a landscape plan which, when completed, will give it a remarkably picturesque setting; it already possesses several buildings of carefully finished construction in native stone that are admirable examples of academic architecture; and its chapel, designed by the eminent ecclesiastical architects, Messrs. Cram and Goodhue, has about it and within it a suggestion of Oxford and Cambridge. Not one of the least interesting things at Sewanee is the University Press, a small building with very modest typographical and mechanical appliances where, however, the director, practised in the art and trade of typography, produces some specimens of his art which would excite the admiration of the members of the Grolier Club. There I saw the title page of a book about Shakespeare by a former member of the Faculty which, because of its faultless design in Caslon type, I should like to have framed and hanging on the wall of my library as a reminder that mass production has not yet wholly obliterated individual artistry in American industrial life.

It was in such surroundings and associations that Archie Butt spent several years at Sewanee in the preparatory department and in the University itself, graduating in the class of 1888. In those days there was military training at the University, and it is a curious reflection on the inaccuracy of history to find that some of his college friends recollect that he had a strong dislike for his military duties while others recall that he ranked high as an officer of the undergraduate military corps, and was an outstanding figure in the selected company which often went to various places in the South for competitive prize drills. There is no difference of opinion, however, about the fact that he early showed a gift for journalism and founded a little paper which later developed into the weekly publication of the University. He was popular, honourable, and reasonably proficient as a student, but his records, which are still in existence, show that he was what would be called at Oxford and Cambridge a pass-man rather than a prize-winner. Nevertheless, he certainly imbibed a love for good books and especially good poetry. He was active in the social life of the University community, prominent in the college dramatic club, and much in demand at social functions as a leader of the cotillion or, as that one-time extremely fashionable dance used to be called, the "German." A member of the Greek letter society to which he belonged speaks of him as "freckle-faced and red-headed, and like most red-headed fellows he was as loyal as they make 'em; let anything be said against a friend and he was up in arms, and in a way, too, that was most discomfiting to the offender."

Archie Butt's career is an actual illustration of the truth of the statement put into the mouth of Hamlet by Shakespeare that "there's a divinity that shapes our ends rough hew them how we will." He wanted to be a literary man; fate wanted him to be a soldier; events proved him to be both; and his college associations prepared him without his being aware of it for the combination. On leaving college through the influence of General John B. Castleman of Kentucky, famous in the blue-grass country as a lover of good horses, he obtained a place on the staff of the Louisville *Courier Journal.* There he stayed three years and then spent twelve months with the Macon, Georgia, *Telegraph.* He must have achieved some reputation in the South as a newspaper writer, for he is next found in

Washington as the representative of a group of Southern newspapers which he jocosely called his "mosquito fleet." He was now fully launched as a Washington correspondent and said in one of his letters that he "would have money for the first time in his life if friends would not borrow from him as fast as the fleet brought it in." His integrity and accuracy in reporting details combined with a genuine talent for entertaining writing gave him a recognized standing in the heterogeneous group of Washington correspondents. Moreover, he had unusual social gifts. These qualities commended him to General "Matt" Ransom, a well-known Confederate officer and Democratic member of the United States Senate from North Carolina, who was appointed Ambassador to Mexico in the second Cleveland Administration. General Ransom took Archie with him as Secretary of the Embassy. While in Mexico he continued his journalistic work, and the unusual mixture of Republicanism and Democracy in his official career is foreshadowed by the fact that while in Mexico he wrote a newspaper article entitled "Where Silver Rules" which was used by the Republican Party as a campaign document during the contest between Mr. McKinley and Mr. Bryan over the question of sound money in the presidential election of 1896. From Mexico he returned to Washington again to take up his newspaper work, but at the outbreak of the Spanish-American War he volunteered for service and obtained an appointment in 1900 as Assistant Quartermaster of Volunteers with the rank of Captain. Thirteen months later he was promoted to the rank of Quartermaster in the regular army with the rank of Captain, receiving both commissions from President McKinley. Thus he became a professional soldier, actuated not only by a spirit of patriotism but by a sense of family honour. He said to his brother at the time that the family had been represented in the American Revolution, in the War of 1812, and in the Civil War, that he felt it should be represented in the war for the liberation of Cuba.

Here we take leave of "Archie," who now becomes Captain Butt. In 1900 he went to the Philippines as Assistant Quartermaster of Volunteers. His first military duty was a responsible one and established his reputation as an officer. He had charge of five hundred and fifty-seven horses and mules which were being transported from Portland, Oregon, to the Philippines for the use of our army in those islands. At that time it was not supposed in the army that such animals could successfully be carried across the Pacific without being unloaded at the Hawaiian Islands for temporary rest and recuperation on land. Perhaps because he had been so lately a civilian and a newspaper correspondent, in which capacity he was accustomed to acting on his own initiative and following his own discretion so long as he successfully attained the ultimate object which his superiors directed him to attain, he ignored his army orders, gave the Hawaiian Islands a wide berth, sailed directly to Manila, and landed all of his precious cargo of animals in such good condition that they went into active service at once. His success in this perhaps rash experiment—rash at any rate from the professional soldier's point of view—was such that the Government abandoned much of the expense which it had previously thought necessary in transporting army animals on long sea voyages. While in the tropics he made a special study of the care and diseases of horses in that unaccustomed climate, wrote about the subject, and had the satisfaction of seeing his system adopted by the British Government in transporting its army horses to Africa during the Boer War. In a memorial address after his death Colonel Henry L. Stimson, then Secretary of War in President Taft's Cabinet, spoke of Captain Butt's military qualities as follows:

It is not always that the terse, dry records of an officer on file in the War Department reveal those dominant characteristics which have brought him success or failure in his profession. Very often it is only from other sources—from the lips of his associates or others—that we can obtain the keynote of his character which furnishes the true picture of the living man. In the case of Major Butt, however, the story told by the records and by all his fellow officers is the same. From the day he landed, a young volunteer, at Manila with his ship-load of teamsters and pack animals, down to his latest recorded service, he made the same simple yet clear and strong impression upon all who came in contact with him.

Absolute and unshaken loyalty to every friend and to every duty, good-humoured tact and discretion combined with efficiency, an ever-gentle and considerate manner coupled with unflinching courage when courage was required—these were the simple soldierly traits which all who met him recognized.

Colonel Miller, the Chief Quartermaster in charge at Manila, has put it on record that he was so impressed with the condition of Captain Butt's cargo when it reached Manila, with the excellent care which had been given to the animals and the skill and discretion shown in handling the unruly teamsters and pack men, that he at once assigned the young quartermaster to the unusually important and responsible position which he held thereafter during the three years of his stay. An old newspaper friend who had known him as a society man and leader of cotillions in Washington went aboard the transport to welcome him at Manila and found him in overalls and shirt-sleeves among his men, pushing mules over the gang-plank. He never seemed to lose his temper or his coolness. He was never loud or boisterous, nor was he ever excited. He was never rough with his men, but was always able to get an unusual amount of work out of them.

Shortly after his arrival during the fall of 1900 a tremendous typhoon or hurricane visited Manila. When the inspecting officer visited the Quartermaster's corral the next morning, expecting to find loss and destruction of animals and property, he found instead that Captain Butt had spent the night there among his teamsters quieting the animals and insuring their protection.

When orders came for the Cuban intervention in September, 1906, instead of waiting to go with his companions by ship, Butt took the train at once for Key West and Havana, reached there two days in advance of his chief, and had all plans ready for the landing by the time that they arrived.

All of these incidents, each comparatively small, perhaps of itself, show that under the pleasant, cheerful exterior of this young officer there lay a keen interest in his profession, a constant ability to cope with men and events, and an ever-ready devotion of self to duty. Lieutenant General Chaffee wrote to him in 1906: "You are an officer always regardful of the Government's interests, loyal to superiors of every rank, honest as the United States Treasury, your integrity unassailable."

And there will be found among the illustrations of this volume the reproduction of a letter by President Roosevelt—one of the last which he wrote in the White House—commending Captain Butt's military capabilities. It reads as follows:

THE WHITE HOUSE
WASHINGTON

March 3, 1909.

To the Secretary of War:

I wish the following memorandum filed in the record of Captain Butt.

Captain Archibald W. Butt has been for eleven months with me as chief aide. In addition to our purely personal association and the performance of his duties in connection with the White House proper, I have treated him throughout that time as a general in the field would treat a staff officer of unusual ability, because I have found that from him I was able to get information of real consequence to me in planning and working for the betterment of the army conditions. He has been an exceptionally tactful and diplomatic aide-de-camp; he is an exceptionally able and efficient officer; and if ever again it should befall me to command troops I should desire him to serve under me.

Theodore Roosevelt.

It is well to bear in mind this testimony to Captain Butt's proficient, courageous, and sometimes dangerous service as an army officer, lest the reader should get the impression from the letters which he wrote as a Military Aide at the White House that he was merely a gifted and brilliant social functionary.

Captain Butt, returning to America in 1904, was detailed as Depot Quartermaster at Washington. In 1906, as Colonel Stimson relates, he was sent to Cuba, where he became Depot Quartermaster at Havana, and remained there in active military service until he was recalled in the spring of 1908 to become President Roosevelt's Military Aide at Washington. He now began writing the letters which constitute the body of this volume.

Service under Theodore Roosevelt in any capacity was extremely stimulating and delightful, but it was also exacting. Roosevelt's abounding vitality and the vigour and enjoyment with which he both worked and played kept his colleagues and subordinates always at concert pitch. He was not a taskmaster in any sense of the word, and there is constant allusion in Captain Butt's letters to his characteristic consideration for his associates. But somehow or other while seldom commanding or reproving or spurring them on, he filled them with an ambition to keep up with him as far as possible—and the pace he set was a rapid one. How Captain Butt managed to write so voluminously and in such vivid detail under these conditions of multifarious and pressing duties is surprising. The letters themselves, when the conditions under which they were written are borne in mind, are effective testimony to the considerateness, courtesy, loyalty, and wholesome balance of his character—qualities upon which his friends, who have written and talked to me about him, uniformly dwell. General Frank Ross McCoy, who is now (1924) on the staff of General Wood in the Philippines, and who preceded Captain Butt as Military Aide in the White House, has this to say of his old colleague:

I knew him best in Washington and find myself usually reminiscing about his doings there, but I have had the satisfaction of following him in Havana and Manila, where after many years his sayings and doings still persist in the best of company, and his kindly deeds live after him amongst old soldiers and employees—not forgetting the oldest ladies who love to laugh and gossip over "Archie's" doings and gayety in the days of "The Empire."

When he came up from Havana in 1908 to relieve me as senior aide of the President, he took over his duties with a boyish delight and a relish for all the gay doings of the White House and the charmed circle in which he was thrown from that time on. It must have given his letters home the finest fillip.

He lived with us bachelors at 1718 H Street that spring, and livened up the old house like unto a favourite son home from college for the holidays, and until he and Frank Millet and Blanton Winship took over another old house near by and made a real home and gathering place where he loved to entertain.

I remember he inveigled Colonel Roosevelt to lunch at this house with some of us youngsters, very much at home in the fun and frolic. Archie was very fond of having his portrait painted, and one of the reasons for this particular celebration was to show the President a labour of love by Frank Millet, who in those days was painting in an old house 'way over in Georgetown. I am afraid we made a good deal of fun of this portrait of Archie. But since we allowed it was a good picture of his uniform, his countenance brightened. For he did love his uniform and had frank and unabashed pleasure in it—the gaudier the uniform the better, the broader and yellower the stripes the better—quite in contrast to the self-consciousness of the average regular officer of the days before the war, when the uniform was seldom worn away from army posts and made the wearer somewhat conspicuous. . . .

Any one writing about Butt naturally turns to his lighter and gayer side, but the reason he was so much enjoyed by his friends was the real character and sturdy personality and loyal gentleness which were happily combined in him and inspired confidence in all those who knew him. One of his most thorough loyalties was his ardent devotion to his church. Wherever he was you found him in touch with the spiritual work of the Episcopal Church. It was true-hearted service that he rendered to his chief, his country, and his church; and that makes us all hark back to him with good green remembrance.

General McCoy's recollection of Captain Butt's kindly deeds to old soldiers and employees and of his resplendent appearance in his uniform recalls one of the most human and genuine tributes that was ever paid to him. One day—I get the story from his sister-in-law—as he was hurrying to the White House for some official function, in full military dress, glittering with gold braid and colour, a really magnificent figure, a grizzled-headed darkey whom he had befriended stopped, looked after him, and said to one of Butt's acquaintances who happened to be at hand: "He's de highest wid de mighty and de lowest wid de lowly of any man in Washington!"

The reader will observe that the letters in this volume cover only the period from April, 1908, until President Taft was inaugurated on March 4, 1909. Captain Butt did not leave the White House with Theodore Roosevelt. Mr. Taft invited him to remain as Presidential Aide, and he did so, serving President Taft in the same capacity in which he served President Roosevelt for three years until his career was cut short by the *Titanic* disaster.

For obvious reasons the letters of the Taft administration are still held in reserve by Captain Butt's family, not, however, because they are lacking in appreciative loyalty to President Roosevelt's successor, who by a turn of the wheel of political fortune had become the letter-writer's chief. One of the striking manifestations of the fine grain of Captain Butt's nature is that he was able to serve two such divergent masters without sacrificing any of his absorbing admiration for the first or of his sincere personal attachment to the second. He saw both men in an official and personal relationship of unique intimacy. The two presidents whom he served were totally different in temperament. They approached life from different angles. Their qualities were complementary. President Roosevelt was quick, active, decisive; President Taft was deliberate. President Roosevelt believed, as he himself once said, that aggressive fighting for the right is the noblest sport that the world affords; pugnacity of any kind was distasteful to President Taft. President Roosevelt was born with the temperament of an advocate; President Taft with the temperament of a judge. Toward the close of President Taft's administration, when Roosevelt and Taft came into political conflict that developed into a bitter struggle, Captain Butt found himself in a difficult position. His personal devotion to Roosevelt had not in the least waned. He felt himself drawn, as so many others have been, to his first chief by a spiritual affinity, if I may use that term, which time, distance, and admitted mistakes or defects could not destroy. But the engaging personality of his second chief had also enlisted his affection. Moreover, he had that high sense of honour which we like to think, and rightly think, is characteristic of the best type of military officer. Here was a dilemma. How could he preserve his sense of loyalty to both friends without taking sides with either? His unpublished letters, without directly referring to the struggle which was going on in his own mind, without comparing the two men, without disparagement of either, without expressing a judgment as to the rights or the wrongs of the conflict, indicate clearly by implication that he found the situation a very harassing one. This was not because any one on either side asked him to declare himself. Indeed, there was no official reason why he should have declared himself, for his position was not a political one, nor did it involve any political duties or responsibilities. But apparently he felt that his own spiritual self-respect would sooner or later call for a decision, even if a private one. He felt, it would seem, that he must either throw himself with wholehearted sympathy on the side of Mr. Taft, thus breaking with the Roosevelt family, which had entwined itself with the deepest and most intimate feelings of his life; or he must resign his position as Presidential Aide, in connection with which he had very high ideals and which he regarded as a place of public trust. To the casual reader who looks upon the position of a military aide as that of a mere social functionary, this may all seem very grandiloquent, but Archie Butt was much more than a social functionary. He was a simple, straightforward, honourable gentleman, and a psychological problem such as he was facing is much more profound and perplexing to a simple and straightforward soul than to the shrewd and calculating man of affairs. Whether my analysis is correct or not, it is a fact that in the spring of 1912 Archie Butt's superb physical health began to show signs of deterioration. He suffered from depression and fatigue, which the kindly eye of President Taft observed, and at the suggestion of the President he planned a trip to Europe for recuperation. To this trip he looked forward with some foreboding, which is expressed in a letter addressed to his sister-in-law about the first of March, 1912. It is the last letter which he wrote from Washington.

Dear Clara:

If my letters suddenly come to an end it will be because I have gone to Rome for a little holiday. I am completely tuckered out, and the doctor advises me to take a rest, and the President is willing that I should go. As it is between seasons and the only time I can get away, I think I shall take advantage of a letter from Frank Millet to go to Rome with him. He is at the head of the American Academy at Rome, and is compelled to be there on the fifteenth of March to take over some property Mr. Morgan is donating to the Academy. He is sailing on March the second on the *Berlin* and has got me in the mood to go with him, although I hate to leave the Big White Chief just at this time. But I will be back before the middle of April. I have come to the conclusion that if I am to go through this frightful summer, I must have a rest now. I drive myself like a steam engine and feel tired all the time. I shall do little in the way of sightseeing. In fact, I think the sight of a train makes me sick. . . . Don't forget that all my papers are in the storage warehouse, and if the old ship goes down you will find my affairs in shipshape condition. As I always write you in this way whenever I go anywhere, you will not be bothered with my presentiments now. I am riding every day and walking with the President every afternoon, but I want to get away from all these devilish dinners and banquets. I still have a little toxin poison in my system, and the doctor thinks a sea trip will put me on my feet for the period ahead of all of us connected with this administration. The President is going to make the fight of his life for the nomination, and I want to be with him when he passes the flag or else be of some support to him should he come in second. I even think that a cessation of these letters will do me good for a time, and think what a rest it will mean to you! When I come back I will take them up with a vim, and the last rounds of the fight will be worth recording even should we lose. The Colonel [Roosevelt] has put himself ahead of any of the radicals and many of his old friends are falling away from him, but he may be making two for every one he loses. He is a good judge, after all, of the people and may know what they want. The President is going to fling his glove into the ring in Ohio the first part of next month, and I wish I could see him do it. He is always at his best when fighting and I am glad he feels aroused to the necessity of a fight at last. He is too easy-going and kindly to contend with the political elements, but when once aroused he becomes dynamic, and you may get a different view of him when he enters for the death grip.

If I go, I shall sail on the *Berlin* on the second of March, and shall be back by the middle of April. I only began to think seriously of it yesterday, but my mind is pretty well made up, and when the travelling microbe begins to work in the Butt brain you generally know in advance how it is going to end. . . . The *Berlin* is a North German Lloyd steamer and takes fourteen days to reach Naples. My address there will be care of the American Ambassador. Good night and good luck. Love to all kith and kin and believe me always your affectionate brother,

ARCHIE.

The brief trip to Europe was made as foreshadowed in this letter. He spent only a month on the other side of the Atlantic, and returned with his friend the artist Frank Millet on the ill-fated *Titanic*, which struck an iceberg on the night of April 14, 1912, and sank with a large part of its human cargo. Captain Butt—now Major Butt, for he had been promoted to that rank by President Taft a year previously—went down with the ship. Survivors describe his quiet, calm, but heroic leadership in protecting the women and children from the insane rush of those who lost their heads and their sense of duty. "On the deck of the *Titanic*," to quote the words of President Taft, "he was exactly what he was everywhere else. After I heard that part of the ship's company had gone down, I gave up hope for the rescue of Major Butt, unless by accident. I knew that he would certainly remain on the ship's deck until every duty had been performed and every sacrifice made that properly fell on one charged, as he would himself feel charged, with responsibility for the rescue of others."

I am glad to have my name associated, even in the minor part of speaker of the prologue, with that of this Georgia gentleman.

LAWRENCE F. ABBOTT.

FOREST HILLS, LONG ISLAND,
July 1st, 1924.

THE LETTERS OF ARCHIE BUTT

THE LETTERS OF ARCHIE BUTT

I

THE first letter is naturally prefatory. The reader may be puzzled by Captain Butt's urgency that the privacy of his letters should be guarded. He meant, of course, that they were not to be made public during his term of service. That he realized the possibility of their eventual publication is clearly indicated in a letter he wrote to his sister-in-law, Mrs. Clara Butt, just before he sailed for Europe in 1912. Writing from the White House he said:

> Remember where all my things are, and in case of accident of any kind you will find all papers necessary in my silver chest which is in storage. I always want you to bear in mind that the letters which I wrote to Mother and those which I have written to you are valuable, and in case of my death I have left provision in my will that they are to be published. Don't ever make the mistake, either, of cutting out names; for letters, if they have any historic value, must be printed as written, barring, of course, all the grammatical and typographical errors which necessarily are to be found in letters written as hastily as I have written mine.

1718 H Street [Washington, D. C.],
April 8, '08.

MY DARLING MOTHER:

I find a hearty welcome on every side and especially from the office of my chief—that is, General Aleshire,[1] not the President. The latter and his wife, with the children,

[1]General James B. Aleshire was graduated from West Point in 1880. At the time Archie Butt took up his duties at the White House Butt was a Captain in the Quartermaster's Department and General Aleshire was Quartermaster General of the United States Army.

are in Virginia and will not be back until Monday. I will report to Mr. Roosevelt Monday, and later will go to see Mrs. Roosevelt.

Everyone I meet congratulates me most warmly on being ordered to the White House, seeming to think it an exceptional honour. I presume it is, but I am not over enthusiastic. It means being very conspicuous in a small way, of course, and so many people will try to pump one dry of White House news, and work their little schemes through me, but I am too old a drake to swim readily into such shallow ponds.

General Aleshire has only given me some nominal work, but I have insisted on being assigned to a regular desk, as I do not want to merge the greater duty with the lesser, which I would feel that I were doing were I to do nothing, or next to nothing, in my own department and spend all my time cooling my heels in the antechambers of the temporarily great.

However, I begin my duties as aide believing thoroughly in the real greatness of Mr. Roosevelt, which opinion I know you do not indorse, but time will show which of us is right. It will be interesting to you to give you my impressions as I form them of the man, and I will write you very freely, but you must be careful to guard what I write, as I have a contempt for those people who serve only half-heartedly their chiefs and who permit their private opinions to become public property.

Your devoted son,

ARCHIBALD.

The above reference to Roosevelt's absence in Virginia means that the President was at his bungalow camp, "Pine Knot," to which he used to flee for quiet and isolation and about which he wrote some of the most delightful of his "Letters to His Children," a book to be read by everyone who wishes to see the many-sidedness, and especially the gentleness, of the wielder of the "Big Stick." In one of those letters, written to his fifteen-year-old son Kermit, Roosevelt says:

Next day we spent all by ourselves at "Pine Knot." In the morning I fried bacon and eggs, while Mother boiled the kettle for tea and laid the table. Breakfast was most successful, and then Mother washed the dishes and did most of the work, while I did odd jobs. Then we walked about the place, which is fifteen acres in all, saw the lovely spring, admired the pine trees and the oak trees, and then Mother lay in the hammock while I cut away some trees to give us a better view from the piazza. The piazza is the real feature of the house. It is broad and runs the whole length and the roof is high near the wall, for it is a continuation of the roof of the house. It was lovely to sit there in the rocking-chairs and hear all the birds by day-time and at night the whippoorwills and owls and little forest folk. . . . As we found that cleaning dishes took up an awful time we only took two meals a day, which was all we wanted. On Saturday evening I fried two chickens for dinner, while Mother boiled the tea, and we had cherries and wild strawberries as well as biscuits and corn bread. To my pleasure Mother greatly enjoyed the fried chicken and admitted that what you children had said of the way I fried chicken was all true.

There is a pleasant picture of "Pine Knot," too, in an account which John Burroughs contributed to *The Outlook* of May 25, 1921, describing a visit which he made to the Roosevelts in their camp in May, 1908:

"Pine Knot" is about one hundred miles from Washington. I think we left the train at Charlottesville, Virginia, and drove about ten miles to "Pine Knot"; the house is a big barn-like structure on the edge of the woods, a mile from the nearest farmhouse.

Before we reached there we got out of the wagon and walked, as there were a good many warblers in the trees—the spring migration was on. It was pretty warm; I took off my overcoat and the President insisted on carrying it. We identified several warblers there, among them the black-poll, the red-throated blue, and Wilson's black cap. He knew them in the trees overhead as quickly as I did.

We reached "Pine Knot" late in the afternoon, but as he was eager for a walk we started off, he leading, as if walking for a wager. We went through fields and woods and briars and marshy places for a mile or more, when we stopped and mopped our brows and turned homeward without having seen many birds.

Mrs. Roosevelt took him to task, I think, when she saw the heated condition in which we returned, for not long afterwards he came to me and said: "Oom John, that was no way to go after birds; we were in too much of a hurry." I replied, "No, Mr. President, that isn't the way I usually go a-birding." His thirst for the wild and the woods, and his joy at returning to these after his winter in the White House, had evidently urged him on. He added, "We will try a different plan to-morrow."

So on the morrow we took a leisurely drive along the highways. Very soon we heard a wren which was new to me. "That's Bewick's wren," he said. We got out and watched it as it darted in and out of the fence and sang.

I asked him if he knew whether the little gray gnat-catcher was to be seen there. I had not seen nor heard it for thirty years. "Yes," he replied, "I saw it the last time I was here, over by a spring run."

We walked over to some plum trees where there had been a house at one time. No sooner had we reached the spot than he cried, "There it is now!" And sure enough, there it was in full song—a little bird the shape of a tiny catbird, with a very fine musical strain.

II

General Frank McCoy, to whom allusion is made in the following letter, gives his estimate of Captain Butt in the Introduction.

[Washington, D. C.]
April 11, 1908.

MY DARLING MOTHER:

It is too funny being pursued by people who want my photograph for publication. You would think that I had just been called into a royal household. I have had four requests from magazines by mail and two from women who write for syndicates and papers.

I am writing you all the trivial details as they come up, for they will help amuse you and to pass the time. They may also be of interest to me in the years to come when reviewing this little portion of my life. So if you keep my letters, keep them together and some day we may go over them for our own mutual enjoyment. I may decide to keep something of a diary of the people I meet and the things I do, but there is little interest in writing things down which are not intended for anybody in particular to see. There is certainly no incentive to be anything but dull and prosaic.

I called on the President this morning and had a most hearty welcome. He expressed great pleasure in having me on his official staff and asked me if I was glad to be with him. Of course I said yes, not thinking for the moment of my protest to General Aleshire against the arrangement. He said he wanted me in Fitz Lee's place until September, then to be his Chief Aide in place of McCoy, who has been ordered to his regiment.

Nothing could have been more characteristic of this first meeting. He came into the office, laid one hand on my shoulder, and with the other wrung my own. . . . He went back to his desk, where he picked up a large picture which he found there, read the note with it and then jerked out:

"How I do hate to accept presents from people I dislike. And this man (I don't know the sender) has sent me a Madonna; more pity, for I cannot use it to break over his head."

He talked with me for a few moments and then began the strenuous day's work for which he is famous. I then called on Mrs. Roosevelt, who is just as gentle and lovely as he is vigorous and emphatic. She was delighted at my coming and begged me to get into harness at once. So to-morrow night I assist at a dinner of seventy, including Mr. Bryan and most of the governors of the states.

Your affectionate son,

ARCHIE.

III

In a vivacious and buoyant address which Roosevelt made to the undergraduates of Cambridge University, during his memorable journey through Europe and England in 1910, will be found a confirmation of what Archie Butt here says of his chief's enjoyment of the job of being President. This characteristically Rooseveltian view of the presidency may be found in a volume entitled "African and European Addresses," by Theodore Roosevelt. It is published by the Putnams.

Washington, D. C.,
May 15 [1908].

MY DARLING MOTHER:

I have not written since the meeting of the governors began at the White House. On Tuesday the President gave a dinner in their honour of seventy covers, and besides being one of the aides to assist in receiving and handling the crowd I was also one of the invited dinner guests. I have seldom seen a finer body of men, and my great regret was that Gov. Hoke Smith of Georgia was not present, for he would have added presence to any Southern contingent.

The most observed governor present was Johnson[1] of Minnesota, the man whom the Democrats are trying to put forward for the nomination in place of Bryan. He is smoothly shaven, but has none of that Pharisaical Methodistical manner of the Peerless Leader and never seems to

[1]John A. Johnson, elected Governor of Minnesota, 1904, reëlected, 1906, died in 1909.

pose or to be self-conscious, even when he must know that he is the cynosure of all eyes—official ones at least. He is most direct in conversation, and never leaves you in doubt for a moment as to what he thinks. I suppose the Democracy must be afflicted with Bryan once more, but it is good to feel that we are training up a few leading men to take his place. Everyone seems to concede his nomination, and concede also his defeat, a bad beginning in a presidential campaign. I believe if Johnson primarily had been known a year earlier that he would have been nominated, with every chance for election.

As it is, the people of this country will not have William Jennings Bryan, in spite of the fact that he has never done anything to indicate that he would make a dangerous president. The President likes him, and after dinner the two got together over cigars and coffee for over an hour. As Bryan was leaving he said to him, with the peculiar hissing emphasis he gives everything:

"When you see me quoted in the press as welcoming the rest I will have after March the 3d take no stock in it, for I will confess to you confidentially that I like my job. The burdens of this great nation I have borne up under for the past seven years will not be laid aside with relief, as all presidents have heretofore said, but will be laid aside with a good deal of regret, for I have enjoyed every moment of this so-called arduous and exacting task."

This is really his feeling on the subject. He bounds in and out like a schoolboy, and except when he is very angry always seems to be in a good humour. The second day of the session he called the Governor of Mississippi to preside over it. I heard him tell his wife that he was going to do this to show in some little way his appreciation of the welcome given him last year in Mississippi. Among the governors it was taken, too, as a high compliment.

I was much impressed with both the Governor of Mississippi and the Governor of North Carolina.[1] The latter I understand comes from the people, but he is a fine-looking man, aristocratic in his appearance and gracious in his manner. I renewed my friendship with Governor Blanchard of Louisiana, and met for the first time Hughes of New York. The latter has about as much magnetism as a Cuban potato and struck me as being always on the alert to be wise and sane. Most of the Southern men I met seemed surprised and pleased, too, to find a Southern Democrat on the President's staff, and Johnson and I had a few minutes' chat on the subject. I met an old-timer from the Philippine days, George Curry, at one time in the Rough Riders, and later in the Eleventh Cavalry in the East. He is from Louisiana, a Democrat, but in spite of these facts the President made him Governor of New Mexico.

We were talking of old times when the President slapped us each on the back and said he was glad to see two of his friends get together. Curry then told him we had been together long ago in the Philippines, and this really seemed to please Mr. Roosevelt, for he said:

"I find all my friends have something in common, showing that I must choose them for some salient traits. I think I must choose men who either have done things or who possess the potentiality to do things."

Are you getting tired of all this? I write to no one else, and I give you a lot of twaddle thinking it may amuse you or help pass the day.

Wednesday I lunched at the White House and saw Admiral and Mrs. Cowles. The latter is a sister of the

[1]Charles B. Aycock, Governor of North Carolina, 1901–04, was the apostle of universal education in his state and though dead for several years is still regarded as the outstanding figure in the phenomenal development of North Carolina in the last two decades.

President and, I think, was the only one of the children born in Georgia. President Hadley of Yale was there; Henry Cabot Lodge and his beautiful wife; Mr. Mills, the father-in-law of Whitelaw Reid, and one or two others. Just a family luncheon such as you or any one might have. The President amused us all by reading a letter from someone to the effect that it was reported in New York that in order to emphasize his imperial way of living he was using gold knives, forks, and spoons, while his family used only silver and old broken china.

. . . .

We had simple food and a good Rhine-wine cup. He said that it always amused him to have big temperance leaders dine with him, for he always made it a point to give them something to drink, and that while they usually partook of it, he invariably noticed that at their conferences, such as the one now in Baltimore, they calmed their conscience by protesting against the bibulous habits at the capital.

Well, enough of this. I have got to go through the stable and look after the horses. I have got my coupé out and will break Lucy in to it for driving purposes this afternoon. Mrs. R. gives a garden party to the governors. It is cloudy and misty and just the sort of weather that falls on garden-party days. All my old friends have welcomed me most warmly. I dined at the Wadsworths' last night and to-day I am going to the Edwardses'.[1] Saturday the Bromwells are giving me a dinner, and Monday I lunch with Maria Duvall.[2] I have seen the Perrys for a moment, and both are looking well, at least better than I

---

[1]The family of Major-General Clarence Edwards who organized and led the 26th (Yankee) Division to France.

[2]Mrs. William Penn Duvall. Her husband became Major-General October, 1907, and was assistant chief of staff in 1908.

had expected to see them. Give my love to all and write me often. Let me know always just how you are, wire if you are feeling bad, don't try to conceal from me.

As ever, your devoted son,

ARCHIE.

The Conference of Governors alluded to in the foregoing letter was a decisive and important step in the conservation policy of President Roosevelt. He describes it in his Autobiography in these words:

> In the November following [that is, following a trip which President Roosevelt made down the Mississippi River in October, 1907] I wrote to each of the governors of the several states and to the presidents of the various important national societies concerned with natural resources, inviting them to attend the conference, which took place May 13 to 15, 1908, in the East Room of the White House. It is doubtful whether, except in time of war, any new idea of like importance has ever been presented to a nation and accepted by it with such effectiveness and rapidity as was the case with this Conservation movement when it was introduced to the American people by the Conference of Governors. The first result was the unanimous declaration of the governors of all the states and territories upon the subject of conservation, a document which ought to be hung in every schoolhouse throughout the land. A further result was the appointment of thirty-six state conservation commissions and, on June 8, 1908, of the National Conservation Commission. The task of this commission was to prepare an inventory, the first ever made for any nation, of all the natural resources which underlay its property. The making of this inventory was made possible by an Executive order which placed the resources of the government departments at the command of the Commission, and made possible the organization of subsidiary committees by which the actual facts for the inventory were prepared and digested. Gifford Pinchot was made chairman of the Commission.
>
> The report of the National Conservation Commission was not only the first inventory of our resources, but was unique in the history of government in the amount and variety of information brought together. It was completed in six months. It laid squarely before the American people the essential facts regarding our natural resources, when facts were greatly needed as the basis for constructive action.

IV

Washington, D. C.,
May 18th, 1908.

MY DARLING MOTHER:

I think I wrote you that I was to lunch with General and Mrs. Duval at Chevy Chase yesterday. While I was dressing I received a message from the White House saying that the President wanted to see me at one o'clock—so, as usual when such requests come, you wipe the slate clean and begin all over again.

It seems that the President had ordered his fine horse Roswell and had been told that it was out of commission, that it had been kicked. This was enough to put any one in a fury, and had it happened to my horse I would have been in a fury and damned every one connected with the stables. So from eleven to one I was somewhat nervous, as you may imagine, for I expected to see his Excellency in a real towering Napoleonic rage. On my arrival in Washington he had asked me to take charge of the stables, which, being in my line, I was glad to do. So I really felt responsible for the horses.

When I reached the White House the President had just returned from the Lutheran or whatever church he attends and was in the barber's chair. He asked me to come in and to excuse the informality. Instead of being angry as I expected and as I should have been, he asked most gently how Roswell was kicked and said he was interested as he had no other animal to ride except an old plug of the orderly. I told him I had crawled the collar of every one at the stables and that I did not think anything like it would happen again.

"Well, I am glad you crawled their collars," he said.

"Continue to crawl their collars and remember that their collars are pretty broad also."

He really was most polite, and I, who have been accustomed to see our military people fly off their heads for much less than this, was charmed at the simplicity of the President's kick—for in my estimation he certainly had one coming to him. One thing he asked me was why I did not report it to him, and I answered that I had received no instructions as to what to do in such cases, that I did not know whether he wanted to be bothered with such details, but that I had reported the accident to Secretary Loeb.

"Then in the future, Captain, come direct to me, especially in the matter of horses." [*Unfinished letter with no signature.*]

V

Washington, D. C.,
May 25th [1908].

MY DARLING MOTHER:

The President takes up a good deal of one's time, but he is always so uniformly courteous and considerate that it becomes a pleasure to serve him. I rather suspect you of smiling when you read that he is considerate and courteous, but such is the case. Instead of rushing around with a bowie knife between his teeth and a pistol and big stick in his hands, he moves softly but swiftly. It is the quickness of the man's physical movements which gives one the impression of bounding in and out of the rooms, as I have so often seen him described by the ever interesting correspondents.

I have had two interviews with him to-day. We are buying some horses for the White House stables, and he, of course, is very interested. This morning I went to his office at nine and found Senator Beveridge of Indiana and Senator Kean of New Jersey there. Beveridge is just the same enthusiastic, youthful looking fellow he was when in Manila. You remember the time when he advocated tearing down the old walls of that city, and you told him that such opinions were the iconoclastic leanings of youth. Well, he referred to that to-day and says he has not changed his ideas. He asked after you and also about Uncle William Boggs. You know he is pushing that case against the Mexican Government for an indemnity for the murder of Cousin Willie. He takes as much interest in it as if we were Republicans and from Indiana, instead of being Democrats and from Georgia.

At any rate, he had just said to me that he thought his rank would admit of his seeing the President before me when the messenger came out and said the President would see Captain Butt. Those others waiting to see the President had a good laugh at his expense, in which he joined. The President makes it a rule always to see his aides before any one else, on the ground that they represent him and that he takes precedence naturally over Senators, *et al.*

I decided to-day, after hearing that there were some good horses at the horse show now being held in Philadelphia, to send over a vet and also the President's orderly, if the latter had no objection. It was 2:50 when I went to the office, but was told that he was having a private audience with the Austrian Ambassador, old Hengelmüller, or, as he is called here, Hungrymuller, on account of his abnormal appetite. So I went to his private rooms in the White House and there found him closeted with the Ambassador, and Secretary Root, with the Commissioners from Liberia waiting in the Blue Room to see the Executive. It looked rather hopeless, for, while I might sidetrack a senator, I felt that the Secretary of State was one degree too many to top. However, as Hengelmüller left and the Secretary of State with the three black Africans entered, the President caught sight of me, and waving the Ethiopians aside, called to me, and while he and I had a confidential chat on the subject of horseflesh the Secretary of State and his party were left to stand in the corner.

This gives you some idea of the method of doing business with those around him. He realized the Secretary of State had more time to waste than I.

To-night I am going to the theatre with Mrs. Roosevelt, which brings me to the point I want to take up with you. You must realize that I cannot let anything interfere with my duties at the White House this winter except sickness. If I undertake this detail I must make a success of it or else hopelessly fail. At the same time I want my own home and I want you in it, and at its head, of course. The next thing to having a wife and children around one is to have one's own furniture and belongings, and especially one's dogs. I am inclined to the house idea, with a small back yard where I can keep my dogs, for I get a great deal of pleasure from them.

I saw Secretary Taft to-day. He is just back from Panama. He asked most solicitously after you. He looks well and seems happy. It looks as if he would succeed Roosevelt. Rather, the nomination is largely conceded. Unless the dinner pail gets a little fuller there is doubt expressed in official circles as to his election. I still believe that if the Democrats would dump Bryan they would carry the next election. But such sentiments are heretical coming from me.

ARCHIE.

VI

Washington, D. C.
[About the end of May, 1908].

My darling Mother:

Last night I dined with the Townsends at the Country Club. There were about twenty and mostly foreigners. Mrs. Townsend is most cordial and very agreeable. Most of the diplomats have come since I left and the names are as yet unknown to me. I went out with Alice Longworth in her electric. She has grown stouter and really pretty. Mathilde has taken on some flesh and is very beautiful. They both asked most kindly after you.

I sat between Mathilde and Miss Edith Wetmore, one of the wittiest women I know. She is quite human when compared to the Newport standard. She has a remarkable way of drawing the best out of one in chit-chat conversation. She pitches her dinner talk a little higher than most of those one meets in society as a rule. You remember their home in Newport. One of the loveliest there.

Yesterday afternoon I walked to the Glover place with Mrs. Roosevelt. That meant several miles each way. The President will not let her go tramping the country alone or with another woman without a man, as there have been so many assaults around Washington. She is a pretty good walker and knew all the out-of-way paths. When we got to the Glovers' we had iced tea and lemonade. On our way out I stopped by my house and I took my pointer dog, Duke, with us. She is very fond of animals and fell in love with Duke. Poor Duke does not understand a word of English and I tried to teach her enough Spanish to call him to her. He minds beautifully, but not in English. . . .

Archie.

VII

Washington, D. C.,
June 2, 1908.

My darling Mother:

In addition to my duties at the White House and in the office of the Quartermaster-General, I have been dining somewhere every night. I have now been here three weeks, and this is the first evening I will not have been out to dinner, if indeed I get through the day without receiving some invitation, which I feel I should accept or else desire to accept.

. . . .

The dinner at the Longworths' was simply a work of art, both as to setting and actual foodstuff provided.

Mrs. Townsend's dinner at the Country Club, not Chevy Chase, was a charming affair. I find the Chevy Chase is not quite exclusive enough to suit the very smart, so they have made it the fashion to dine at the old Country Club in Tennallytown. The club house is an old-fashioned, rather dilapidated country place, but the dinner room has been done up in crimson velvet and the galleries have been made large, so that it adapts itself most wonderfully to a dinner. The hostess receives on the verandas, and no one enters the house except to eat, and then adjourns promptly to the lawn or verandas again. But what it does accommodate itself to, especially, is the necessary exclusion of everyone that the Washington millionaire does not want to see about. Members take the club for one evening and do what they want with it. There is a good chef and, as in the case of Mrs. Townsend, she simply takes a part of her ménage with her so that her table appointments are just as handsome as if the dinner were in her own home.

I do not think this desire for privacy is snobbish, as I once did. It is what every old family in the South in the old days tried to have. In the North and in the crowded cities publicity was part of the social game; it was a means of advertisement, of flaunting wealth and of climbing. That every millionaire and climber wanted to have their dinners put in the paper, with the names of the guests whom they chloroformed to get there, was a method they adopted to awe the innocent. That there has been a reversal of this method seems to be a good thing. They may be carrying it to an extreme now, but certainly it is a comfort to go to a dinner and not feel certain that the next morning everybody in Washington would know just where you dined and often what you had to eat.

When I was here before there were certain families who not only gave the names of the guests but even the names of those who had been invited and who had not accepted. So, of the two systems, I much prefer the hostess who errs in the direction of privacy, even if snobbery is at the bottom of it.

There is a good deal of interest just now as to who will succeed Secretary Taft in the War Department. I have not heard the President say anything, so I feel at liberty, therefore, to indulge in my own speculation. I think Luke Wright, former Governor of the Philippines, will come to the War Department. I *have* heard the President say that it was his earnest desire that the South's best class should have its voice in the national Government. Of course up to the present time politics has forced the uncultured class from the South into prominence; the remarkable condition has been forced upon the national

Government of calling the lower element of a great section to pass upon questions vitally affecting its interest. I think Mr. Roosevelt, when he did not have to play politics, has tried to do what was best for the South's interest, and whenever possible he has consulted its leaders in Congress rather than Republican politicians from the States.

I have had some strenuous days with the President since my last letter. Friday he asked me to play lawn tennis. Secretary Garfield, Captain McCoy, the President and I made the foursome. We played seven sets and came out about even, Mr. Garfield playing the best game, I next, and McCoy and the President about evenly matched, I should say. I wore my Jai Jalai[1] shoes, which the President greatly admired. I have several extra pairs and offered him one pair, but when we went to examine his feet we found the shoes several sizes too large for him. I have not got a large foot myself and wear only a seven, but his foot is absurdly small, he wearing a number 4 or 5.

It was a pleasant afternoon. He was in his best humour, and during the afternoon Longworth and his wife, Mr. Pinchot, the forester, and some others came in. The President had already ordered four mint juleps, but before they were served they had got up to eight. As each guest would arrive he would say to someone inside:

"One more mint julep, please," and then laugh with glee.

Finally, when they were served on the lawn by the side of the tennis court, he offered a toast to his new aide.

"Wouldn't dear old Fairbanks give a great deal to be able to sit down and enjoy one of these without fearing that a photograph fiend was hidden behind the bushes?" he said. "It is almost worth being called a drunkard by

---

[1]An extraordinary Spanish game, played usually by professionals—a combination of gigantic hand-ball and court tennis. Pronounced Hy Ally.

Wall Street to feel free to take a julep such as this without shocking the public."

Just then Secretary Garfield said hurriedly:

"Look out, here comes a sightseeing automobile by the White House."

The President grabbed his glass, and with mock fear put it under the table.

"That is the first evidence of fear I have ever seen in you, Mr. President," laughed the Secretary.

"Not for *my* reputation, Garfield, but for you. After all Wall Street has said about me mine can't be injured, but you, my dear boy-faced Secretary, you may yet need the vote of the teetotaller."

The juleps were certainly good, especially after the seven sets of tennis. The President and I finished ours first, and looking up, I said:

"I am glad to see that the Georgia glasses are empty, Mr. President."

"That's so, Butt," he said, "but we can't expect the New England Yankees and Middle West people to drink with us old Southern gentlemen; it would be asking too much."

Pinchot, Longworth, and Garfield and the others promptly took up their glasses and finished them before putting them down again.

I am really amused to hear the reports so often made and more astonished to find that many believe them: namely, that the President is a hard drinker. I have dined with him several times and lunched most informally with him, and he never serves at luncheon, even when he has guests, anything but a Rhine-wine cup, and at dinner he takes hardly anything himself, usually confining himself to white wine.

Yesterday at his request I rode all his riding horses. I

had them taken to the park and there took each one in turn, including a new one we are buying for him. He likes to have them ridden so that he will know just what to expect. He is not afraid of anything, but naturally he has not the time to train his own horses. I am going riding with him to-morrow, but with Larry under me I can follow him anywhere.

This morning while I was with him Fitz Lee came in on his way from the West. He is going to the French Cavalry School at Saumur. [The President] showed the greatest affection toward Fitz, and going over to his desk got out a beautiful leather case and told him it was a souvenir of his services at the White House. When Fitz opened it up it proved to be a magnificent pistol, ivory handled, with his name engraved on it, with the token of esteem also from the President. He is devoted to Fitz, finding in him so many of the fine manly qualities which have always appealed to him in the Southern character. He told Fitz that "Butt is making good" and then laughed and said:

"I see by the papers that I chose him not for any personal qualities, but in order to do honour to my mother's state. As much as I love and revere my dear mother's state, I do not think I would allow it to affect me in the choice of my personal aides." . . .

ARCHIE.

After events add to the interest of the foregoing letter. The irresponsible and often malicious gossip about President Roosevelt's drinking habits, to which he jocosely alluded while in the midst of his "tennis cabinet," finally culminated in a suit for libel which he brought in 1912 against a Michigan editor who had stated in his paper that Roosevelt habitually "got drunk." A large company of witnesses testified to Roosevelt's temperance and

Photograph of the famous painting by Gari Melchers

abstemiousness; the defendant had nothing but hearsay evidence to present; and Roosevelt won his case triumphantly, the defendant withdrawing his charges in open court. All through these letters runs a thread of Roosevelt's interest in the South and his desire to break down the prejudices growing out of the Civil War and the almost fatal mishandling of the race problem by the Republican party during the period of Reconstruction. Luke Wright, a distinguished Democrat of Tennessee, who left the Bryan wing of the party during the campaign for sound money in 1896, was appointed Secretary of War one month after this letter was written and served to the end of Roosevelt's administration. Fitz Lee was a member of the famous Virginian family of Confederate soldiers.

VIII

Washington, D. C.,
June 8, 1908.

My dear Mother:

I have not had the time to write since I came from Leesburg, for my strenuous chief has rather kept me on the go. You were right in your surmise that the horse that dumped the President was the one I had written you about.

I had purchased the horse in Philadelphia and the animal seemed perfectly kind and gentle. I rode him through the park, up and down the embankments, into the water and through the fords, and he did nothing to excite my suspicions. So I reported to the President that he was safe, and that afternoon he ordered him saddled for himself. It seems that the horse balked when the President tried to take him through the creek and wheeled about to come up the bank.

That the President likes to have his own way with horses as well as men is accepted now as a fact, so he tried to wheel the horse about again, which he succeeded in doing, but the horse wheeled again, and in doing so went over backward and both fell into the creek. Fortunately the water was deep at that point and no great harm was done, but it would have been serious had the water been more shallow. Unfortunately, some people were near and reported the matter to the newspapers, so greatly exaggerated accounts of the accident were published.

I thought the President would be chagrined, as he is rather proud of his horsemanship, and he has a right to be, for he now rides a different horse every day, and horses, moreover, that he knows nothing about, and has to rely on me or someone else for the fact that it is safe. Our Government is most parsimonious as to the allowances for the White House. As long as men were Presidents who only wanted horses to drive from one place to another, and cared nothing for horseflesh itself, the allowances for the stables were ample, but the President has to furnish his own mounts, and when they are sick, as they frequently are, he has to beg, borrow, or, as he says, steal from the Quartermaster's Department for a mount.

Governor Magoon in Cuba has far more in the way of automobiles and carriages than has the President of the United States. In fact, the President has no automobiles at all, and while he has never said so much, yet it is evident that he thinks it a piece of cowardice on the part of Congress not to give to the Chief Executive what he may actually need in the way of horses and vehicles, no matter how many he may require. It would be a pretty expensive business if the President were to be maimed or killed by some unknown horse. I know one thing, it places a big responsibility on the aide on whom he relies to recommend his mounts.

Well, the morning after the accident I went to the White House and found Secretary Taft there waiting for the President also. We heard for the first time of the accident there and did not know the results. But as the clock struck 9:30, his hour for arriving at his office, he bounded in through the door, and before any one could say anything caught sight of his Secretary of War and, standing at mock attention, exclaimed, "Viva Grant!" This was in reference to the remarks which the Secretary had made at the tomb of Grant on Decoration Day, namely, that the great general had proved his greatness, as in his military victories, by overcoming his tendency for drink and for which all the old timers like ex-Senator Chandler, Dalzell, Mrs. John A. Logan, and the ones who were once all powerful had flayed him, and which his political opponents had used [in an attempt] to defeat his [Taft's] nomination. The President said:

"Don't worry, Taft, it is not going to hurt you. I have got the public accustomed to hearing the truth from statesmen or politicians, whichever we might be termed, without it changing the destinies of the nation. But before I go into that and the best way of meeting the hypocritical horde which is trying to camp on your trail I want to ask Captain Butt to get me another horse. I do not mind so much being dumped out of my saddle, but Mrs. Roosevelt has made me promise not to get killed until after the 4th of March, and Ethel would be distressed, as the next winter will be her only chance to give a party in the White House."

"If you do ride any more fractious horses, Mr. President," said Mr. Taft, "I wish you would take Fairbanks with you."

This was just after the interviews purporting to come from Fairbanks that the Administration wanted to put Fairbanks on the second place on the ticket, which rather convinced me that the Secretary would prefer him anywhere else than there. Certainly he will be a misfit with Taft, for one seems to be as crafty and shrewd as the other is open and genial. I think the Secretary will rely on his "open and cordial" methods, and the old type of politician, such as we used to think necessary to win by saying nothing, would hamper his campaign. The President added:

"No need to do away with Fairbanks. I think I shall ask Senator Knox to go with me if Captain Butt can provide the suitable mounts, such as I rode yesterday."

This reference was beyond my ken, but he and the Secretary seemed to enjoy the reference, for they laughed immoderately. However, the President was most jovial about his fall, for I had expected him to be ill-humoured, as I had feared the publication might touch him on a weak spot—namely, his horsemanship. I offered him my horse; General Aleshire and Postmaster-General Meyer telephoned putting one of theirs at his disposal. He said:

"Well, it is worth losing one horse to find out one's friends, for only a friend would lend another man his razor or his horse."

Well, he rode my horse, old Larry, yesterday, and this morning told me that he liked him as well as any animal he had been on for a long time. Such is my faith in things going wrong that I kept telephoning to the stables last night until the horse returned and I knew that he had not cut up any capers with the President.

By the way, this morning he asked me to visit them at Oyster Bay this summer and named the 25th of July for the date of my arrival. Mr. and Mrs. Beekman Winthrop are to be there at the same time. He[1] is a fine fellow and Mrs. Winthrop a most charming, gracious young woman.

Last night I dined at the Shoreham with Oden Hoerstman, whom you met in Cuba. There was Elinor Terry and Miss Cockrell, old ex-Senator Cockrell's daughter; the Longworths and one or two of the others, including a rather chic little person, a daughter of Admiral Emory. Miss Terry looks like Kate Deering, now Mrs. Ridgely, without her marvellous colouring, however, but with more temperament.

It was a most enjoyable dinner and the conversation was pitched on rather good lines. Clelland Davis or General Edwards offered to make a bet with any one that no one at the table could name all the States of the Union. Everyone felt certain that he or she could do so, and we all got pencil and paper and began to write them down. I, for instance, left out eight; General Edwards failed to mention five, although as one of the Taft boomers he has been figuring on the votes of the states for the last three months. Alice Longworth came nearer than any one else, naming forty-five states and two territories, thus missing one state only. She read and reread the list and not one of us could see which one she left out. A careful check by the World Almanac revealed the fact that she had left out the one of all others she had thought to name first, namely, that from which her own husband is a Representative—Ohio. Of course this created a good deal of fun. . . .

I think I have given you all the news and possibly bored you, but your statement that you enjoyed my last letter encouraged me to reel off a lot of this gossip to you—of course, for your own consumption. I would not mention that invitation to Oyster Bay, for I do not want anything

[1]Beekman Winthrop, who had been Governor of Porto Rico from 1904 to 1907, was at this time Assistant Secretary of the Treasury.

connected with the President's business to come from me, even when it affects only myself.

ARCHIE.

Although the most notable of Roosevelt's feats of horsemanship will be described in a later letter, this may be an appropriate place to mention another episode in which he "did not mind so much being dumped out of the saddle."

In October, 1885, while riding across country near Oyster Bay in a fox hunt he had a fall which he described at the time in a letter to Henry Cabot Lodge as follows:

The weather was glorious, and everything went off without a hitch; the entire neighbourhood turned out in drags, tandems, etc. The field was only about thirty-five in number, mostly in red; but at least twenty-five were as hard riding men, mounted on as good hunters as are to be found on either side of the Atlantic; every crack rider of the Meadowbrook and Essex clubs was here, each mounted on his very best horse and each bound to force the pace from start to finish. The country was too stiff for any timid rider to turn out.

We opened over a necessarily small field with fences by actual measurement from 4 feet 6 to 5 feet; and the fun grew fast and furious very rapidly. The run was for ten miles with one check, over the country you saw. Douglas[1] took my sister's mare out to school her; at the third fence she turned a couple of handsprings and literally "knocked him silly," and took half the skin off his face; he rode along the roads the rest of the way. A great many men had falls and almost halfway through I came to grief. Frank is stiff and the company was altogether too good for him; I had pounded the old fellow along pretty well with the first rank but he was nearly done out. Then we came to a five-foot fence, stiffer than iron, that staggered the best; my old horse, completely blown, struck the top rail, didn't make an effort to recover, and rolled over on me on a lot of stones. I cut my face to pieces and broke my left arm (which accounts for my superordinarily erratic handwriting). After that I fell behind, as with one hand I could not always make Frank take his fences the first time; after three or four miles farther on a turn in the line enabled me again to catch up, and I was in at the death, not a hundred yards

[1]The late Douglas Robinson, Roosevelt's brother-in-law.

behind the first half dozen. I looked pretty gay, with one arm dangling, and my face and clothes like the walls of a slaughter house. I guess my hunting is over for this season, as my arm will be in splints for a month or six weeks. . . . My face will not be scarred except across the nose—which will not, however, be handsome. The accident did not keep me in five minutes. I rode straight through the rest of the hunt—the arm hurt very little and indeed I did not know it was actually broken until going about six fields, when the bones slipped up past each other—went out to dinner that night, and next day took a three hours' walk through the woods. . . . I wouldn't mind the broken arm a bit if I was engaged in some work so that I was occupied; I wish I had got started on the Mexican war,[1] but I am afraid my bolt is shot, in literature as well as politics.

Roosevelt was just twenty-seven years of age when he met with this adventure.

IX

Washington, D. C.,
June 10, 1908.

My dear Mother:

Yesterday I played tennis with the President again, but this time got licked by him. I think after he trains down a bit he will improve very much. You know there has always been known what is termed the Kitchen Cabinet. Well, the Washington wags have added a "Tennis Cabinet" to Mr. Roosevelt's official family. The Tennis Cabinet is supposed to be that coterie which plays tennis with the President and between plays gives him points on people and things. If some of them could see how little talking there was at these alleged tennis cabinet meetings and how much real work, they would be surprised. In fact the only way for one to make himself solid with this man when doing anything is to do it hard.

I hit him a heavy blow on the head with a ball the other

[1] A book which he had planned.

day and began to apologize when he stopped me and said:

"If I hit you, Captain, I am not going to apologize, so you just bang away at me as much as you like and say nothing in the fray."

This comes from my policy of smashing direct at my opponent.

By the way, the White House grounds are looking simply lovely these days. There is a great preponderance of yellow flowers over the grounds, a colour which Mrs. Roosevelt loves. She said the other day that when she came to the White House there was hardly a yellow flower to be seen anywhere, for the reason that Mrs. McKinley disliked yellow to such an extent that she would not have even yellow wild flowers around her. It was almost an obsession with her, it seems, and she liked blue as much as she disliked yellow. In consequence, the grounds were literally covered with blue flowers. Blue seemed to soothe her always, while yellow had the opposite effect. Strange, wasn't it?

. . . .

ARCHIE.

X

Washington, D. C.,
June 11, 1908.

MY DEAR MOTHER:

I have got my eye on a lovely old-fashioned house on the corner of Eighteenth and K, near the Marlborough, for which they ask $60. I have offered $50, but I have not heard whether they will accept it or not. It is just what I want and I am sure you would like it so much for the fall and spring months anyhow. It has a furnace and the rooms are very large and Colonial in type. It has sufficient room for me to fit up two to rent to army officers, which would make it very easy for me. My idea would be to rent the two small rooms for $25. Before I do anything, however, I will let you know. I must have a place where I can have my dogs and friends who are passing through.

Yesterday I took the new horse which I have purchased for the President and took him over every one of the jumps in the park. The best jump is a little over five feet. I, or rather he, took every one of them as clear as a bird, and I feel that he will in every way answer the call to be made on him. This jockey business is new to me, but what pleases me tremendously is that I have not even felt nervous in taking a new horse over those jumps. When you think that I took up horseflesh so late in life, fate and finances prohibiting it in the earlier years, I feel that I have some reason to feel satisfied with my record in this respect. Don't be worried, for I have finished now and the President takes over the horse this afternoon. In order to divide the responsibility, Fitz Lee is going to ride him this afternoon, and to-morrow we both accompany the President so that he will be well looked after.

I find that I have got to get a pistol. If I am accountable for this man when alone with him I must be armed at least. For if anything should happen to him and I was not armed I would never forgive myself. He carries a pistol himself and would be able to look after himself pretty well, but merely as a matter of precaution I ought to be armed at all times.

To-morrow afternoon a choral society is coming over from New York to sing for the President and Mrs. Roosevelt. It ought to be good, for there are some fine voices in it. Mrs. R. has invited only fifty of the "Very Smart" to hear it. The occasion will be rather pleasant, I imagine. It is very interesting to see how wisely Mrs. R.

segregates society in Washington and the wisdom she shows in sending her invitations. She has some entertainments in which the "inner or smart set," so called, predominate; then others when the political element is in the majority; others again when she invites only those whom she really likes and whose society she herself enjoys. The people invited do not know that they have been segregated in this fashion, but it has the effect of making her gatherings very pleasant for everybody.

The ultra smart love to meet each other and when they parade together they imagine that the entertainment is most successful and the White House pitched on very high social lines. Then the political crowd meet and deal in big gossip and think that they are most favoured. But the entertainments which are truly enjoyable, are those where the list is prepared by Mrs. Roosevelt herself and each invitation means something more than mere conventional social routine. The atmosphere is different. Where every person present has something in common with the hostess they naturally have something in common between themselves. . . .

XI

Washington, D. C.,
June 15, 1908.

My dear Mother:

Saturday was a very busy day for me and a very delightful one, as it brought me into more intimate contact with my chief than any day since I have been connected with him officially. At the time of Alice's marriage, when he appointed me a special aide, I saw something of the personal man, but it was not the same as now, for between himself and his aides, or rather those whom he admits to his intimacy, there is a total lack of formality, and it is a privilege to see the man as he is in his own family, robbed of his official dignity.

I took official charge of the White House on Saturday when the Arion Chorus, consisting of 150 male voices, sang. They were mostly German, and I have never heard such wonderful effects with the human voice. There were only fifty or sixty guests invited, and Mrs. Roosevelt received them informally in the Green Room, saying a word to each. The President came in late, and as is the custom, he had to choose some woman to sit with him, two seats being always placed in front of all the others for him and his wife, or for any one he may select. Mrs. Roosevelt seldom sits in front, but usually takes a chair on the side, just within the East Room.

The President on this occasion chose Mrs. Dewey. The Admiral was ill and could not come. I have seen him once or twice at the club, and it seems to me that he is breaking rapidly. He still remains one of the most observed and sought-after men in the capital. By the way, they have moved out of the house which the public gave them and into a large one, the house formerly occupied by Secretary Hitchcock. They were so afraid of comment that they moved into their new home overnight, so it is said, but whether it be true or not, they were settled in it before the press could raise a howl about it.[1] Mrs. Dewey is very gray, and it is becoming to her. She looks delicate, but has great loveliness and a very refined kind of charm.

The entertainment was informal and very lovely. At my suggestion, much to the relief of the other aides, the

[1]For some reason explicable only on the ground that the American people are subject to sudden ebullitions of petulance, Admiral Dewey was so overwhelmed with criticism, some of it vituperative, for leaving the "gift house" that he and Mrs. Dewey seriously thought of leaving the United States and going to Europe to live. The story is told somewhat fully in my "Impressions of Theodore Roosevelt."

President permitted us to wear the white uniform. It was the first time the white uniforms were ever worn in the White House, and you have no idea how they brightened the scene. It was my first suggestion since being attached to the White House, and the President and Mrs. R. were so much pleased that I think it will become the recognized uniform for all functions there during the warm weather. It was the first time Colonel Bromwell had ever had on his white duck, although he had it made when it was ordered to be a part of the prescribed uniform a number of years ago. Fitz Lee was the only aide who did not have a white uniform, and when I told the President that he could not wear it, he said:

"Then tell Fitz to come in pajamas and a sword, after Cuban fashion."

Fitz appeared in blue.

The musicale was over by four o'clock. It had been set at an early hour, so as not to interfere with the horseback riding later. I think I wrote to you that he had set Saturday for testing the new horse I bought for him at the Leesburg horse show. I had tried him several times and had jumped him until I felt that he was safe. I did not want to have another fiasco. I really felt very much chagrined about the other horse going over backward with him, so I felt that my reputation was largely at stake and, as you may imagine, I was somewhat nervous.

Fitz and I met the President at the White House at 4:45 and drove with him to the head of Seventeenth Street, where we found the horses waiting for us. I watched his Excellency cast his eye over the brute, and I could not tell whether he was pleased with him or not. However, he had not gone far before he threw him into a trot and then into a good swift canter. His face broke into a smile and he said:

"I think he'll do, don't you, Captain?"

I tried to be noncommittal, for I knew there was plenty of time for him to change his mind, especially as the jumps were yet to come. We took it slowly and rambled at will through the by-paths and had some interesting chit-chat. He spoke of "Dixie" and then told me that he had asked the leader to have it sung, and had been surprised to find that it was in their repertoire.

"That is our only piece of martial music. It is the best battle music in the world, even more than the 'Marseillaise,' for it goes with more of a jump and dash. It does not fit to voices well, and the words are inadequate, but for a bit of martial music there is nothing finer."

I agreed with him as to "Dixie," but said that we did not have a single national anthem that men could sing marching; that "Dixie" was impossible; that not even trained sopranos could sing the "Star-Spangled Banner," but that there was one anthem that should be our national hymn, for it was the grandest one ever written, namely, the "Battle Hymn of the Republic." You know we have often discussed this point, and you have never agreed with me, but it has always been a hope with me that some day it might supplant all the other nondescript national anthems which we now have. As I said this the President's face lighted up and he said:

"I am de-lighted to hear you say that, Captain, and especially as you come from the South, for as you say" (for I had aired myself at length on the subject), "there is not a sectional line in the whole hymn. The line, 'As He died to make men holy, let us die to make men free,' is universal, catholic, as true a hundred years ago as it is now, equally true of Anglo-Saxon or Hindu. Yes, that hymn ought to be our national hymn, but how can we bring it about?"

Then he began to repeat it; every now and then he would get stalled, and I would correct him, for every line of it I knew, and as he finished he said:

"Archie, I am glad you know that hymn."

It was the first time he had ever called me anything but Captain Butt, so I felt that I had touched some hidden spring in him. We rode on in silence for a few minutes, and then, checking his horse, he said:

"I have it. I will write to Joel Chandler Harris, Uncle Remus, you know, and get him to start the movement in the [Atlanta] *Constitution.* Then I will write to others in the West and get them to take it up and we may live to see it our national hymn. The movement must come from the South, and it had better come from someone not connected with politics at all. Would it not be fine to have a hymn that this great nation could sing in unison?"

He talked at length about it and seemed possessed with a desire to do something at once. He then told me that when he had talked with Kipling once about his Recessional Hymn the poet had said to him that the Battle Hymn was the greatest hymn ever written, that it would never be touched.

"It has always been my favourite short poem. My next favourite is——" Here is where I lost connection. It was one of Scott's shorter poems, and he repeated it, but to save my life I could not remember the first line of it, nor could I find it later when I hunted through a volume of Scott I found at the house. I will ask him some time, as it would be of interest to know what are his two favourite short poems. In the meantime, we were approaching the hills, and Fitz, who had not said a word, here stated that he would take a shorter cut and see that the bars were all up on the high jumps for we were coming to them. The

President and I rode by the road while Fitz darted off through the bridle paths. As he passed out of sight the President said:

"Fitz is a lovely fellow, but he has a good deal of contempt for you and me just now for talking literature. I don't think books are his strong point. I do not think, however, I could be much fonder of him if he were our own son."

I said that everyone liked him; that he was a lovable fellow, and that personally I was very much interested in him, as I felt that every Southern man should feel interested in seeing the name kept on a high plane.

"Never say that again, Captain. This nation is big enough now to revere the name of Robert E. Lee without sectional distinctions. He is no longer Southern, he is American, and he belongs to the nation not to the South alone."

Later he added:

"The two names which will stand out as the great ones of the civil war period are Lee and Lincoln."

He placed Lee first, but I thought more by accident than design.

"The dignity of Lee after the close of the war is awe-inspiring."

Just then we came in sight of the jumps, and the President put his spurs to the mare and she pointed her nose straight at them and I knew she would take them. He went over the bars and then straight for the stone wall with the brush on top of it. She cleared both like a bird, and I felt that my reputation was safe for the moment anyhow. Just as he cleared the second we heard someone applaud, and looking up saw his daughter, Ethel, and Miss Marion Oliver come out of the woods where they had been hiding. I had told Ethel that the President was going to try the new horse, and she and Marion Oliver had decided to watch it without letting any one know. He was enthusiastic over the mare and said:

"You could not have pleased me better had you taken a year to find a horse. I feel independent now, for when Roswell is sick I will have—by the way, what is her name?"

"She has not been named," I said.

"Then we will christen her Georgia, for this has been a regular Georgia day."

So now she has that name over her stall. We then went across country, and being sure of her, the President took her over ditches, up and down hills, and we had a good time following. Once as he pulled up he said again:

"I cannot tell you how much I like Georgia. I never had such a feeling of perfect safety on an animal before."

"I am so glad, Mr. President," I said, "for that wipes the tear out of my eye over the other horse."

"There was no need to have the tear there, for no one in the world could have known that the beast would rear."

He rode her again yesterday, and to-day he telephoned me to come over and play tennis with him at 4:30.

I am writing you at length about these matters, for I think they are of interest. You have always been set against him, I fear, on account of the Booker Washington episode, and I would not have you change your opinions merely for me for anything, for after all it is your steadfastness in all matters of conviction which makes you an interesting personality to us besides being our mother.

Your devoted son,

ARCHIE.

XII

June 16th [1908].

My dear Mother:

Yesterday afternoon Fitz Lee and I went over to the White House to play tennis, the other two players being the President and Postmaster-General Meyer. The latter is an exceedingly finished New England product of the Harvard cult. But he is very much a man and goes in for all sorts of sport. He was one of the President's classmates and intimates, yet he is most punctilious always to call him "Mr. President."

Just as we began to play it began to rain, and it did not cease during the afternoon. We thought, of course, that the President would stop as soon as it began to rain hard, but on the contrary, he played all the faster. We could not make any suggestions about stopping and the second set was played in a driving rain, with water over the entire court and the balls so wet that they would not bounce. The court being dirt, we had great fun trying to run, for at every step one would slip and someone go down. The third set was farcical, but he said that while people looking on might think us insane, yet we could get just as much exercise playing water tennis as water polo, and since exercise was the ultimate object of all sport there was no use stopping on account of the elements.

He gave us a good mint julep when we had finished, and while we were drinking it in the office, with the water pouring off us, Mr. Loeb came in with some dispatches from Chicago. We heard him say that Taft should know that at once and he began to dictate dispatches about two planks in the platform to be adopted, saying "that Taft had always stood for them," etc., etc.

I looked at Fitz and we hastily withdrew, for there is a

thing of knowing too much and hearing too much. It is safer sometimes to be out of reach. He has such perfect confidence in those around him that he never cautions any one to secrecy and takes it for granted that he is safe with those who serve him.

. . . .

Your devoted son,
ARCHIE.

XIII

The casual allusion in the following letter to President Roosevelt's naval aide, Commander Sims, is of more than passing interest. It is hardly necessary to say that this was William Sowden Sims, who as Admiral of the United States Navy was in command of all our naval operations in European waters during the World War. Few, if any, American naval officers have been so honoured with decorations and university degrees, both at home and abroad, as he. In his Autobiography Roosevelt speaks of him thus:

> When the *Maine* was blown up in Havana Harbour, war became inevitable. A number of peace-at-any-price men, of course, promptly assumed the position that she had blown herself up; but investigation showed that the explosion was from the outside. And, in any event, it would have been impossible to prevent war. The enlisted men of the navy, who often grew bored to the point of desertion in peace, became keyed up to a high pitch of efficiency, and crowds of fine young fellows, from the interior as well as the seacoast, thronged to enlist. The navy officers showed alert ability and unwearied industry in getting things ready. There was one deficiency, however, which there was no time to remedy, and of the very existence of which, strange to say, most of our best men were ignorant. Our navy had no idea how low our standard of marksmanship was. We had not realized that the modern battleships had become such a complicated piece of mechanism that the old methods of training in marksmanship were as obsolete as the old muzzle-loading broadside

guns themselves. Almost the only man in the navy who fully realized this was our naval attaché at Paris, Lieutenant Sims. He wrote letter after letter pointing out how frightfully backward we were in marksmanship. I was much impressed by his letters; but Wainwright[1] was about the only other man who was. And as Sims proved to be mistaken in his belief that the French had taught the Spaniards how to shoot, and as the Spaniards proved to be much worse even than we were, in the service generally Sims was treated as an alarmist. But although I at first partly acquiesced in this view, I grew uneasy when I studied the small proportion of hits to shots made by our vessels in battle. When I was President I took up the matter, and speedily became convinced that we needed to revolutionize our whole training in marksmanship. Sims was given the lead in organizing and introducing the new system; and to him more than to any other one man was due the astonishing progress made by our fleet in this respect, a progress which made the fleet, gun for gun, at least three times as effective, in point of fighting efficiency, in 1908, as it was in 1902. The shots that hit are the shots that count!

Washington, D. C.,
June 19 [1908].

MY DARLING MOTHER:

Politics is sizzling, and everybody in the Republican party not on the Taft band wagon seems to be getting on it as rapidly as possible. The President alone seems poised and unconcerned. Having set up the Taft cards he knew that they were going to fall as he had planned, and of everyone here during the past few days he seemed to be the only one certain that the programme was going to be carried out as planned. The second day of the convention, the day after his name had been cheered for forty-nine minutes, he came to the office in as gay a humour as I have ever seen him. By accident four of his aides had met there—McCoy, Commander Sims, Fitz Lee, and myself. Someone said something flattering about the reception his name had been given.

[1]Executive officer of the *Maine* when she was blown up, later rear-admiral with a record of distinction.

"Yes, but that is all. It gave them a chance to let off steam. Taft will be nominated on the first ballot."

He then proceeded to talk horses with Fitz and me, the War College with McCoy, and listened to Sims. Sims is a great talker and an interesting one, too, and even the presidential presence does not stem his flow of anecdotes.

I asked him [the President] for a photograph of himself for General Aleshire, which he gave at once and paid a high compliment to the latter. The General had asked me to try to get him one signed, but I was not sure how it could be done, and the fact that I was able to secure one the day after he asked the favour has given him a very exalted idea of my influence. The fact is the President is so free with those about him that there is little in reason that one might not say. I took the opportunity to say how Aleshire had decentralized his department and that he had his remount stations under experiment now.

"I am glad to hear you say that, Butt, for I appointed Aleshire quite over the advice of my advisers. Root told me that he knew nothing except about horses, and I told him then that any man who knew everything about horses must know a good deal besides. Everything has been too much centralized in Washington. I shall never forget dear old Admiral Ramsel telling me with pride one day when I was Assistant Secretary of the Navy that he could look in a certain pigeon-hole, which he showed me then, and tell exactly how many bottles of red and how many bottles of black ink each ship had on board. I never got over the horror of that statement. So if Aleshire has decentralized his department it carries out my opinion of him and I congratulate myself on my choice of a Quartermaster General."

I find that his opinion of General Bell[1] as Chief of Staff

[1]Chief of Staff, 1906–1910, commanded 77th (Rainbow) Division in World War.

has undergone a change. In fact, General Bell talks so much that he gets on people's nerves. He always seems to be talking for the benefit of someone in the adjoining room. I do not see how he is going to last much longer. He has crossed swords, too, with General Ainsworth,[1] a fatal thing for any one to do, especially one who does not handle a rapier. Ainsworth attends to his duties so perfectly that it is a relief for any one to approach his office. He is deep and wise and kind, except where he is crossed, and then the Assyrian could not come down more swiftly or more deadly. But all his influence in the War Department is for good, and discipline is his religion.

Well, I have got a long way from the White House, possibly a relief to you. The President went on to talk of the merits of the volunteers and the State militia. He said, among other things which I thought worth remembering, that the volunteers represented the men of the militia who wanted to fight. "I think, for instance," he said, "that Forrest would have made a very poor militiaman."[2] But his accent and manner said much more than his words.

He was in a gay, impersonal humour, and this on the day that the nominee was to be named. He did not seem to be even thinking about it. In fact, all the talk of a stampede to him did not worry him at all, for he had said one morning, the day before, I think it was, that should such a thing occur he would decline it before it could be made official. He has never for one minute thought of

[1]Adjutant-General, 1907–1912, when he retired.

[2]General Nathan B. Forrest, the Confederate cavalry leader, was famous for his native genius rather than for his education. It is said that when asked for his theory of cavalry strategy he replied that it was "to git there fust with the mostest men," a formula quite as sound and effective as if it had been expressed in the most polished West Point phraseology.

accepting a third term. In fact, he said the last time we were out riding that this African trip was the only thing which would probably break his fall.

"It will let me down to private life without that dull thud of which we hear so much. I will be away from it all, and by the time I come back it may be that I will have been sufficiently forgotten to be able to travel without being photographed."

At this he leered through his glasses and smiled sardonically.

It will be interesting to watch his career. I feel sure that he is going to Africa as much for Taft as for himself. If he were anywhere near telegraph lines it would be hard for the public not to suspect that Taft was being managed by him, and I think he wants to leave his secretary absolutely free with his own fate. It is pretty hard on Mrs. R., but she says that even wild-animal hunting in Africa will have its compensations when she thinks of her anxiety when he is appearing in public, a target for every crank who comes to these shores.

While there he sent for his orderly, old Sergeant McDermott. McDermott has had twenty years of service and only five years more to serve before retirement, yet he wants to resign and take a civil position. In the midst of all this convention talk and excitement the President found time to send for the Sergeant, and while he kept Assistant Secretary Bacon and one or two other public men waiting, spent over a half hour trying to get Sergeant McDermott to change his mind, and finally said:

"Sergeant, you must know that my advice is only for your own welfare. Now you go home and think it over, and don't let your wife have too much to say on the subject. But whatever you want to do I will agree to, although I think it a pity to throw away all you have gained by such a long service and splendid record."

Really nothing escapes this man once his interest has been aroused. . . .

He leaves to-morrow morning for Oyster Bay, and this afternoon I am going over to have a final game of tennis with him.

I dined with the Olivers last night and Ethel Roosevelt was there. She told me that her father had read a letter out to them all at the table that he had written to Harris[1] about the "Battle Hymn of the Republic," and that he had said a good deal about me in the letter. She said her father had also written a private note to Uncle Remus to publish his letter in his magazine if he thought it worth it. He discusses a lot of things with his children, so Mrs. R. says, mentioning only those things which he thinks will do them good or which he thinks they ought to know. This is how she knew about the "Battle Hymn" incident, evidently.

Well, next week my letters will grow strangely short and, possibly, more personal and interesting to you. I find that the President fills a good deal of the minds of those around him. He is mental and physical energy personified, and you find yourself caught up in his whirl and go skimming through space with him without any will power either to stop the machinery or even to slow it up. How your Robertson ancestors would have delighted in this man! They have the most terrific energy of any people I know, and even you, my dear mother, jumping about the world as you do, must admire it.

Good-bye, with a lot of love,

Your devoted son,

ARCHIE.

---

[1]Joel Chandler Harris, the author of "Uncle Remus"; see Letter XI.

XIV

Washington, D. C.,
June 22 [1908].

MY DARLING MOTHER:

You have got somewhat mixed up on the two favourite short poems of the President. The first was the "Battle Hymn of the Republic," beginning:

Mine eyes have seen the glory of the coming of the Lord,
He is trampling out the vintage where the grapes of wrath are stored;
He hath loosed the awful lightning of His terrible swift sword,
His truth is marching on. . . . .

I have found the second poem which he likes so much, and which is from Scott. It is "Elspeth's Ballad," written in 1816, and appears in "The Antiquary." The first stanza begins with "The herring loves the merry moonlight," but this is not the real beginning, for the poem proper begins at the second stanza:

Now haud your tongue, baith wife and carle,
And listen great and sma',
And I will sing of Glenallan's Earl,
That fought on the Red Harlaw,

I confess that I do not think of it as the President does. It has a lot of action in it, and when repeated by him seems to possess tremendous vigour, but I could name a dozen short poems which I think are equally vigorous and possessing finer poetic qualities. . . .

I have certainly got to overcome the fault of never remembering names unless I particularly like the owner, before next winter, for if I do not the Ambassador from Russia may go down the White House lines as the Minister from the Netherlands and Mrs. Archibald Hopkins pass in review as Mrs. Slater or some equally haughty dame whom I happen not to remember. Edwards[1] is trying to teach some of the naval files to ride, and, considering it was the first time McCauley and Davis were ever on a horse, they sat their saddles pretty well. I find that McCauley has left the most wonderful records of all White House functions. No records were ever kept until he went there as aide and since then every entertainment, no matter how insignificant, has been recorded and precedents laid down as decided.

Some new problem (social) is always coming up, however. For instance, at the dinners to the governors, when William Jennings Bryan was present, we were in a quandary where to seat him. No such complication had ever arisen before. The Speaker and Chief Justice and other justices and certain senators were also there. Usually when the Speaker is invited to dinner the Chief Justice is not, as both claim precedence. So McCoy and I took the matter up, and after a conference with the President and the Secretary of State, Mr. Root, it was decided to settle this matter once for all by putting the Chief Justice on the right of the President and the Speaker on the left, thus, of course, giving the place of honour to the Chief Justice.

Cannon appeared to be rather sulky the entire evening, and I noticed that when he left the White House that night he did so without saying good-bye to the President.

In the matter of Mr. Bryan the question was not so easily settled. The others thought that as he had no official position he should sit after the governors, but I took exception to this, as I felt sure that the President would want to pay some signal attention to the Democratic leader. So finally we took the matter to the Presi-

[1]General Clarence Edwards.

dent, and he said offhand that Mr. Bryan must sit next to him, but to this Secretary Root and others declaimed, and so the President finally compromised by putting him next to the Supreme Court and ahead of all senators and governors. But if the President had had his way he would have smashed all form and seated the "Peerless One" next to himself. As it was, he talked with him the entire evening so as to even up the honours. The governors were seated according to the dates on which the States entered the Union. But no more.

Good-bye.

Affectionately,
ARCHIE.

In spite of Roosevelt's personal interest in Mr. Bryan —an interest which is revealed in the foregoing letter— he was never deluded by the economic and political fallacies of the "Peerless Democrat." In his Autobiography, written in 1913, he made the following estimate of what may be called the Bryan doctrines: "Mr. Bryan's candidacy in 1896 on a free-silver platform had threatened such frightful business disaster as to make the business men, the wage-workers, and the professional classes generally, turn eagerly to the Republican party. East of the Mississippi the Republican vote for Mr. McKinley was larger by far than it had been for Abraham Lincoln in the days when the life of the Nation was at stake. Mr. Bryan championed many sorely needed reforms in the interest of the plain people; but many of his platform proposals, economic and otherwise, were of such a character that to have put them into practice would have meant to plunge all our people into conditions far worse than any of those for which he sought a remedy. The free-silver advocates included sincere and upright men who were able to make a strong case for their position; but with them and dominating them were all the believers in the complete or partial repudiation of national, state, and private debts; and not only the business men but the workingmen grew to feel that under these circumstances too heavy a price could not be paid to avert the Democratic triumph. The fear of Mr. Bryan threw almost all the leading men of all classes into the arms of whoever opposed him."

XV

Washington, D. C.,
June 24 [1908].

My dear Mother:

I have not heard from the proposed landlord whether he will accept the price I have offered for his house on I Street. I feel toward it as Moncheur, the Belgian Minister, did toward his house on H Street, which is very large and commodious and for which he only pays, I think, some ridiculously small price, something like a thousand dollars. When asked how he could get it so cheap he replied: "Because no American would live in it." I have to get the I Street house for sixty a month because no Northerner would live in it.

Good-bye, with much love, as ever,
Archie.

XVI

Of the *dramatis personæ* in the following letter the reader may be interested to know that Logan is Colonel James Logan, now the American observer on the Reparations Commission; that Captain Cheney is Colonel Sherwood A. Cheney, who, after serving with distinction in the World War, is now military attaché in China; and that Mrs. McLean is the mother of the present proprietor of the Washington *Post*, Edward B. McLean, whose name was unhappily connected with those of ex-Secretary Fall and Attorney-General Daugherty in the Tea-pot Dome Scandal.

Washington, D. C.,
June 25 [1908.]

My dear Mother:

The spring season has always been delightful to me here because of its informality. One does not have to keep track of dinner engagements made thirty days ahead. But the system of inviting dinner guests has somewhat changed of late years in Washington, or rather among a very few in Washington. Even when I was here before I have received invitations through butlers and on arrival felt certain that my hostess did not know who was coming until the guests arrived.

The Pattens, for instance, have been known to direct their butler to call up the Metropolitan Club and ask any diplomat who might be in the club to come to dinner. I was present one afternoon at Mrs. Longworth's when she was trying to get up a dinner and bridge party for that evening. As we were leaving the house here were her instructions to the butler:

"Call up any of the gentlemen who dine here and ask them for dinner for this evening. Only ask those who play bridge. You know who they are. After you get the gentlemen, then get four ladies without husbands, if possible."

That evening the dinner was really charming and the guests carefully selected. Each guest thought he or she had been asked to fill a place that day.

I had an experience last week that was really comical. After four o'clock I hurried to the house to dress for tennis. I found a note on the hall table signed "Logan," saying that Mrs. Townsend presented her compliments and asked if I could dine there the following evening. As both Mrs. Townsend and Mathilde knew I had an engagement for that evening with the Pattens, I realized that I was being asked by the butler. The 'phone message also asked me to let Mrs. Townsend know as soon as I came in. As I was in a hurry I did not stop to 'phone, and when I came in in a rush to dress for a 7:30 dinner I found another note, this time signed by Captain Cheney, another of the mess in Poverty Flats, as we call our ménage. Cheney, with a sense of humour, wrote:

"Mrs. Townsend's butler wants to know if you are coming to dinner to-morrow evening and wants to know as soon as you come."

I was late in dressing, so I made a dash out of the house, still without answering the butler. When I came in after 11:00 that night I found a message on the hall table from McCoy, which read like this:

"Why have you not answered Mrs. Townsend's butler's invitation for to-morrow evening? He is mad as hell and wants you to call him up no matter what time you come in."

I then called up and told the irate menial that I was unable to come, to which the well-trained man replied:

"Mrs. Townsend will be very sorry, sir, as she was particularly anxious that I should get you."

In laughing over this matter with Mrs. Townsend later, she said:

"I ought to have told him that I had already asked you myself, for James is so careful to have my dinners successful."

It is said that Mrs. McLean's maid invites all of Mrs. McLean's guests; that she never knows who are coming until she sees them in the house; that she does not even take the time to read the list over before they come.

Affectionately your son,

ARCHIE.

XVII

Colonel William Murray Black, a distinguished army engineer, to whom this letter is addressed, had been on the staff of Governor-General Leonard Wood in Cuba and at the time was American adviser to the Cuban Provisional Government in the Department of Public Works. He attained the rank of Major-General in the World War, was awarded the Distinguished Service Medal, and was retired in 1919.

Washington, D. C.,
[About end of June, 1908.]

MY DEAR COLONEL BLACK:

Colonel Edwards tells a very good story apropos of Symons which illustrates some of the funny incidents which can and do occur at the White House. It is worth repeating to you as an engineer, especially as it is in line with some of our talk on the same subject before:

He said he went with Secretary Taft one afternoon late to keep an appointment with the President. It was the summer time, when the family were away somewhere, and grounds were being loaned once or twice a week for the sick or other charities. That as he and the Secretary entered they heard the greatest racket on the grounds, and inquiry developed the fact that Colonel Symons had loaned the grounds to the Society for Fallen Women. Just at that moment the President entered. He had not seen them before, and hearing the noise he went to the window, where, as Edwards described, large yellow-haired women were rolling up and down the lawn pulling at each other's blondine wigs and pink ribbons and making an awful racket.

"In Heaven's name, what is this going on?" he asked.

By that time the Secretary was convulsed with laughter and between gasps he explained:

"Only Symons has loaned the White House to the Society for the Rescue of Fallen Women, Mr. President. Come to this window and watch them fall. They are falling in great numbers here. Watch that last one fall"—as a two-hundred-pounder rolled down the hill.

"Where are the rescuers?" exclaimed the President.

"Falling, too, no doubt," laughed the Secretary.

"Well, let's send for Symons, then," said the President, and a messenger was dispatched for the officer in charge of Public Buildings and Grounds. Before the conference ended, Symons came in and the President, red with anger, demanded of him what he meant by turning the White House into such a pandemonium.

"Aren't we near enough to the fallen district without having it moved into the grounds?"

Poor Symons was very much flustered, but replied as best he could:

"Knowing how charitably inclined both you and Mrs. Roosevelt are, Mr. President, I loaned the grounds to the Society for Fallen Women, thinking it a charity which you wanted to encourage."

"Encourage not to fall, Symons, but here we are encouraging them to fall. I never knew it was possible for so many large and ugly women to fall as rapidly as they are doing out there. Rescue them, Symons, before it goes too far. See if you can save that one who is about to fall over there. Tell them, if they must fall, to fall nearer the fence and not so close to the office. Go and help to rescue them, Symons"—and the crestfallen officer made a dash out of the side door to find Charlotte Walker, the main rescuer, who had them in charge.

By this time the President saw the humour and as Symons left the office he was joining the Secretary in bursts of laughter. Edwards thinks that this scene was the straw which was thrown into the scales and which finally brought about the appointment of Colonel Marshall as Chief Engineer instead of Colonel Symons, who everybody thought had the post nailed down. . . .

With best wishes, most sincerely your friend,

A. M. Butt.

XVIII

Washington, D. C.,
June 30th [1908].

My dear Mother:

We have had rather an interesting day saying good-bye to the retiring Secretary of War [Mr. Taft] and listening to the predictions of his election to the Presidency. He seems perfectly happy and smiles at everything and everybody. . . .

While I was in his office he saw at least a dozen people on business and settled many questions. He has a wonderfully well-trained mind and seems to have none of the trouble of so many people in deciding questions. He is capable of a great amount of labour, but those of us who have served with him in the Philippines have seen this capacity for work almost overworked at times. I have seen him in the Philippines, lying on his back and suffering intense pain, transact business from his bed with a cheerfulness which many of those on top do not exercise in their comfortable offices. He thinks he is going to be elected, but does not feel at all certain.

"What are you going to do in New York?" he asked old Michael J. Dady, who came into his office.

"We are going to carry it without doubt for you," he replied.

"Don't be too certain," said the Secretary, "for there is a very uncertain vote this year and this election is going to turn largely on the labour vote. I have been trying to impress it on Charley Taft, my brother, that he had better take nothing for granted, but to fight as if he were making a losing fight, to contest every inch in every state and not to look on Ohio or any other state as certain."

But he was smiling all the time, yet his fighting qualities show in his blue eyes, which are close together, and his lips, which are thin. . . .

You tell me I have written nothing about Miss Hagner.[1] Well, she is the same open-hearted, generous friend as ever. I am simply astonished at her executive ability. She really is the chief factor at the White House, and the fact that everything has gone as smoothly as it has is due more to her than every one else put together about the Executive Mansion. During the season her mind is active every minute of the day. Before the aides are up in the morning Miss Hagner is telephoning to McCoy or Bromwell to remind them of some big dinner at the White House for that evening and to ask if it has been ordered, which in five cases out of seven has been forgotten.

The large dinners are prepared and cooked by Rauscher at so much per plate. Last year he got $10 a plate, but this past winter they cut him to $8. This includes all the wines with the exception of champagne. There is no entertainment fund, so you can see how rapidly the President's pay is eaten up. He could cut down his expenses by cutting down his guests, but he has a horror of trying to save any money out of his pay, and I heard him say to Mrs. Roosevelt once that while it was more expensive to

[1]Mrs. Roosevelt's secretary.

have Rauscher serve the dinners, yet all the salary had to go anyhow, so it had just as well go in dinners, for then it at least reflected credit on the Government.

But his chief reason for not having the dinners prepared at the White House is to take the worry off his wife. He tried the other plan and found out that the day of a dinner every one was running to her for orders, and no matter how competent a chef and butler one had, still it was to Mrs. Roosevelt that all matters were referred.

Mrs. Taft loves the worry of housekeeping, and if her husband is elected I think you will see a very domestic administration. But this is a long skip from Miss Hagner, when I started out to tell you of her at your own request. . . .

The entire force rely on Miss Hagner, and it is really humorous to see her conducting the affairs of that big establishment. She went there merely as the social secretary of Mrs. Roosevelt, but her sphere has broadened until it is sort of head aide, general manager, and superintendent. She keeps Mrs. R. informed as to everything, and Mrs. Roosevelt relies on her to see that her wishes are carried out in detail. Mrs. Roosevelt herself is a splendid executive, and attends to a vast number of things without seeming to trouble herself or any one else very much, but I hardly see how she would get along without Miss Hagner. The latter never seems to play any favourites or have any axes to grind. She does not let her likes or dislikes play any part, and her advice is always sound and impersonal. Yet she keeps her weather eye open for her friends. After I had been to a dinner and a luncheon she suggested that I leave a card at the White House.

"But why?" I asked. "I am in and out there every day."

"But when you come to dinner you come as a guest, and

I know Mrs. Roosevelt appreciates it if you pay her the same respect that you would to other women who invite you to dinner."

So after each meal at the White House now I leave my card, and I know that it is appreciated, just as Miss Hagner hinted. . . .

Good-bye, lots of love,
ARCHIE.

XIX

Mr. Taft, who had been President Roosevelt's Secretary of War for four years, resigned from the Cabinet in the summer of 1908 in order to direct the campaign for the Presidency to which he had been nominated by the Republicans. General Luke Wright, a Tennessee "gold Democrat," had been Governor-General of the Philippines under Roosevelt's administration. Roosevelt not only liked Southerners but he had a deep-seated desire to replace the feeling of political solidarity and antagonism in the Southern States, the heritage of the Civil War, with a sense of National confidence and responsibility. The thread of this fine purpose may be found running through the seven years of his Presidency.

Washington, D. C.,
July 1 [1908].

MY DEAR MOTHER:

All the officers went by orders to pay their respects to the new Secretary of War this morning, Luke Wright. The retiring Secretary presented each in turn and the introductions were very happily made by Mr. Taft. As General Aleshire and his staff were waiting in the hall to go in Captain Parker called to me, who was nearer the head of the column, that there was a photograph with my name on it near him. I went back and there found a splendid likeness of Mr. Taft, and under it was written in his own handwriting: "To Capt. Archie W. Butt, with the warm regards of Wm. H. Taft." He had remembered a request I made to him in Cuba for one of his photographs.

As we filed by the Secretary, Frank Cheatham and I were together. Secretary Wright caught us both by the shoulders and gave us a kind of hug. Cheatham is the son of General Cheatham, and both of us had been very close to Secretary Wright when he was in the Philippines. People never get over that old feeling of friendship for those who have served with them in times which are at least trying. Of the eight or ten assistants to General Aleshire only two are Northern men. He laughed as he introduced them, and added:

"Mr. Secretary, you see I have a reconstructed brigade from your part of the country."

"You could not have a better," added General Wright.

Aleshire is from an old Democratic family in Ohio. He often laughs and says it does not mean anything for us to be Democrats, but that his family were Democrats when it meant almost ostracism in the state he comes from. His appointment to the office of Quartermaster-General only shows how little politics cuts any figure with Mr. Roosevelt where the good of the army is involved. It certainly did my heart good to see an old Confederate soldier head of the War Department, and many were thinking about it also, although I did not hear a comment on the subject. . . .

As ever, your devoted son,

ARCHIE.

XX

The office of Adjutant-General is an important one in the American Army or, indeed, in any army. In the

United States Army he is the head of a department which manages recruiting and has charge of all the voluminous army records. General Ainsworth, who figures in this letter, was born in Woodstock, Vermont; was graduated from the Medical School of New York University; and entered the army as an assistant surgeon at twenty-two years of age. He was the first officer who had never commanded troops to hold the office of Adjutant-General and attained his high rank and responsibilities because of the successful system he devised for keeping individual historical records of soldiers in the Pension Bureau, a gigantic task of clerical compilation. The letter is addressed to Clara Doughty Butt (Mrs. Lewis F. Butt), Archie Butt's sister-in-law.

Washington, D. C.,
July 16 [1908].

My dear Clara:

Being in the humour to write, and Mother being with me, I have picked you out as the victim.

We went to the Warm Sulphur Springs to remain most of the summer there, but found that the altitude was too much for Mother's heart and the doctors advised us to come to the sea level again, so back we came. We had all sorts of invitations to stay with people. The Duvalls wanted us with them again, and General Aleshire offered to turn over to us his house, with a cook alive and ready to work besides. Colonel Bromwell wanted to take us in, but we declined all invitations and took a suite of rooms at the Gordon, on the corner of Sixteenth and I streets. As I had only two months' leave, I hated to fritter it away in railroad travel, but Mother's health, of course, was first consideration. When I first took leave I would have arranged to go at once to Europe had not the President's invitation to visit Oyster Bay during the latter part of July intervened to put a stop to all plans. When one stands in the ante-rooms of the great, one has to make plans according to their wishes, I find.

However, we came back to Washington and every one about here had a good laugh at my expense. Having a leave and not to know what to do with it is one of the standing jokes in the army. Of course, with a large balance sheet there would never be any trouble to know where to go, but when one has got to make army pay reach out from the regular tent the travelling necessarily becomes limited.

I went with my troubles to General Ainsworth, the Adjutant-General of the army, the man who rose from a young surgeon to the post of Military Secretary and now Adjutant-General. If every one knew his business as this man knows his the army and the Government wherever he touches it would run smoother. He still has the air of a medical man and looks at one as if he is deciding whether it is a case for real treatment or merely a neurasthenic to be handled. He gives one the impression that he is looking you through and through, and he manages to get at the bottom pretty soon. I should hate to be a malingerer and stand before him for five minutes. The fact that I was A. D. C. to the President would cut little ice if the justice of the case did not appeal to him. Not that he would buck the President, but routine to him is righteousness and order in military affairs his religion.

In the first place, he said that an invitation to visit the President was an order, and while I was there that time should be deducted from my leave. Then he said that while I was waiting on the President's orders—otherwise, the nod from Jove—I should not be called to waste my leave, so he decided that my leave should be suspended until after my visit to Oyster Bay, and that it would continue at whatever day I desired, to run on then until the two months should be up.

So our present plans are to leave for Europe the first week in August. I will leave Mother there and return about the middle of September, get the house in readiness, and have things running smoothly by the time she comes. . . .

I was much amused to see the fashionable Virginia resorts turned into a political headquarters. There is some method in Mr. Taft going to Virginia with his family for the summer. Something else than climate appeals to him. In the first place, he knows that the South is almost in open revolt against Bryan and that form of Socialism he has lassoed and dragged into the Democratic party. He has hitched up with Socialism every other ism under the sun, and is dashing over the country in a chariot trailing the South after him, literally tied in chains. The South made him and it is hard to get away from him. The South is no more allied to the West than I am with the average bronco buster. Though I may admire the tricks of the latter on horseback I should not like to follow him. After the stand that Mr. Taft has taken on the Negro question and the Brownsville affair, it would be a great thing for him to break the solid South and carry several states. Even if he lost the Presidency, it would be a memorable thing to do. The North is getting very tired of the Negro, and Mr. Taft is the only man at present who can unload him.

When the Republican convention was being held the platform committee had intended to put into it a plank pledging the party to continue the fight to cut down the representation from the South. Mr. Taft himself wired his managers that he would not have this plank in the platform and would not advocate it if it was inserted. A pretty brave thing to do at that juncture. Bryan cannot put him in the unenviable position of a corruptionist, for his life is too clean and pure to admit of such charges. His very poverty, for it is hardly anything more than that now, is like a badge of honour on him when you think of the length of public service he has had and the multitude of chances he must have had to enrich himself during his career. . . .

I saw him while at the Springs and he was the same jovial, cheerful man as ever. The cares of the campaign sit lightly on him. He believes in his destiny, and, should he be defeated, the campaign he intends to make will leave the political atmosphere clearer and better for his having been in it. I went over to the hotel, where he is staying very little, for I did not want to appear that I was in any way anxious to keep in touch with him. Until he is in office, I will see much less of him than ever before. If he wants to change his aides, as it is natural for him to do, I do not want to hamper him by hanging about his neck. I hope that the end of this Administration will end my tour as an A. D. C., for the duties are not the pleasantest in the world. Only the kindly consideration of Mr. Roosevelt makes them possible.

The fact that one serves the President makes one a target for all the envious tongues in the army, and so many slighting remarks can be made. Luckily my long tours of foreign service would dull the point of any criticism aimed at me from that direction. I will always be proud that I have served with Mr. Roosevelt in that capacity, but I should hate to become a professional aide at the White House. Here I have done nothing but talk about myself and link myself with all the greatness which seems to be going, but this being in the limelight for a minute,

I fear, makes one exaggerate his own importance. I imagine that each planet revolving around the sun thinks him or herself the main centre of the orbit. As long as I realize the tendency I will at least remain normal and not lose knowledge of my relative position.

Your affectionate brother,

ARCHIE.

XXI

The four letters to which we now come constitute a chapter by themselves and present a characteristic picture of Theodore Roosevelt's family life; without a knowledge of this side of his life no one can form an accurate or just estimate of his personality. Roosevelt himself has also described the life at Sagamore Hill in one of the best chapters of his Autobiography—the chapter entitled "Outdoors and Indoors." In this chapter he says:

> There are many kinds of success in life worth having. It is exceedingly interesting and attractive to be a successful business man, a railroad man, or farmer, or a successful lawyer or doctor; or a writer, or a President, or a ranchman, or the colonel of a fighting regiment, or to kill grizzly bears and lion. But for unflagging interest and enjoyment, a household of children, if things go reasonably well, certainly makes all other forms of success and achievement lose their importance by comparison.

In the latter part of July, 1908, Mrs. Roosevelt wrote to Captain Butt from Oyster Bay confirming her verbal invitation given in Washington and saying that he was expected on the twenty-fourth. She added: "I sometimes feel doubtful about my guests, but I know that you will like Sagamore Hill. The President is glad to have good news of Georgia."

> Sagamore Hill [says Roosevelt in his Autobiography] takes its name from the old Sagamore Mohannis, who, as chief of his little tribe,

signed away his rights to the land two and a half centuries ago. The house stands right on the top of the hill, separated by fields and belts of woodland from all other houses, and looks out over the bay and the Sound. We see the sun go down beyond long reaches of land and of water. Many birds dwell in the trees round the house or in the pastures or the woods nearby, and of course in winter gulls, loons, and wild fowl frequent the waters of the bay and the Sound.

Oyster Bay, L. I.,
July 24 [1908].

My dear Mother:

The greatest surprise to me so far has been the utmost simplicity of the home life at Sagamore Hill. I am constantly asking myself if this can really be the home of the President of the United States, and how is it possible for him to enforce such simplicity in his environment. It might be the home of a well-to-do farmer with literary tastes or the house of some college professor. . . .

There was no one at the house when we [Captain Butt and Beekman Winthrop] got there. Mrs. Roosevelt had been out to see some sick neighbour and the President was playing tennis. They both came in together, however, he in tennis garb and she in a simple white muslin with a large white hat of some cloth material, with flowers in it, a wabbly kind of hat which seems to go with trees and water. He welcomed us with his characteristic handshake and she most graciously and kindly. The President was so keen for us to take a swim that he did not give us time to see our rooms before we were on the way to the beach.

I do not know when I have enjoyed anything so much. I could not help remarking how pretty and young Mrs. R. looked in her bathing suit. I did not admire his, however, for it was one of those one-piece garments and looked more like a suit of overalls than a bathing suit, but I presume he did not think it dignified for the President to wear one of these abbreviated armless suits which we all think are so becoming. I confess to liking to have as much skin surface in contact with the water as possible.

Dinner was at 8:00 and we hurried home to put on evening clothes. I had asked Mrs. R. if the President dressed for dinner and she said that he always wore his dinner jacket, but to wear anything I wanted, as the only rule they had at Oyster Bay was that they had no rules or regulations. I finally wore white trousers and white waistcoat with the dinner jacket and black tie. He said it was a costume he liked more than any other for summer and that he often wore it himself. He put Mrs. Winthrop on his right, and I sat on his left. There was no special formality, the only deference which was paid to the President was the fact that all dishes were handed to him first, then to Mrs. Roosevelt, and after that to the guest of honour, and so on.

Miss Ethel was late in coming to dinner and every one, including the President, rose. From the conversation which followed I learned that it had always been a rule in the household for the boys to rise when either their mother or father or their sister came to the table. In fact, Kermit said that since such was the custom the girls ought to make it a rule to be on time for their meals, and this remark started the Roosevelt ball rolling. The President said that he thought Ethel ought to try to be on time, too; that he preferred that no notice be taken of him when he came to his meals late, but that since Mrs. Roosevelt (with a deferential wave of the hand toward her) insisted upon this modicum of respect being paid to the President he always tried to be on time to his meals. Mrs. Roosevelt said that she did not insist upon the mark of respect being paid to the President but to their father, whereupon all laughed, and Ethel said she would try to be on time to all her meals except breakfast.

I was very hungry and enjoyed my dinner, being helped twice to nearly everything. We had soup, fish, fried chicken, and corn on the cob, and jelly. There was nothing to drink but water. The President asked me if I would have something, but as it was not the custom I declined.

"We often have something," said the President, "so do not hesitate to take what you want. We are not the tipplers that our friends in Wall Street would make us out, but don't mistake us for prohibitionists."

I was much interested in meeting the family in this way and never saw less restraint than at the President's table. Every child has something to say, and when one makes a remark it is certain to bring forth a volley of denials or contemptuous rebuttals from the others. In fact, there was nothing studied or formal, and every member came in for a little fun before the dinner was over. Even the guests did not escape.

When Mrs. Roosevelt reproved Kermit for putting his elbows on the table the President said that his children were well behaved as a rule, but that when he saw me do the same thing he felt that the example would be quickly followed. I then told how you had urged me to mind my table manners, especially while at Oyster Bay, and how you had no faith in me even at this late day. The President said he would not give a hang for a boy, no matter if he was forty, in whom his mother could not find something to reprove.

I forgot to mention the fact that the fried chicken was covered with white gravy, and oh, so good! The President said that his mother had always said it was the only way to serve fried chicken; that it gave the gravy time to soak into the meat, and that if the gravy was served separately he never took it.

Ted is now grown up and, while not handsome, has a keen face and is certainly clever and with a splendid sense of humour. Kermit is very attractive in manner and in appearance, and I have an idea that he is his mother's favourite, though, of course, she would deny it, just as you do when accused of favouring me over the others. Archie is the one who was so ill, and still looks very delicate. He is the pugnacious member, evidently, for he takes up the cudgel at every chance. Quentin[1] is the youngest, and a large, bouncing youngster, who brought in his last-made kite to the table to show his father, and who explained to me the merits of the newfangled kites for flying purposes, which controversy would not interest you in the least.

There, I have introduced you to the family, and will stop, as lunch is nearly ready, the first bell having been rung some ten minutes ago. By the way, the bell is a cow bell, just the kind you hear on cows in the cow lot, but sounds as sweet as any other if one is hungry.

. . . .

I shall resume where I left off before lunch. After dinner we all went on the broad veranda which runs around part of the house, and which affords a beautiful view of the Sound. The house sits on top of the hill and there are only one or two trees in its immediate vicinity. The ground slopes in all directions from the porch, and near the foot of the hill the trees grow in great profusion

[1]Quentin was an aviator in the World War, and fell with his plane in action in France, where he is buried. Just before his own death Roosevelt said to a French friend who had asked him for a message for France: "I have no message for France; I have already given her the best I had. But if over there they speak of me, tell them my only regret is that I could not have given myself."

and in many varieties. What charms me especially about the location is that there is not another house visible from it and nothing to mar the landscape. As the President says:

"We have no one looking into our pantry and there is no need to close a shutter."

We smoked and chatted on a hundred different subjects and made plans for the following day. Mrs. Roosevelt finally took her knitting inside and was soon followed by Mrs. Winthrop. Miss Ethel evidently found us dull, and went walking with her dog Ace, and the boys went to the *Mayflower* to spend the night. The President, Winthrop, and I sat and talked on every subject which three men knowing something of the affairs of the day (I have only a smattering, perhaps) can talk. The talk naturally drifted to Taft's nomination and the chances for his election. The President seems to think that he will be elected, though there are certain elements of danger.

"If the people knew Taft there would be no doubt of his election," he said. "They know what he has done, but they don't know the man. If they knew him they would know that he can be relied on to carry out the policies which I stand for. He is committed to them just the same as I am and has been made the mouthpiece for them as frequently as I."

He did not think Mr. Taft would break the South.

"You know," he said, "my chief regret in not making the race this year is that I am not able to demonstrate the fact that I can carry Georgia. I am convinced that I would carry Georgia, Virginia, and possibly Louisiana. I doubt if I would carry Tennessee or Kentucky, but I am certain about the others. I would make my opening speech in Savannah or Macon and would fight my way out from there. I would carry those states for the reason that I am not sectional; I have not got a sectional bone in my body. I imbibed the traditions and the folk lore of the South from my mother; my earliest training and principles were Southern; I sought the West of my own accord, and my manhood has largely been fought out in the North."

He spoke of his popularity as I would speak of riding ability. I said that to me the great danger to Mr. Taft came from the residuary legatee idea, but that I thought this would be counteracted by the fact that Mr. Taft would also be the legatee of the President's popularity.

"Yes," he said, "I think so. I do not think Taft would be as aggressive as I have been, but there will be no backward step under Taft."

He then referred to the recent decision in the Standard Oil case and added:

"Like Andrew Jackson, when the enemy gains some advantage I advance a foot nearer. I have never betrayed the people yet, and I don't propose to do so now by default. If a technicality protects the criminal we must overcome the technicality. I am popular because I am trusted and I believe my policies to be best for all classes. If ever the unidentified class in this country feel that the legislative class is not to be relied upon then may the wealth and culture really expect trouble. In this country we have got to play the game squarely, for if we don't we will not be allowed to play it at all. The people are too well educated to be fooled."

We talked of this man and that man, and he had something of interest to say about each name as it was mentioned. Winthrop asked him if he did not think Garfield a very ordinary man.

"Not at all," said the President. "His great fault lay

in the fact that he had no horror of corruption. He cared nothing about it, while a perfectly honest man himself. . . . But next to Jefferson, Garfield was the most brilliant President we have ever had.

"Hoar," he said, "was always small, inasmuch as he was sectional." He said that because the Declaration of Independence declared that all men were free and equal, and that Massachusetts had approved it for personal reasons, so Hoar really thought the Negro could be legislated to be as good as the white man, forgetting the natural limitations of the Negro.

"I am afraid I have not got as much reverence for the Declaration of Independence as I should have because it has made certain untruths immortal." . . .

He said that he thought Senator Platt of Connecticut, Senator Lindsay of Kentucky, and Senator Cockrell of Missouri, the three best men he had ever met in public life, and that old Sayers of Texas did not come far behind them.

He then talked of Monroe and I fear he has a very poor idea of him. He took us into the library and read us a number of speeches of President Monroe made on a trip through New England. It was an old volume he had dug out of some obscure library. One speech he almost knew by heart. It was made in answer to an address of ministers and preachers in Portland, Maine. One sentence he recalled with great glee. It was to the effect that all religion in general would have his hearty approval and support.

"Why, by the side of these speeches the remarks of our estimable Vice-President, Mr. Fairbanks, would seem most indiscreet, if not positively indecent."

Well, I have rambled on, incoherently at times, but possibly with some interest to you. The fact that you tell me you have kept all my letters and that they will be a sort of diary some day inspires me to write more fully than I otherwise would. The only interest I have in writing is the hope that you will be entertained by what I say, so that when I have not you to write to I fear that my diary will come to a sudden close, for the simple record of facts to me has always been most distasteful. I should like to convince you, too, that the President is all that I think him, but when I read what I have written it seems to me that I have brought out facts which might put him in an unenviable light rather than in a favourable one, for I remember that one of the things you stored up against him was his criticism of the Presidents: just, possibly, but you thought in bad taste.

One thing he does do most successfully, he makes you forget that you are in the house with the President, and that you are merely the guest of a very charming, witty, and hospitable gentleman. I will remain over Sunday; at least I think that is as long as my invitation lasts. The life is going to be strenuous and healthy. I see endless tennis and swimming and boating and riding ahead of me, and I am keen for it. Why was I not born a countryman instead of a horrid city type from which I cannot escape?

Good-bye, with much love,
ARCHIE.

XXII

Sagamore Hill, Oyster Bay,
July 26 [1908].

MY DEAR MOTHER:

This is the end of a very busy day and a very delightful one also. Our other guest arrived soon after breakfast this morning, and while I am writing he is sleeping. I think I may have spoken of him before. He is a Mr. Phillips—William Phillips, I think. At any rate [he] is a Harvard man and a New Englander.[1]

I feel toward New Englanders as a friend of mine did toward the Democrats of New York. He said he knew there were some good Democrats, but that he thought he knew them all. I feel that there are some mighty nice New Englanders, but I think I know them all. At any rate, I am constantly surprised how many more nice ones there are to meet. Phillips is one of them. He is rich, has a motor yacht, and yet works hard. He was in the diplomatic service somewhere in the East and then came to Washington, where he has been put at the head of a bureau on Eastern affairs in the State Department. He was expected last night with us, but did not arrive until this morning. He came by boat and anchored while we were in swimming. I know him chiefly as a friend of Captain Logan, which is a good recommendation in itself to any one. I am not jealous of his yacht, but I am of his English travelling bag, one of the biggest and clumsiest ones I have ever seen, but holds a complete wardrobe.

It rained all the morning, but that did not prevent us from going in swimming and playing tennis. We started off with a good breakfast and every one was keen for it. Peaches and cream, handed twice, and fried liver and bacon, and, strange as it may seem, hominy, served as we serve it in the South. Not big hominy but grits, as they call it in the North.

"Why, Mr. President," I exclaimed, "this is a Southern

---

[1]William Phillips has had a diplomatic career that is encouraging to those who believe in a permanent Department of State based on merit, training, and service. He began as private secretary to Ambassador Choate in London, has passed through various ranks, including Under Secretary of State, and is now (1924) Ambassador to Belgium. At the time this letter was written he was Chief of Division of Far Eastern Affairs.

breakfast. I have never seen hominy served anywhere out of the South in this way before."

"What did I tell you, Edith? Yes, it is just the breakfast my mother always had, varied as to the meats, of course. I have the hardest time with most of my guests, who usually want to eat the hominy with sugar and cream, and some think it a fruit. We eat it just as you do in the South with salt and butter and nothing more."

The President has his own coffee pot and slop bowl and cream pitcher and sugar. I think it is a complete set in itself. Mrs. Roosevelt says that it is next to impossible to get his coffee to suit him, and as he is a great coffee drinker she provided him with a service of his own, and if the coffee is not right he has no one to blame but himself. He drinks several cups at his breakfast and makes each one a matter of great formality. It is really interesting to see how much pleasure he gets out of it.

I note with some hesitancy to speak of it that the President is a good eater. You think me a large eater; well, I am small in comparison to him. But he has a tremendous body and really enjoys each mouthful. I never saw any one with a more wholesome appetite, and then he complains of not losing flesh. I felt like asking him to-day: "How can you expect to?" He does not smoke, and the time when other men take to the weed he gets the papers and magazines and for about ten minutes is absorbed in them. He takes only the New York *Herald* and New York *Tribune*. He knows he will not find anything in them to upset his digestion.

"I could not stand the *Evening Post* or the *Sun* after a hearty meal," he said.

Secretary Loeb sees that he hears what evil is published of him just before meal time. He says he could never fight on a full stomach. But while he does not take any of the other papers at his home, everything reflecting on him or which would be a guide to him in any way he has laid on his desk.

"I always want to see the laudatory things, so I think it my duty to read the contrary."

After breakfast we went on the porch and shook our fists at the rain. The President said the rain would not bother us, as we (he and I) had played a record game with the Postmaster-General one afternoon in the rain. While we were sitting there Quentin was seen scuttling around the corner. His mother said:

"I know what that means."

She called to him and when he came she whispered to him and I heard him say:

"Oh, Mother, I thought you would forget."

"Mothers never forget these things, even if little boys do," she laughed, and he went out as we all have done on similar occasions to clean his teeth. Oh, horrors of boyhood days!

We all went in swimming after tennis and a lot of fun we had. Every one joined in the water fight and sides were chosen to see who could clear the float.

I cannot help but think that Mrs. Roosevelt feels anxious over this forthcoming African hunt. The President talks about it continuously and spends much of his spare time studying maps and reading up jungle literature. What makes me interpolate something about it now is the thought of Kermit, the second son, whom the President is going to take with him. He is a splendid fellow, but looks more musical and literary than a huntsman. It may be that the President thinks he needs just this experience, though he says that Kermit has more endurance than any child he has. But if he were mine, I should say good-bye to him with a good deal of anxiety. There is some beautiful understanding between him and his mother. He always stands near her with his arm around her waist, and he never comes in a room that he does not go up and kiss her. I asked Miss Ethel this morning if he was not Mrs. Roosevelt's favourite. She said that it makes Mrs. Roosevelt angry to be accused of it, so evidently it has been noticed before. But in talking to Mrs. Roosevelt later about it, I told her what I had said to Miss Ethel, but she said she had been accused of being fonder of Kermit than the others, but it was due solely to the affectionate nature of Kermit, that he gave more affection and in the same proportion invited more display of affection.

As I came out of the water my leg was bleeding from a number of scratches from barnacles under the float. The President noticed it and asked how it happened. I laughingly said that Phillips had done it. The President then told the crowd that Phillips had worn his spurs in the water and that I had said that if Phillips was a gentleman he would cut his nails. Poor Phillips, who is the most ultra-type of a cultured Bostonian, could see no humour in the remark at all. All during the day the President would refer to it and ask me solicitously if I had used any antiseptics, as he heard poison from nail scratches was considered very dangerous.

There were a number of persons to lunch, several magazine editors and an artist, a sculptor and Dr. Lyman Abbott. The conversation was on more conventional lines and the charm of the informal meal was missing. I noted that a Rhine-wine cup was served and that the President only took one cup of it. It was not bad, either. When I think how seriously the people of Newport asked me if the President was drunk every night I simply get boiling. He does not seem to mind these reports at all. He told me this morning that when they are not saying that he is insane, they sadly admit the drunken theory.

"What difference does it make?" he said. "Only that which is true is going to last. The people have their own methods of finding out the truth."

But for all that, I should like the roof of this simple home to be removed for twenty-four hours and that the eighty million pair of eyes could be focussed on Sagamore Hill. What a revelation would be its simplicity, its naturalness, its moral poise, its genuine family life, and above all its united love and happiness! I am beginning to be affected by it. I keep forgetting that this is an historic visit I am making, that my host is the President of the United States and that I ought to try to chain in mind the things which are happening about me.

If he should come back from his African hunt, and the South with the rest of the country should call him to the Presidency again, what a vindication for his life and policies! Or if he should never return, what a priceless memory will be theirs who have served with him as I have, and who have seen this phase of his life!

In the afternoon Miss Ethel gave her much-talked-of Coney Island party. We went by motor along the Shore road, through Prospect Park, Brooklyn, and then to Coney Island. There were just the Winthrops, Phillips, Miss Ethel and myself. We did everything and took in the Bowery. It was my first trip to the island. We went there in two hours and a quarter from Sagamore Hill and made the trip back in two hours and a half.

I started this letter last night after coming in and got up at six o'clock, took a fresh-water bath and while waiting for breakfast have finished it. This is Sunday and I may or may not go to church. Whether I go or not, I am sure you will be there, so in thy orisons, dear mother, be all my sins remembered. Good-bye.

Your affectionate son,

ARCHIBALD.

XXIII

Sagamore Hill, Oyster Bay,
July 27 [1908].

MY DEAR MOTHER:

It is well on into Sunday night, but I will not go to bed before giving you some idea as to how the day has been spent. I have been to church, seen something of the religious side of the President and watched the marvellous character of Mrs. Roosevelt itself. She seems so perfectly unconscious of herself that one can study her at length without being balked in this study by conscious moments or anything resembling pose. She really constitutes the atmosphere of the house, a sort of feminine luminiferous ether, pervading everything and everybody.

The President with his rugged personality, the children with their Rooseveltian characteristics, might easily convert this home into a disorderly household if it were not for the ever-softening influence of Mrs. Roosevelt. She is perfectly poised and nothing seems to annoy her, and she permits nothing to disturb the routine of her housekeeping. I had noticed her routine at the White House, but there everything is so ordered and governed that it would run of its own momentum, but here one sees Mrs. Roosevelt just as she is, and her life and order at Sagamore Hill make me doubt whether after all the routine of the White House would be run so smoothly without her influence and guiding hand.

She came down Sunday morning to breakfast, breakfast being a half hour later than usual. Everybody was in a gay humour and each had to give an account of him or her self of the night previous before the President was satisfied. Mrs. Roosevelt announced at table that she and the President and the children were going to church and that they would not expect any of their guests to go unless urged to do so by their conscience, but that she would ask Mrs. Winthrop, but there her invitations would end. One by one the men spoke out and each had some excuse to offer for not going. At each excuse there was a burst of merriment, and when Ted finally said he had to remain to look after me, I dumfounded them all by announcing my intention to go. Kermit at once said with characteristic cynicism that if I was going only to make character with his mother it was unnecessary; that she was already committed to me.

I held my own against the onslaught of good-natured banter of the table, and it was finally agreed that I should have a seat in the automobile, in spite of the fact that Ted said my going to church would upset all arrangements, for the reason that every seat was already taken and the detective would have to be left behind, in which case the President might be killed and his death would be due solely to me. Long before this we had seen that Ted had mapped out a morning in which I was a chief actor. I did not tell them that I had received your letter only the night before expressing the hope that I would go to church and that it was with a feeling somewhat of loyalty to you that I had decided to do so. I did not regret it later, for it turned out to be a very delightful experience.

Before getting ready for church we began to make plans for the afternoon, and I soon saw that the President was not to be included in any of the arrangements for the day. He told me later that he did not regard it as either wicked or careless of holy things to play tennis or golf on Sunday, but he simply did not do any of these things on Sunday on account of the effect it might have on other people.

"I never want to see the observance of our American Sunday changed," he said. "There is a great deal to condemn in it, possibly, from a foreign standpoint, and a great deal that is narrow, but I believe it is wholesome and strengthening. It is very hard not to be able to shoot, for instance, on Sundays, but then the majority of our people believe it is wrong and I certainly would be the last to try to change their opinions. If I were a private citizen I would possibly join you to-day in tennis, but were I to do so as President all the papers in the country would have something to say about it and the example might be harmful to many. I am afraid that I sometimes shock the sensibilities of our people, but I never want to do so in any matters pertaining to the morals or the religious prejudices of the people."

All this sounds rather prosaic, but everything he says is accompanied by such exuberance and vivacity that he never seems to be preaching or moralizing. There is always a perfect abandonment in the way he gives out confidences and I often stop to wonder if it is the President of the United States speaking or some intimate chum of my college days. But when one remembers the way he stamps people liars when they repeat or betray these confidences one is careful to retain a certain silence regarding them. Of course, he is perfectly right, for what kind of honour has a man who will repeat private conversations or betray confidences? I have no doubt but that the President did tell Hobson just what Hobson repeated in the Democratic convention, for it sounds just like him; yet to let a statement like that go undenied or unchallenged would mean possibly a war with Japan. There is nothing for a man to do but deny it.

After all, a man is a liar who gains knowledge under false pretences and then betrays it, just as much of a liar as one who makes up conversations or repeats things which have never been said. . . .

The motor car came sooner than I had expected it; in fact, the presidential family had to be kept waiting while I put on shoes instead of the pumps I had slipped on for breakfast. I explained to the President as I took my seat that my tardiness was due to the discussion I had just had with Beekman Winthrop over Catholicism, I claiming that the Catholic rule in the world had done more harm than good, that without it we might have advanced in education and culture far beyond what we had already done; that in Cuba, after centuries of hierarchic rule, the only feeling that the Cubans had for the Church was one of intense hatred and contempt. He cited the Philippines and claimed that great good had been done there by the Catholic Church, etc., etc. The President, looking rather quizzically at me, said:

"Archie, when I discuss the Catholic Church, I am reminded that it is the only church which has ever turned an Eastern race into a Christian people. Is not that so?"

I did not know whether that was so or not, but I knew there was a rebuttal and I told him so, but that I would think the matter over before answering him.

Mrs. Roosevelt then asked what I thought Bishop Brent was going to do about the call to Washington.[1] I said I had no way of knowing, but that I hoped he would accept, as I thought he had the wisdom of the serpent if nothing else, and I believed that we should have ecclesiastics in

[1]The Rt. Rev. Charles H. Brent, now Bishop of Western New York in the Protestant Episcopal Church. His great service to his church and, indeed, to the world, was as Bishop of the Philippines. He declined the election to the Washington bishopric.

Washington who were capable of fighting Rome on its ground. The President then added:

"The great trouble Brent is going to have in changing his mind is that he put his declination on the Lord, so changing his mind now means changing the Lord's also. The trouble about these high church people is that they get so accustomed to putting everything on the Lord that they leave nothing for themselves to decide. Now if Brent had not said that the Lord had told him to do so and so he would have no trouble in changing his opinion, but it is a more serious thing when you take Jehovah into your confidence and then change without letting Him know."

The President expressed great admiration for Bishop Brent, however, but regretted that he was a celibate.

"You know as between a faith which admits of celibacy and one which admits of polygamy I infinitely prefer the one which proclaims polygamy in its tenets. That is why I have no sympathy with the Roman Catholic faith or the extreme ritualistic end of my wife's faith," this latter with a smile at Mrs. Roosevelt.

She then added that she was opposed to what was known as high church and thought the simpler you kept the form the purer you kept the faith, and that I would find in the little church at Oyster Bay just such a service as I would like. By that time we had arrived at the church door, where we found a row of boys, possibly forty in number, drawn up in line in front of the main entrance. They saluted as the President stopped in front of them, and he said:

"Boys, I am glad to see you; where do you come from and what are you doing here?"

"We are from Grace Church, New York," said the oldest, "and we came to see you."

"Well, I am mighty glad to see you, also, and the next

time you come to Oyster Bay you must come out to my home and see me."

The way he said it was cordial and emphatic, and each boy will carry in his mind as long as he lives this fleeting picture of the President.

The President has two pews on the side aisle, he and Mrs. Winthrop and I occupied the first one, and Mrs. Roosevelt, with Kermit and Miss Ethel, occupying the one behind us. The President bowed his head in prayer just as all good Episcopalians do on entering church, and so did each of us. As the service proceeded I noticed that the President followed the service without the use of a Prayer Book, singing the chants, even going through the Te Deum, without notes, as it were. He sang all the hymns and said the creed aloud. But I noticed that he did not bow his head in the creed nor did he at the Gloria. I suppose this was too much form for a member in good standing of the Dutch Reformed Church.

He has a poor idea of music, I imagine, for while he sang all the choral parts of the service, he was usually an octave lower than the choir in the hymns, but he did fairly well in the difficult Gregorian chants, much better than I who had sung in a choir at Sewanee, and I recognized the impossible formations of the syllables in the Te Deum and remembered, with a smile, how I used to work my jaws in it so that the precentor would not know that I was not singing. Well, the President got through it in the most wonderful manner. I came to the conclusion before the service was over that the President was at heart an Episcopalian, whatever his earlier training might have been. The hymns were evidently those sung in the North and not in the South, for I did not recognize one. I think the South likes strong, sentimental hymns, while every one which was sung at Oyster Bay had some poetic value.

They had an extra hymn interpolated without any reason, "Ten Thousand Times Ten Thousand," and as we left the church the President said:

"Why do you suppose, Edith, that they put in an extra hymn, and if they do put it in, why in the name of goodness don't they put in one which people can sing?"

"That is too funny," added Mrs. Roosevelt, "for they have added another hymn because they heard that you liked more singing."

"Did I ever say so?"

"Yes," said Mrs. Roosevelt, "you did in the presence of one of the choir last summer, so you have no one but yourself to blame."

"Well, then, please suggest to them if they do me the kindness to add more hymns to sometimes put in 'Jerusalem the Golden,' or 'Oh, Paradise; Oh, Paradise,' or something in which I can lift up my voice and praise."

This led to a discussion of hymns, and it was with some interest to hear each one mention his or her favourite hymn. Mrs. Roosevelt likes such hymns as "Nearer, My God, to Thee" and "Art Thou Weary," etc., while the President said his favourite hymn was No. 457,[1] beginning "Christ is made the sure foundation." His second favourite is "Holy, Holy, Holy, Lord God Almighty." He also expressed great admiration for "Jerusalem the Golden" and "The Son of God Goes Forth to War." For the first time I realized that I had no favourite hymn, but I think at my funeral I should like to have sung "Nearer, My God, to Thee." I have thought of it during the day and I believe

---

[1]A translation by John Mason Neale of a Latin plain song of the 7th century. The tune to which it is generally sung is by Henry Smart, a well-known English composer, and is one of the most stirring processionals in the Episcopal hymnal. It may have been the marching rhythm that appealed to Roosevelt, for he was not interested in the high-church theology of which this particular hymn is an expression.

that I shall take "Nearer, My God, to Thee" as my favourite. It appeals to the sentimental side of me at least.[1]

We left the President and his family at the West Roosevelts, where they go every Sunday to see "Aunt Emily," a charming elderly woman who seems to be sort of prophetess of the clan. Often after playing tennis we go over there, and we have never failed to find a large pitcher of orange or lemonade on the back porch. Whether any one comes for it or not, it is always kept there for the boys who care to come in for it. It is not necessary to speak to any one, and once, coming from swimming, Ted and I drank the entire pitcher and there was none for Kermit a little later, and to have heard the row it raised one would have thought the ten tables of commandments had been broken. As fast as the pitcher becomes empty it is supposed to be refilled immediately.

I went to Oyster Bay in the motor, as I felt I would be *de trop* at Aunt Emily's. I got out my pipe and borrowed some tobacco from the detective, Mr. Sloan, and enjoyed the ride back to Sagamore Hill. Mr. Sloan is the head detective, and a fine gentlemanly appearing man he is, too. There are several, and two are always on duty at Sagamore Hill. They station themselves night and day at angles where they can cover the entire house, and there is always a feeling of protection, though the President says it would have no effect at all on a really first-class anarchist.

"It would be a pretty poor anarchist who could not get me any hour he wished while I am playing tennis, riding horseback, and swimming."

The detectives try to do their duty, but it is impossible for them to know what the President will do. He never

[1]It is said by survivors of the *Titanic* that as the ship was going down Captain Butt ordered the band to play the music of this hymn.

takes them into consideration, and he darts from the house sometimes and is well a mile away before they have a chance to follow him. He will be on horseback and he says nothing to them, so that they cannot follow him. He seems to be utterly devoid of fear and never takes the possibility of accident into consideration. Sloan tells me that fifty detectives could not keep him covered, and that he really gets angry at times being followed, yet they do not allow his feelings in the matter to change their orders at all and one always tries to keep him in view. I seldom saw the detectives myself and often wondered what use it was to have them at the house when he was not there, but one day when we were all out of matches the President, who was playing tennis while two of us were not, there being six on the lawn, said:

"Why not see if the detectives have any? You will possibly find them with a weather eye on me from that clump of bushes over there."

I followed the directions and found the detective just where the President said they would be, lying in the grass smoking a pipe himself. He laughingly told me that while they were supposed to guard the President most of their time was taken up hunting places to conceal themselves in as he hates to be spied on all the time.

"If we did not keep out of his sight we would soon lose our jobs. He only lets us come here because the Madame wants us. If it was not to please her he would ship us away."

I found later that Mrs. Roosevelt not only insists upon the detectives, but keeps tab on them to see that they do not yield to the wishes of the President and keep too far out of sight.

To-night it was almost like fairyland. The air was soft and the President in a perfect gale of good humour.

Hardly any one talked but he, and he filled the evening telling of boyhood days and the fun he has had when he goes camping with children. It was almost as if Uncle Remus were among us to amuse us with stories, except that there was no dialect. He spoke of the fact that the boys never seem to remember that he is growing old and "shame upon me to have to admit it—fat." He recounted, for instance, last summer when they had dug or burrowed holes through all the haystacks and that nothing would do but that he should go through some of them. Also he said they ran in odd directions and once he got so badly mixed up that he had to burrow a new way for himself.

"The next day Justice Moody came to visit me and I put Kermit up to taking him through them. Of course he did not want to go and saw little fun in it at best, but to please them he went, and so did I to see the fun. Well, he got stuck in one hole and it was with some difficulty that he was gotten out. It was one of those circuitous routes which go up in the hay and then down. It would have been an easy job for Fairbanks, but Moody's build was not exactly made for quite such sudden turns. Next to Phillips going in swimming with his spurs on, I think it was as funny an incident as we have had here."

He talked a great deal about his proposed African trip.

"You know," he said, "how you feel when you have all but finished one job and are eager to get at another. Well, that is how I feel. I sometimes feel that I am no longer President, I am so anxious to get on this trip."

He told us where he was going, the route he would take, and so on. He has seen many hunters and has many maps laid out.

"If I were younger," he said, "I would do so and so, but I will never be the same man I was and I will have to

To the Secretary of War:

I wish the following memorandum filed in the record of Capt. Butt.

Captain Archibald W. Butt has been for eleven motnhs with me as chief aid. In addition to our purely personal association and the performance of his duties in connection with the White House proper, I have treated him thruout that time as a general in the field would treat a staff officer of unusual ability, because I have found that from him I was able to get information of real consequence to me in planning and working for the betterment of the Army conditions. He ~~is an exceptionably able and efficient officer; he has~~ has been an exceptionally tactful and diplomatic aide-de-camp; he is an exceptionally able and efficient officer; and if ever again it should befall me to command troops I should desire him to serve under me.

T. R.

President Roosevelt's official opinion of Captain Butt

cut my work to my capabilities. I shall avoid now what I would eagerly have sought ten years ago."

"Don't you think, Mr. President, that after you are out a month or so all your old vigour will return, and that you will be as good physically as you were in the Spanish War?" I asked.

Before he could answer, Kermit, who simply worships his father, said he felt sure that he would be as strong as ever. The President said he would like to think so, but he knew that he could not stand as much now as he could stand in the Spanish War; that he often felt inclined to stop and rest, and such a thing was unknown to him in the past. When asked by Winthrop what was the most dangerous animal he would find to hunt he promptly said: "the lion." He thought that most hunters thought the elephant, others the tiger, and many more the hippo, but from what he had heard and read he felt that the lion was by far the most dangerous, because it was the quickest.

"Others do not think him so, for the reason that you can kill the lion by shooting him in any part of the body, but his alertness and agility make him the most dangerous to me."

He said that Mrs. Roosevelt would meet him in Cairo as he came out of the desert, that he expected to be gone a year, and by that time he would be sufficiently forgotten that he could return to the United States without being a target for the newspapers. He said that he was not going near a capital in Europe, that he had decided to abandon the trip rather than be made into a peripatetic show. He was going to stay out of Abyssinia for the reason that he wanted to avoid the entertainment which he would get there.

"The King of Abyssinia has already sent me a lion and cubs and other pet animals of his, and he would expect me to come laden in such fashion were I to enter his domains. No, I want to keep entirely from sight if I can. I do not suppose it will prevent the papers, in the same shameless way as they did when I went West as Vice-President to hunt for game, from describing just what I had killed and what I had every night for supper. In that Western trip I never saw a newspaper man and none ever saw me, yet when I came out I found that my day's doings had been heralded right along, and even such men as Cabot Lodge were so taken in by the accounts that he wrote me, hoping that I would get the letter, that, if it were possible, to be less advertised, that it gave me the appearance of seeking too much notoriety. Yet not one of these papers ever contradicted one word of all the lies they had published."

He said that he would take only a few volumes with him, such as he could carry with ease.[1]

"I will not come on deck with the Bible in one hand and 'Vanity Fair' in the other, as a noted statesman from Indiana did on the Philippine trip, and then proclaim them 'my favourite bits of literature.' In spite of the fact that I do not care for Shakespeare I will take him, because I can get all of him in three pocket volumes. I don't care for dramatic poetry, but, of course, you get a lot of compressed thought in Shakespeare. I will take him just as the soldier takes the emergency ration, not for the quality, but for the largest amount of sustenance in the smallest possible space. I will see that Kermit takes his Bible, and I presume his mother will conceal the Book of Common Prayer somewhere among his underclothes."

And so the night wore on, and I am here trying to think

[1]Roosevelt eventually took into Africa a carefully selected list of books, specially bound for durability, which he called his "Pigskin Library." It is fully described in his "African Game Trails."

of some of the many things he said which made us all roar at the time, but nothing seems to come back to me. His humour is so elusive, his wit so dashing and his thoughts so incisive that I find he is the hardest man to quote I have ever heard talk. His style of narration is so peculiarly his own that it is hard to reproduce it. In fact he does not reproduce it himself in writing. He cannot follow himself with pen in hand. In conversation he is a perfect flying squirrel, and before you have grasped one pungent thought he is off on another limb whistling for you to follow. I can do all he does physically; I think that is one reason why he finds me agreeable to have about him, and I can follow him at times in conversation, even adding my share, but let him have the reins once between his own teeth fairly and squarely and he simply runs riot with the conversation. The only person I know who is his equal at all is Alfred Henry Lewis, and in conversation they remind me much of each other.[1]

By the way, to-night at dinner Kermit announced that I thought of going on Monday, but that he asked me to remain longer; but that I had declined to do so, as I had not been invited. This took some retraction on the part of Kermit and some explanation on the part of myself, but finally I agreed to stay, after which Kermit said that he had put the matter that way as he knew it was the only way to keep me.

"People are always afraid of staying too long in this house, so they hurry off as if they had not enjoyed themselves."

The President and Mrs. Roosevelt both told me after dinner that they wanted me to remain as long as I could,

[1]Lewis was a gifted, versatile, but somewhat erratic newspaper correspondent and story writer whose tales of frontier life had considerable vogue during his lifetime.

that while they felt that Sagamore Hill would bore many people they were conscious I was enjoying myself and that was all they wanted to know. As we went to bed that night Phillips said:

"What a wonderful man and what a still more wonderful woman! What a privilege it is to have seen this household as we have seen it."

"Yes," I added, "that is the greatest thing he has yet done, to hold his family simplicity and homelike love and surroundings as he has done here. It cannot be said of him as was said of Gladstone, that he hews the forest merely to be gazed upon. I think Mr. Roosevelt cuts down trees merely for the pleasure of hearing them fall. Just as he swims and plays tennis merely for the pleasure of straining his muscles and shouting. Yet when he reads he has such powers of concentration that he hears no noise around him and is unable to say whether people have been in the room or not. He is fondest, he says, of history and biography, and when he goes to light literature he wants ghost or detective stories. He says that he loves "The Upper Berth."

"Because," he says, "I want ghosts who do things. I don't care for the Henry James kind of ghosts. I want real sepulchral ghosts, the kind that knock you over and eat fire; ghosts which are ghosts and none of your weak, shallow apparitions."

Affectionately,
ARCHIBALD.

XXIV

Oyster Bay,
July 28th [1908].

MY DARLING MOTHER:

I can keep up with the President in all his outdoor sports, but I confess to being tired out and wanting to sleep when I come in, especially after eating the large old-fashioned meals which are most temptingly served in this house. I would have no trouble in keeping pace with the President, but when he is busy I do some stunts with Ted, then possibly walk late in the afternoon with Miss Ethel and ride with Kermit. I might say, as did General Castleman of Kentucky when they tried to get him intoxicated in Washington one winter, that he could put the whole of the District of Columbia under the table, but he could not meet the other states represented there in relays and still remain as sober as a Kentuckian should when off on his holidays.

By the way, the President told me this morning that Uncle Remus had printed our letter, as he called it, regarding the adoption of the "Battle Hymn of the Republic" as our National Anthem. "And I fear a few bricks coming our way, Captain Butt." The Jews, he said, had already protested against having a hymn as the national anthem with the name of Christ in it. But Julia Ward Howe was a Unitarian, and the Jews acknowledge the Saviour as a leader.

However, I suppose all the papers who oppose the President will take a fling at him and incidentally at myself. If one buzzes about the throne he must expect to get scorched occasionally. The President fattens on criticism, but I confess to liking to remain in the shadow. Did I ever repeat to you the witticism of William Kenley[1] about those who are stationed in Washington? It shows what the attitude of the rest of the army is to those who are stationed here. He came in my office when I was Depot Quartermaster and after chatting over Philippine times, said:

---

[1]Chief of Air Service and Commander 2nd Field Artillery Brigade in France, Director Military Aeronautics, April 26, 1918.

"Well, Butt, how do you like it here, anyway?"

"Well, Kenley, I don't give a damn to be in the light which beats around the throne."

"And I don't give a damn," he added quickly as lightning, "for the beats who light around the throne."

So there is no use to try to prove to anybody that you don't like to be stationed in Washington, for they simply take it for a pose and set you down as a liar.

I have got the President very much interested in Ty Cobb, the famous baseball player from Georgia. I told him I had given Ty a dinner at Clarence A. Edwards's house, and he wanted to know all about him and the others whom we had invited to meet Ty. Ty is only twenty-two years old and neither drinks nor smokes, and neither did any of the ball players who were there. That interested the President greatly, as he saw in this the perpetuation of the game in this country and its higher development.

Yesterday when I tried to get a smash over the net I landed the ball on the President's head.

"If you would emulate your statesman Ty more in placing your hits your partners would be in less danger," he laughed.

I think the President begins to feel worried about the political outlook for Taft. He does not like the lack of enthusiasm which is evident, or the situation as it is developing in Ohio and New York. I think it will be decidedly against his interest to have Taft elected, for should Bryan come in, and with his avowal that he would not take a second term, it would almost certainly mean Roosevelt again in the next four years, whereas if Taft is elected Mr. Roosevelt will have to stand out of his way for a second term. I do not think he weighs this side at all, or he will not allow himself to weigh it, for he is certainly going to do all in his power to have Taft succeed him. He has no fear for the country under Bryan. He says the latter has never been rightly understood in America and that it is absurd to class him as a Socialist or a dangerous character. He says he is a wonderful man and would make a strong, able President.

"And he is not a charlatan, either: he is a splendid politician and a wonderful leader. He has met with nothing but defeat so far, and yet he is stronger to-day than ever and will be the hardest man to beat, whatever the papers may say to the contrary.

"I believe that Taft will be elected, but if he is not the interests of this country could be entrusted and have been entrusted to much worse hands than those of William Jennings Bryan. Both parties, it seems to me, are breaking up, and it would not surprise me or any one else to find in the next few years an entirely different alignment. I should like to see the South broken and the parties so divided that each would have to put forward the best men they could find and on platforms which would represent the best and most honest opinions of the country, without regard to sections or petty interests or political advantages." . . .

Your affectionate son,

ARCHIBALD.

Captain Butt's impressions of Roosevelt's estimate of Bryan must be taken, I think, with a grain of salt. I had some correspondence and one long conversation with the President at the White House about Mr. Bryan during the summer of 1908. He did not doubt Mr. Bryan's sincerity, integrity, or good intentions, but he was far from having "no fear for the country under Bryan." His interpretation then was what it was in

1913 when he wrote what I have quoted under Letter XIV.

XXV

Washington, D. C.,
July 29, 1908.

MY DEAR MOTHER:

I spent the last night at Sagamore Hill with the President and sat until late talking on every subject under the sun, or rather the moon, for it flooded everything. I shall always remember this visit with the greatest pleasure. The individuality of each member of his family is indelibly impressed on my mind. . . .

The President . . . predicted, that last night we were together, that we should have war with Japan, not as soon as it was suggested as being in his mind, but he said it would be sure to come.

"No one dreads war as I do, Archie," he said. "As President I would go far to avoid it. The little that I have seen of it, and I have seen only a little, leaves a horrible picture on my mind. But the surest way to prevent this war with the East is to be thoroughly prepared for it." . . .

Your affectionate son,
ARCHIE.

It was this belief in preparedness which led Roosevelt to send the battle fleet round the world, a naval adventure which experts at home and abroad said was bound to end in disaster. In reality, it was an unprecedented success.

Of the purpose and achievement of this American Armada Roosevelt writes as follows in his Autobiography:

In my own judgment the most important service that I rendered to peace was the voyage of the battle fleet around the world. I had become convinced that for many reasons it was essential that we should have it clearly understood, by our own people especially, but also by other peoples, that the Pacific was as much our home waters as the Atlantic, and that our fleet could and would at will pass from one to the other of the great oceans. . . . Many persons publicly and privately protested against the move on the ground that Japan would accept it as a threat. To this I answered nothing in public. In private I said that I do not believe Japan would so regard it because Japan knew my sincere friendship and admiration for her and realized that we could not as a nation have any intention of attacking her; and that if there were any such feeling on the part of Japan as was alleged, that very fact rendered it imperative that the fleet should go. . . . In a personal interview before they left I explained to the officers in command that I believed the trip would be one of absolute peace, but that they were to take exactly the same precautions against sudden attack of any kind as if we were at war with all the nations of the earth; and that no excuse of any kind would be accepted if there were a sudden attack of any kind and we were taken unawares. . . .

It was not originally my intention that the fleet should visit Australia, but the Australian Government sent a most cordial invitation, which I gladly accepted; for I have, as every American ought to have, a hearty admiration for, and fellow feeling with, Australia, and I believe that America should stand back of Australia in any serious emergency. The reception accorded the fleet in Australia was wonderful, and it showed the fundamental community of feeling between ourselves and the great commonwealth of the South Seas. The considerate, generous, and open-handed hospitality with which the entire Australian people treated our officers and men could not have been surpassed had they been our own countrymen. The fleet first visited Sydney, which has a singularly beautiful harbour. The day after the arrival one of our captains noticed a member of his crew trying to go to sleep on a bench in the park. He had fixed above his head a large paper with some lines evidently designed to forestall any questions from friendly would-be hosts: "I am delighted with the Australian people. I think your harbour the finest in the world. I am very tired and would like to go to sleep."

The most noteworthy incident of the cruise was the reception given to our fleet in Japan. In courtesy and good breeding, the Japanese can certainly teach much to the nations of the Western world. I had been very sure that the people of Japan would understand aright what the cruise meant, and would accept the visit of our fleet as the signal honour which it was meant to be, a proof of the high regard and friendship which I felt, and which I was certain the American people felt, for the great Island Empire. The event even surpassed my expectations. I cannot too strongly express my appreciation of the generous courtesy the Japanese showed the officers and crews of our fleet; and I may add that every man of them came back a friend and admirer of the Japanese.

This battle-fleet cruise marks a high point in the international recognition of American authority in the Pacific Ocean which was crystallized in the Four-Power Treaty of the Washington Conference.

XXVI

The hiatus of nearly two months in Captain Butt's diarial record is the result of the "leave," referred to in Letter XX, which was spent chiefly in England. The allusion to Foraker in the following letter recalls one of the dramatic incidents of Roosevelt's presidency. In August, 1906, a shooting affray and riot occurred at Brownsville, Texas, in which the chief participants were soldiers of a Negro regiment stationed at an army post in that city. As it was a Southern city, feeling against these Negro soldiers was intense. President Roosevelt held an investigation and as the individual offenders would not confess or were shielded by their fellows Roosevelt discharged an entire battalion. Senator Foraker of Ohio who, although a Republican, was bitterly and, it was alleged, pecuniarily opposed to Roosevelt's policy regarding "big business" or the trusts, espoused the cause of the Negroes. He hoped to use negrophile influences to beat Roosevelt's administration measures. He failed, as most of those did who attacked Roosevelt by methods of political ambush, and died a few years later a disappointed and discredited man.

Washington, D. C.,
Sept. 23 [1908].

My darling Mother:

I am once more in harness and very busy. I arrived by steamer on Sunday night after a most frightful voyage. We were in the same gale of wind that so bruised up the *Mauretania*, so you can imagine what it did to our little craft.

The President arrived last night at 6:00. There was a great concourse of people to meet him, and as he passed through the station the crowd broke into a yell of cheers. Mrs. R. is looking very well, and they both gave me the heartiest kind of a welcome. I went to his office this morning and entered as usual without being announced. He looked up and saw me and said: "This is the first time I am not glad to see you. I am going to devote the entire morning to answering Mr. Bryan's letter-telegram of last night. I have not the time even to ask you what you have been doing since your trip to Oyster Bay." I did not wait for any more, but went at once.

He is really carrying the whole weight of this campaign on his shoulders. He came out yesterday with a letter which appears to be a powerful blow to Foraker. The latter has been divorced from the Republican [campaign] entirely, as it is shown that he has been a regular paid attorney for the oil trust. Mr. Bryan sent him a telegram last night which seemed to put the President in an awkward position, but it is this communication which he was answering this morning when I went into the room.

Bryan is making a wonderful campaign and the Republicans are very anxious. Mr. Roosevelt is the only person who can save the day and so he has really taken the entire burden of it on himself. He is not half hearted for Taft, and there is nothing personal in his attitude.

He only wants to see his policies continued. He wants no let up until he has driven corruption out of public life. It is almost an obsession with him, and while he admires Bryan, he has not that confidence in him that he has in Taft. The whole fight seems to be centring about him. Both Taft and Bryan are trying to convince the people that each is better fitted to carry out the Roosevelt policies. That seems to be the only issue. Isn't it remarkable to see a campaign conducted on such lines?

I spent some time with Mrs. R. to-day talking of plans for the White House next winter. She feels worried about the President, for, as she says, this conducting the campaign for someone else is far more trying than having his own to look after, for if he makes a blunder they can lay the blame of failure on him.

. . . .

This is all of interest to-day, except possibly that on my return I found a very interesting letter from Julia Ward Howe telling me how much she thought of my opinion in the matter of the "Battle Hymn." She also sent me a most interesting history of how she came to write it. She also gave me the information that she had Southern blood in her veins and that she was related to Gen. Marion and that there were strains of the South in her. . . .

As ever, your devoted son,

ARCHIE.

XXVII

Oak Glen, Melville Station.
Newport, R. I., Aug. 8, 1908.

CAPT. A. W. BUTT:

My dear Sir: I am much obliged for your letter and inclosure. I had only heard vaguely of your conversation with the President when a Boston paper telephoned to me, asking how I felt about it—the conversation.

I have taken time to write for you a little screed relating the circumstances under which my "Battle Hymn" was written. A very similar account is given in my volume of "Reminiscences," published some years since by Houghton, Mifflin & Co. of Boston. With it is printed a facsimile of the hymn as I scribbled it, without much swing, on that early morning. It would gratify a dear wish of my heart if the South would adopt my verses. Like our beloved President, I have in my veins a strain of Southern blood. My maternal grandmother was a niece of Gen. Francis Marion. A Mrs. Bullock, who lived in Savannah, Georgia, was her niece.

Believe me, dear sir, very cordially yours,

JULIA WARD HOWE.

In the memorandum inclosed in her letter to Captain Butt Mrs. Howe describes a visit which she made to Washington during the Civil War not long after the first battle of Bull Run. Her husband, Doctor Howe, the great teacher of the blind; Governor Andrew, the famous war governor of Massachusetts; and the Rev. James Freeman Clarke, an eminent Unitarian clergyman of Boston, were her companions. Her "little screed" reads partly as follows:

Between Baltimore and the capital my husband pointed out to me the pickets, groups of soldiers, gathered about a fire, who were set to guard the railroad from attack, the enemy's forces being in the near neighbourhood.

In my mind a little spirit seemed to be saying to me:

"You can't be of any use here. You can't leave your nursery full of young children to help on the battlefield or tend patients in the hospitals."

It chanced that a number of us went out, one day, to be present at a review of the Union troops. While it was still in progress, the manœuvres were interrupted by an attack on the part of the enemy. We saw the re-enforcements gallop to the assistance of their comrades, but the holiday function was perforce suspended. Troops and spectators were to return to Washington. We were obliged to drive very slowly, as the troops, marching to quarters, encumbered the road. To beguile the tedium of the way, we began to sing some of the songs familiar at that time, among others the well-known one:

> John Brown's body lies a-mouldering in the ground;
> His soul is marching on.

This seemed to please the soldiers, who shouted, "Good for you."

Presently Mr. Clarke, who was with me in the carriage, said:

"Mrs. Howe, why don't you write some good words to that tune?" I replied that I had wished to do this, but had not found it possible.

I went to bed that night as usual, and slept quietly, but in the gray of the early dawn I suddenly found myself awake, and the lines of my Battle Hymn began to suggest themselves to my mind. It was as if they had written themselves out before me.

"I must get up," I thought, "and write this down."

I had long been accustomed to write without looking, when, in my darkened room at night, one of my dear babes lay sleeping. This made it possible for me in the dim light to scrawl the long lines which I made haste to copy in the later morning. After writing out the hymn I went back to bed, as it was still very early.

The poem was published in the *Atlantic Monthly* magazine for February, 1862.

Thus was born the "Battle Hymn of the Republic," which, as is related in Letter XI, Roosevelt, the Northerner, and Archie Butt, the Southerner, conspired to make, not a sectional, but a national hymn of patriotism.

XXVIII

Washington, D. C.,
September 25 [1908].

MY DEAREST MOTHER:

I have come into the sunset of this Administration, but I fear that it will leave an afterglow that will be seen for many years to come. The President has taken on himself the entire burden of the Taft campaign, and while I regret he has done this I realize fully that he could hardly have done otherwise, he being Mr. Roosevelt. . . .

He really puts his policies over any individual interests he might have. If he would leave things alone and disappear for four years, at the end of that time, I believe, and so does every one here, I think, believe, that the nation would call him to the Executive chair again, but as he said to me yesterday: "There must be no let-up until grafters and dishonest people are driven from public life." He seems to have driven Senator Foraker to the wall, but behind Foraker there is a large crowd of friends who resent the exposé of their idol and they will remain hidden until later.

He has attacked Haskell, the treasurer of the Democratic campaign committee, and forced his retirement, and in doing so has let loose the flood gates of Bryan's eloquence against him.

Bryan, by the way, is making the most wonderful campaign, clean, sound, and vigorous. At the present time it is a toss-up as to who will win. It was the fear of the Republicans which forced Mr. Taft to appeal to the President.

Mr. Roosevelt gets the credit of "butting in," but the fact is that Mr. Taft made the appeal to Mr. Roosevelt to help his cause. Mr. Taft did not want the odium of expelling Foraker from the Republican ranks, and nothing would give the President more pleasure. But the day he forced Foraker and Haskell out of prominence he also forced Du Pont from the Republican committee. I never saw the President in such a rage as he was the day that it was shown up that Du Pont was as much in touch with the trust as Haskell. He waded into every one who came near him. He said he advised that Du Pont should be ousted a month ago, but the Republican committee did not act; then a week ago he said to the committee again that Du Pont must go, but still it hesitated, and it was only after his indictment of Haskell that the Republicans let Du Pont go, so nothing was gained politically.

The President still seems to be the idol of the nation, but whether he can continue his fight for Taft and retain his ascendency I do not know. He feels that he has made no mistake, but that is because it gives him the opportunity to continue his fight for political purity. I dined with him night before last and went with him and Mrs. Roosevelt and Postmaster-General Meyer to the theatre to see "A Gentleman from Mississippi," a play founded on politics and showing up the corruption which is said to exist in the Senate. . . .

During one of the entire acts he spoke of his enjoyment but added, "It makes me very melancholy to think that such things can exist." . . .

Then he began to call the roll of the Senate, and as each name would come up he dismissed him as either being capable of such grafting or as not being. His indictment of some of the senators was simply terrific. He spoke of Aldrich, and said that while he knew nothing definite against him his whole life in politics made him a man to be shunned. Hale, he said, was without conscience, whose motives were always petty and spiteful. Yet there is Tillman, he said, whose blatant radicalism offsets his sturdy honesty and minimizes the power of his brain. He said he would not trust the word of Gallinger, and Bacon only had to know what someone else wanted to oppose it.

He was getting so confidential on the subject of the Senate that I was glad when the curtain went up. But on the way back to the White House he kept harping on the Senate.

"The Senate will never clean itself," he said. "It can only be cleaned by making any form of grafting so obnoxious that the nation will drive from politics any one even suspected of dishonest motives."

He then referred to the investigation of the Senate when a number of senators, especially Senator Quay, was shown to have speculated in sugar while the tariff bill was in the Senate under consideration, and that after a half-dozen senators confessed to being interested in sugar they were allowed to continue in their seats.

"We have progressed so far," he said, "that such a state of affairs is unimaginable now. Those men would have been scourged from public life now."

He liked the play so much that the next day he had some of the company presented to him at the White House.

He has not taken any exercise since he came to Washington this time. He is suffering from an old wound he received several years ago in a trolley accident when one of his detectives was killed and Mr. Cortelyou was injured also. At that time it was thought the bone of his leg was injured, but he apparently recovered. He told me yesterday that whenever he gets tired or gets a jar it pains him again. I am afraid he is going to have trouble with it in Africa, for I have seen cases like this one develop most seriously in the tropics. It would not surprise me if he had to have a part of the bone taken out later. He is still keen on his African trip. He asked me to come to the White House to see him at 5:00 yesterday, and when I got there he sent word that he might be delayed, so if I had anything to do not to wait. I hung about for an hour and it was 6:00 before he came in looking tired and worn out. When he saw me, however, he clapped his hands together and exclaimed, smiling:

"Poor old De Graffenried! I certainly feel sorry for you, to be forced to be around that man Roosevelt, who never keeps his engagement."

He has found a new name for me. He read Al Lewis's sketch of Archibald De Graffenried Butt, and so he now insists upon calling me De Graffenried. I told him it was one of our family names and—well, I suppose I will always be De Graffenried to him now. I don't think he liked the name Archie, for he says that Mrs. Roosevelt never knew whether he was talking about me or his son Archie.

We talked for an hour about his African trip, and I gave him my experience in the tropics with woollens and cotton goods, and I am to purchase his outfit largely for him. He has decided to stop in England on his way home, as he has been invited to deliver some famous lecture at Oxford University. The university is going to bestow on him the same honour as it did on Gladstone and Emperor William. He says he does not care so much about the degree as he does for the opportunity to deliver the address. I told him what had been my impression while in England and how the English people seemed to admire him.

"Yes," he said, "I do seem to appeal to the imagination of the British, but just why I do not know. The Germans have apparently some enthusiasm for me, but it always strikes me as if it is worked up, while that in England seems to be sincere.

"I do not like the idea of touring the world. I thought it a mistake in Grant, and in the case of poor old Seward it was pitiful. For, after all, we are only private citizens and have no right to expect anything. I had intended to avoid all European countries, but this invitation offered makes it not only permissible for me to go into England but proper. Just how I can pay a visit to Edward and not to Nephew William, I hardly see, but I shall not go into any country without an invitation which I can accept with dignity."

And this leads to a very funny incident. At dinner the other night he said that while abroad he might be called upon to attend functions where it would not be proper to go in ordinary citizen clothes, and he seriously objected to wearing knickerbockers and black stockings, and that, while he had never owned a dress military uniform, he thought he would get me to order him a uniform of a colonel of cavalry, and asked my advice as to the justification he had to use it. I told him he had the legal right and it was so prescribed in orders, and that the uniform as it existed when he was a colonel was brilliant with yellow plumes and gold lace: in fact, the handsomest and most showy uniform we have ever had in the service. He said he would order one of Hasas and wear it with patent leather boots.

I saw at once that Mrs. Roosevelt disapproved and she began laughing at the idea.

"Theodore, I would never wear a uniform that I had not worn in the service, and if you insist upon doing this I will have a vivandière's costume made and follow you throughout Europe."

He took it good-naturedly, but she told me afterward that his weak spot was disliking to be laughed at in the family. "I will not have him wear a uniform in Europe, for they would ridicule him in this country."

She then told me not to encourage it and to keep postponing it if he should refer to it again. He did the next day, and he says he sees no reason why he should not wear the uniform he was entitled to wear as Colonel of the Rough Riders; and I must confess I do not either. He will certainly make a more imposing figure than in our abominably ugly frock coat. She usually has her way with him in such matters, and it remains to be seen what the outcome will be. I hope, however, he does not get me to order it for him should he persist in this fancy. . . .

Your devoted son,

ARCHIBALD.

Roosevelt did not "persist in this fancy" but during his European trip wore whatever the customs and manners of an American gentleman in private life required. In my "Impressions of Theodore Roosevelt" will be found an account of the amusing complications that arose about his costume at the funeral of King Edward, his cordial conformity to the antiquated and somewhat absurd requirements of the Court officials, and his reply to the American military attaché who protested against these requirements, "Why, Mott, if the English people want me to, I'll wear a pink coat and green-striped trousers!"

The inception of Roosevelt's plan for his African expedition is entertainingly described by Carl Akeley, the African explorer and sculptor, in his introduction to the new edition of "African Game Trails." Akeley, at a dinner at the White House, told a story of an African cave from which he had seen sixteen lions emerge. Roosevelt, turning to a Congressman at the table, remarked that he wished he had those sixteen lions to turn loose in Congress with which august assembly he was just then having some difficulty. "But, Mr. President," said the Congressman, "aren't you afraid they might make a mistake?" "Not if they stayed long enough," replied the President amid general laughter.

XXIX

Washington, D. C.,
September 30 [1908].

MY DARLING MOTHER:

Since I last wrote I have had a birthday, but did not remember it until it was too late to drink my own health. I am beginning to feel old, but the fact that the club begins to bore me, rather than my looking glass, warns me of approaching age. . . .

Yesterday I had rather a strenuous day of it. I had what I should call my first ambassadorial day. Bromwell is away and, in fact, there is no one here to help me, and the entire business at the White House devolves upon me. I had a chat with the President in the morning about Africa, and at 2:30 was at the White House in the full-dress uniform, in spite of the fact that the thermometer was over eighty, to present the Japanese Ambassador and the Swedish Minister. They both arrived within five minutes of each other, so I put the Jap in the Blue Room and the Swedish Minister in the Red Room. When both were safely behind doors I went for the President, who was not in the best of moods because Bryan had once more taken up the pen.

But whatever his humours, I must say that I have never seen him in bad temper with a member of his family household and he is always courtesy itself to his aides. He reserves his ill humours for those deserving them. I had never seen him as the diplomat, and it was therefore rather interesting to watch him playing the game with the Japs.

The Ambassador had made an appointment to present a Prince Kara, a very remarkable man, it seems, and who either now [is] or at a former time [was] Secretary of what would be the Interior in this country. I never saw such a polished Oriental. He did not look Oriental, and as the President afterward remarked to me, "He looks far more Parisian than the French Ambassador himself." He could not speak English, but said that he spoke French.

Whereupon the President began to speak French in the softest accent. It seemed to me that he spoke much more fluently than did Prince Kara, and I felt considerable pride in his accomplishment. As we went into the room I walked in ahead of the President and simply announced, "The Japanese Ambassador—the President." The Ambassador then presented the Prince, and the President waved them to seats and turning to me said, "Captain, will you please draw up a chair and be seated?" I paid not the slightest heed to him, but walked back about three yards and stood like a statue until the interview was over. I have a perfect horror of sloppy military etiquette and nothing could be more sloppy than sitting in the presence of the President on such a formal occasion. I have made up my mind never to be anything but most formal on formal occasions.

The President was most diplomatic, and when the Prince referred to the regret his nation felt over the exclusion of the Japanese, the President added yes, that it was unfortunate that the labouring classes could never live amicably, but that he felt it was better to keep the labourers of the two nations apart so that they would have no opportunity to involve the nations themselves in trouble. The friendship of Japan was too valuable to this country to have it impaired by petty labour squabbles.

Each time the President met this wily Oriental in just such a reply, and I seemed to see my chief in a new light. There was nothing of the big stick, but only the gloved fingers. As I bowed them out the President said, pleased as pickles with himself:

"I don't claim to be a perfect French scholar by any means, but did you notice the Prince putting up signals of distress and finally abandoning his French altogether? I don't think he thought I could speak French, so I was glad to run away with him in our 'court language'."

We then had a half-hour session with Baron Lagercrantz, the Swedish Minister. The President seemed to know what a time they were having in Sweden, for he said how sorry he was to see the growth of Socialism in that country. Then with tears in his eyes the poor Baron told how he had always had the devotion of the labourers on his place, yet when he went home this summer, the young peasants on his estate would not even lift their hats to him.

"What is the cause of it? I cannot understand it," said the President.

"It is the newspapers," said the Baron. "In our country as in your own, in fact, as it is in every country now, the newspapers tell all of the evil and none of the good, so that the unenlightened have begun to think that there is nothing but rascality and corruption in public life."

"And so it seems to be here," added the President, "but this is the age when the public demands to know everything about its affairs, and the press will continue to abuse this privilege until the public is better educated, and then the press will find its level and simply purvey the news."

Lagercrantz is a very simple type and seems to take everything very much to heart. He said he was a member of the Salvation Army, which struck me as being very incongruous, for he is very elegant in manner and exquisite in dress. . . .

The night before, De Koven opened here with his new opera, "The Golden Butterfly," and sent a box to General [Clarence] Edwards and Charley McCauley. They had a dinner at the Edwardses and afterward occupied a box, I being one of the party. The opera is not up to "Robin Hood," although De Koven thinks it is his masterpiece. It may be, from a musical standpoint. So last night I had the same crowd to dine with me, giving them a simple wholesome meal. There were Fred Chapin, Oden Hoerstman, McCauley, Colonel Denny, Clelland Davis of the Navy, and they were quite as noisy and hilarious as my party to-night was sedate and dignified.

They did not leave here until late and then, as they were starting, Hoerstman bet Davis that he could not make the distance from my house to the Metropolitan Club at golf in ten strokes. The bet was ten dollars, and Denny took another ten that he could not do it in fifteen. I loaned a putter and balls, and so they started out, the rest of us being judges and caddies. You can imagine what an absurd spectacle they were. A policeman came up to see what it all meant and agreed to go with us to give countenance to the performance. While it was only three blocks away, yet he lost both bets, but I think another match is to be played from the club to the Capitol in the daylight. Davis lost two balls in sewers, and one disappeared in John Baker's deserted house on H Street.

It is now after 12:00 and I am sufficiently tired to go to sleep. Good night, dear mother. I miss you very, very much.

As ever, your devoted son,
ARCHIBALD.

XXX

Washington, D. C.,
October 2 [1908].

MY DARLING MOTHER:

. . . Yesterday afternoon we played tennis at the White House, and the President, choosing me for a partner, called Captain McCoy and Captain Van Horn. We beat them three sets, but two of the sets were love sets. As we went in to have tea we met Mrs. Longworth [Alice Roosevelt] and she asked who won. The President said:

"The two old Southern gentlemen whipped the two Yankees."

Whereupon Mrs. Longworth quickly retorted, "I should put it that the Cracker[1] team won out." [*Unfinished letter, not signed.*]

XXXI

[Date and address missing.]

Well, my luncheon went off very well, although I was there only during the first two courses. Besides the Duvalls and their guest, there were Captain McCoy and Mrs. Garlington, wife of the Inspector General. She is from the West, dresses rather well and is a good talker, keeping things on the move. Just before luncheon was announced a message came from the White House that the President would have a conference with the Belgian Minister, presumably about the Bulgarian squabble. So in the midst of the luncheon I had to excuse myself and don full-dress uniform. I left Captain McCoy in command of the table, and they remained over an hour longer, and the butler tells me they had an awfully good time.

To my horror, when I got upstairs, I remembered that I had sent my dress-suit trousers to have the gold lace renewed and that they had not come back. So I had to wear undress trousers of a different shade of blue and different quality of cloth. I did not think the President would notice this makeshift of a uniform, but I stole out of the house to avoid saying good-bye to my guests, as I did not

[1] "Cracker" is a local term for the uneducated and poverty-stricken whites of some of the Southern States. It is derived from the supposed fact that they live so largely upon cracked corn.

want General Duvall to catch me in such a mixture. I share his horror of badly uniformed officers, and while he would have understood my dilemma, still he would have felt shocked just as I would have done under similar circumstances.

When I got to the White House the President was having a conference with George R. Sheldon, Treasurer of the Republican committee. One by one the campaign managers seek the advice of the President. Some of the old leaders are fearful that his participation in the campaign may be harmful, but they would be at sea without him now. The old-line politicians have been swept off the board, and the new crowd with Hitchcock have proved entirely inadequate to the demands up to the present time.

Mr. Roosevelt is the greatest force in the Party to-day, far and away the most expert tactician, and without his personality there would be an awful slump in the matter. I heard him tell one of the managers the other day that he could not continue to be "butting in" and the best thing for him to do would be to keep hands off, yet whenever they get in a tight place they come to him, and he simply sacrifices himself for what he believes to be the good of the country. If he had not renounced the Presidency, he might be in a more difficult place, but he voluntarily waved aside this tremendous honour in order to remain true to his word and to the really important tradition established by Washington. The moment he voluntarily put aside the Presidency, that moment he had the same right as any other patriotic citizen to advise the people of the country the best policy to follow. That is the way I look at it, and I feel rather indignant when I hear people about me question his right to take part in the campaign.

Well, I did not mean to enter into a political discussion with you. At any rate he was telling the treasurer how to run this campaign when I reached the White House. The Belgian Minister arrived and was shown into the Blue Room. His engagement was for 2:45, and at that time the President was sitting on the edge of the sofa in the Red Room pounding his fist on the arm. Whether to interrupt or not was questionable, and Mr. Stone, the old factotum at the Executive Mansion, advised me not to do so as he might be angry. However, I thought it his duty to be prompt with the representative of another country, and whether it was his duty or not, it was mine to remind him of the engagement, so, much to the horror of Mr. Stone, I stepped into the room and simply waited.

"I will be with you in a moment, Captain," he said, and continued to talk.

I stepped out of the door into the corridor about two feet and there remained standing until he finally cut the interview short and came out. I thought he was a little irritated, but I knew I was right and I knew he would know it, too. He puts himself too thoroughly in the hands of those about him not to be rigid in handling him. I entered the room and announced him, and I heard him start off with: "I sent for you, Mr. Minister." I took this as my signal and disappeared into the corridor, for I knew by the set of his mouth and the intonation of his voice that he had something to say of importance and that no witnesses should be present. . . .

Enough. Good-bye,

ARCHIE.

XXXII

Washington, D. C.,
October 6 [1908].

MY DEAR MOTHER:

Bryan and Taft are hammering at each other in the West. Of course my horizon is that of the White House and if the President looks worried I feel anxious for Taft, but if he is in a rollicking humour I take it as a sign that he has heard something to the detriment of the Democratic cause. . . . I never did take much stock in the reports that he was constantly doing things without giving them thought—in other words, going off half cocked. He thinks most rapidly and reaches conclusions while other people are stating the premises, but there is thought, and deep thought, in every act of his, whether it is merely which horse he is going to ride or which candidate he is going to appoint, or what policy he is going to adopt. I have seen enough of him to know that he does not do things unadvisedly. They may be regarded as ill advised and he may make serious mistakes, but whatever he does he does after thinking, and hard but very rapid thinking. He is not as impetuous as he likes to appear. He was talking last night after the tennis game and was rehashing some of the San Juan Hill gossip, especially that bit about the proposed retreat.

"When the matter was brought to my attention," he said, "I not only did not agree to the retreat, but told General Wheeler that if a retreat was ordered that I did not know whether I would obey or not. I do not now know whether I would have obeyed it, but I would have done some quick thinking had the order been actually given. Had I disobeyed the order it would have been regarded as an impetuous act, I presume, but it really would have been the result of careful thought after carefully weighing the pros and cons."

This furnishes a very fair illustration as to his method of coming to conclusions. . . .

I am going to lunch at the White House to-day and I will have to go in full regalia, as I am to present the Austro-Hungarian Ambassador at 2:30 and at 2:45 the

Secretary of the German Embassy, Prince Hatzfeldt, presents Doctor Koch to the President. This Hatzfeldt is the cousin of the Prince Hatzfeldt whom I met at Ostend and [who] played such monstrous stakes at baccarat. Cloman[1] and I watched the baccarat game for several nights, and I never saw Prince Hatzfeldt make a bet of less than three thousand francs and more often between eight and twelve thousand. He married, you may remember, the adopted daughter of Collis Huntington. It was about Hatzfeldt that the latter made the famous remark, "Princes come high but we must have them." They really came higher than even old Huntington suspected, for at his death Prince Hatzfeldt threatened to break his will and finally compromised for another three million.

Don't suspect that I am beginning to like this life overmuch. It has certain compensations, chiefest of which is the association with the President and his wife. The more I see of them, the more I see in them to admire. I am kept busy, though. I sometimes change my clothing five and six times a day. I find that I have little time to accept invitations out, so when I am not at the White House I am at home and really I am more at home than if I were accepting invitations out to dinner every night. [*Unfinished letter, not signed.*]

XXXIII

October 7th [1908].

MY DEAR MOTHER:

We had such a delightful luncheon party at the White House yesterday. The guest of honour was Mr. Zangwill, the Jewish author, who is now in Washington to witness the initial performances of his latest play, "The

[1]The late Lt. Col. Sydney B. Cloman, who saw service in the Philippines, at Panama, as attaché in London, the author of "Myself and a Few Moros."

Melting Pot." The Secretary of War, the Secretary of State, the Secretary of Commerce and Labour, Mr. Straus and Mrs. Straus, and a few minor personages like myself. The Straus family are Jewish, of course, and so the luncheon had a decidedly Semitic flavour.

I was much interested in Zangwill. I had always heard that he was slouchy and ill kept and inclined toward soiled linen. On the contrary, he was extremely punctilious as to his dress and he had the air of always being clean and well dressed. He was very easy in his manner, far more so than most persons coming to the White House. He has the typical Jewish cast of countenance, is ugly but extremely intellectual in appearance. His wife looks only slightly Jewish, more English than Jewish, and was dressed in a rather artistic style, with a low sweeping hat with feathers and a sort of Empire gown.

The conversation was carried on largely by the President and Zangwill, the latter quite talking back at Mr. Roosevelt when he disagreed with what he was saying. The President criticized severely certain passages in his play, which gets its name from the fact that America is a pot where all the nations of the world are melted down and become as one. In fact, as Zangwill said yesterday, the Jewish problem breaks to pieces as soon as it comes to the United States; the Jews cease to be Jews as they are Jews in Germany, Russia, and France, but become simply citizens of the United States.

In one passage of "The Melting Pot" Zangwill makes one of his women say, when they tell her it is not necessary to keep her vow to her fiancé, that not being an American she still regards her marriage vow as sacred. The President told Zangwill that he had not a right to take advantage as an author to indict a whole people. Zangwill replied that it never hurt to indict a majority, that it was only when a small minority was indicted that it cut; that persecution was only persecution when applied to a small people like the Jewish nation. The President said then that an indictment was wrong where particular or peculiar conditions were made to apply to the whole and that, whereas there were too many divorces in America, yet there were only a little more than 1 per cent. of the whole which were divorced, leaving $98\frac{9}{10}$ of the marriages in America pitched upon much higher planes than the marriage state anywhere else in the world. He added that if he, Zangwill, had said that this woman not being a native-born member of the four hundred, etc., he would have found no objection to the statement. Whereupon Mr. Zangwill said he would change his play to this extent. When the President incidentally referred to his African trip and to the fact that he would be out of a job after March 4th, Zangwill said:

"I can offer you a kingdom somewhere in the East, Mr. Roosevelt."

"I am not unmindful of the fate of the last man to whom you offered a kingdom," said Mr. R., laughing, but added seriously: "I fear I have not enough sympathy with it. I believe in amalgamation of the Jews, letting them hold to their faith, but only as a denomination of faith such as a Roman Catholic, Episcopalian, Methodist, etc."

"That is very well as far as the States are concerned, but in the meantime I want to see the Jewish people taken out of bondage of Europe."

The President was most interesting and no one else did any talking but these two, even Secretary Root listening intently to the discussion which was carried on across the table. After lunch the Austro-Hungarian Ambassador was presented by me to the President, by appointment, and as I presumed the interview was on the subject of

Turkey and Austria and the Balkan States, I hastened out of earshot. After this conference was over we went into the Green Room, where was Prince Hatzfeldt with the eminent German doctor of science, Doctor Koch, and his wife. Koch spoke English badly, but his wife, a large, well-groomed blonde Teuton type, spoke English fluently and interested the President more than most women seem to do. She and her husband had been in Africa for two years—he investigating the sleeping disease there and other microbic troubles indigenous to that climate.

Doctor Koch had hunted a good deal, and he seemed to know as much about hunting as did the President, and the President in turn seemed to know as much about Doctor Koch's specialties in science as did the doctor himself. Every now and then the President would lapse into German and carry on an animated conversation with Koch. I noticed that the President took occasion to tell Koch, as if Prince Hatzfeldt were not present, that he would deliver the Romanes lecture at Oxford University and that he had been invited by the French Academy to deliver some equally famous lecture in France. I could see Hatzfeldt calculating how quickly he could apprise the Emperor of these facts, and I feel sure that in less than a month the new German Ambassador will be inviting the President to do some stunt in Germany.

With much love to all,

Archibald.

XXXIV

Washington, D. C.,
October 9, 1908.

My dearest Mother:

Imagine my surprise when in leaving the White House yesterday the President said to me:

"I understand that my wife and daughter have been

asked to lunch or dine with you some time. I wish you to know that I am not accustomed to be left out on such occasions, and unless I am specifically 'not wanted' I shall expect an invitation also."

I merely laughed, thinking he was joking, for it is an unwritten law almost that he never dines or lunches outside the White House save with members of his cabinet. However, when I saw Mrs. Roosevelt later after the musicale she opened the subject herself by saying that she had merely mentioned to Ethel at luncheon that same day I wanted them in to a family dinner, and that she thought it would be nice to go. Whereupon the President entered the conversation by declaring that he wanted to go also. I told Mrs. Roosevelt that I would, of course, feel greatly honoured, but that it could hardly be expected that the President would find time to come. She seemed to think he was in earnest, however, and so it has developed.

When I went into his office this morning he greeted me with the remark:

"I have accepted your solicitous invitation to lunch with you on Tuesday next," and proceeded to write it down on his calendar.

What I will give them to eat I have not decided, but it will be the simplest of luncheons, not very different from what I have every day. I shall make it Southern and will give him, among other things, a huge dish of rice. I hope it will not get in the papers, for it is breaking a precedent for him to lunch out in this fashion, and it would look to many that I was using my position as aide to exploit myself, whereas I have done nothing of the kind, and merely while out walking with Mrs. Roosevelt one day I asked her if some time she would like to dine with me to look over the old things I had picked up here and there.

She is what she calls a great "snooper" herself, and says I must be one from what she hears of my house. "Snooping," as she defines it, is the art of finding quaint and valuable things in junk heaps and the ability to get them cheap. The day we were out walking she said, with that inimitable little laugh of hers:

"Snoopers are born, not made. Now Ethel thinks she is a snooper, but she really isn't, and does not know the first principle of snooping. No amount of training would make the President a snooper. He would possibly pass over the most charming articles of china or bronze and end by buying a brass bedstead. Alice is better, but of all my children Kermit is the ideal snooper. He has the nose of the perfectly bred snooper."

We went riding yesterday, McCoy, Ethel, a friend of hers, Miss Alexander, and I. We went to Chevy Chase, where the finals in the tennis tournament were being played. The Marine Band was there and a crowd of people. We came in early, as the President had asked us to have tea with him in his office after his game. We were a little late, and when we arrived we found the President, Ambassador Jusserand and his wife, Postmaster General Meyer and Billy Phillips. Mme. Jusserand had come down for her husband in the motor car and was pouring tea when we entered. It seems that the President and Phillips had been badly beaten by Jusserand and Secretary Meyer. Seeing me, he said:

"We will challenge them, Archie. I think the Cracker team can beat this Ambassador and ex-Ambassador."

We spent about an hour talking, I falling to the lot of Mme. Jusserand. She is an American, but looks French. She is not pretty, but frail and high-bred looking. Her husband is a bearded little fellow, full of enthusiasm and vim and a great chum of the President, playing tennis with him often and quite his equal in the walking contests.

Yesterday afternoon he and the Ambassador and Mme. Jusserand got on the subject of "Alice in Wonderland," and it seemed to be a contest as to which of the three could remember the most of this book. . . . [*Unfinished letter—no signature.*]

Ambassador Jusserand, now in his seventieth year, has served in the French diplomatic service since he was twenty-one and, having been French Ambassador to the United States for more than twenty years, is the dean of the Diplomatic Corps at Washington. He is one of those rare men of letters, like Carl Schurz and Joseph Conrad, who can write in a foreign tongue as skilfully as in their own. At least three of his books, "English Wayfaring Life," "The English Novel in the Time of Shakespeare," and "A Literary History of the English People" are the envy of English stylists and literary explorers.

XXXV

Washington, D. C.,
October 10th [1908].

My dearest Mother:

I went walking with the President this afternoon: rather I should say climbing and swimming, for there was far more of that than walking. I had an engagement with the Carpenters to dinner at 7:30, but as I did not get in the house until 7:15 I had to beg off from the dinner. I had often heard of his walks, and tradition about the White House tells of this or that general or ambassador or cabinet officer who had dropped out and fallen by the way. In fact, the President himself told me that what made him begin to investigate the physical condition of the officers of the army was the fact that General Bliss,[1] General Carter,[2] and Colonel Scott[3] and others were unable to keep up with him in walking, and that they showed such evident fatigue and distress as to make them unfit, he feared, for active service in the field.

He told me of one Assistant Secretary, Newberry I think it was, who not only had to fall out but took a car home and was laid up in bed for several days. I can easily imagine this, for Mr. Newberry is a very heavy man and leads a sedentary life, I should think. On one occasion he [the President] and General Wood and the French Ambassador were out walking, and coming in sight of the Potomac River, the Ambassador remarked how inviting the water looked, whereupon the President suggested that they swim to the Virginia side, which they did, not only swimming over but back to the District shore. Of course the papers have cartooned these walks and made great sport of them, and I would have felt quite out of it had I not had an opportunity to take one. I shall not be as eager a second time. I enjoyed it thoroughly, however, and I have never known him to be so talkative or communicative. He was like a schoolboy, kind of dancing all the way, eager to try every cliff, and once, plunging into the creek, swam to the other side. As it had been raining hard and the water was high, it took real swimming, too, to get over it.

We drove from the White House at 4:15 and reached the boulder bridge near the centre of the park in less than

---

[1]Major-General Tasker H. Bliss, chief of staff, 1907, American member Supreme Military Council at Versailles, member American Commission to Negotiate Peace, 1918–1919.

[2]Major-General William Carter, retired, 1915; recalled for active service, 1917, in command Central Dept. Chicago, August '17—February, 1918.

[3]Major-General Hugh L. Scott, chief of staff, 1914–1917, became Commander of the 78th Division December 26, 1917.

a half hour. I had on heavy marching shoes, leggings, and a flannel shirt. He was dressed in what appeared to me to be a handsome cutaway coat, but wore a campaign hat. I thought, therefore, that we would have a mild walk, especially as he had been laid up with his leg and Doctor Rixey[1] had advised him to take it quietly for a while. I think this very advice inspired him to test his strength and see what his leg could endure.

As we got out of the carriage he dismissed it and told the two detectives who had followed us on wheels not to attempt to follow us, and so we started. We made a circuitous route through the underbrush and at length came out farther up the creek, where there were no paths and few openings to the water and many overhanging cliffs and rocks. He pushed through the brush like an Indian scout and when he got to the water's edge he began to clamber out on the ridges and overhanging rocks. Sometimes we had to pass ourselves along the outer faces of rocks with hardly enough room in the crevices for fingers or feet. Each time I made it after him he would express his delight and surprise that I had done it so nimbly. I did not tell him how each time I thought it would be my last, nor did I show the real fear I had of falling.

My chief anxiety was for him. I felt that he had no right to jeopardize his health and life as he was doing. Finally we reached one cliff that went straight up from the water, made a turn, and the ledge he would have to make hung over some very nasty and jagged projections, so that if he should fall it might prove most serious to him.

I watched his ascent, therefore, with alarm. The rocks were slippery, and just as he was on the point of

---

[1]Surgeon-General Presley Marion Rixey, U. S. N., became Rear-Admiral, 1902, official physician to President McKinley and President Roosevelt.

making the highest point, imagine my horror when I saw him lose hold, slip, and go tumbling down. He went feet foremost fortunately, and he showed great presence of mind by shoving himself away from the rocks as he fell. Had he swerved his head would have been certain to strike some projection.

I stood paralyzed with fear. I could see what it would mean to have him meet with any accident of this kind. However, he missed all sharp projections and fell straight in the water. It was deep, but he did not go over his head, the water only reaching to his shoulders. With a laugh he clambered to the bank again and started once more. I knew that there would be no use trying to dissuade him from the effort, so I watched him with more anxiety the second time than I had felt the first time. He made it on the second trial and then came my effort. I felt so relieved about him (and I knew he felt chagrined at having fallen) that it was really a matter of indifference to me whether I went into the water or not. On the contrary, however, I went over the ridge like a cat. It was the best climb I made during the afternoon.

But his innings were coming later. We trudged on for about an hour more, sometimes crawling, sometimes climbing. Just about dark we reached a point on the creek where we had to swim it.

"Are you willing to try it?" he laughed, and plunged in.

I followed. He called back to swim hard and straight, which I did, and soon we were on the other side, shivering but laughing, and then he told me how near Fitz Lee came to drowning at that point one afternoon; that after three efforts he had refused to permit him to make another effort and made him take the detour. We then skirted the Zoo and finally came to a ledge of rocks that rose, I should say, forty feet in the air and was much higher when taken in conjunction with the sloping and rocky surface below it. He said it was dangerous and he doubted if it could be made on account of the rain and darkness. All these rocks and climbs were familiar to him, and he knew what could be done. He started up, and to my surprise he made it. I began the ascent and got midway and could not budge another inch. I could not see anything and when I glanced below it appeared about as dangerous to go back as to try to go over. I could hear him calling from above not to attempt to follow, that it was too slippery and that it would be fatal to fall. I made one or two more efforts and then decided that I was beaten and started back. But I had better gone on. I simply had to slide down and when I reached the bottom I was pretty nearly used up. He made the detour and joined me about fifty yards further on, coming out of the precipitous jungle like a bear, but laughing and evidently buoyed up over his prowess. Indeed I felt proud of him, too. I told him how chagrined I was not to have been able to follow him.

"Never mind," he said, "you did not fall into the water. So we are quits."

That was the only reference that had been made to the mishap.

This all sounds like hard work, doesn't it? and yet it was one of the most enjoyable afternoons of my life. If I could only remember half he said and how he said it. But when I read what I wrote about him to you, I find so much missing, his mannerisms, his incisiveness, and above all his enthusiasm.

There is no subject in which he does not seem to be interested, from baseball and balloons to the ethics of nations. He asked me where Ty Cobb had ended in the batting record and showed an intimate knowledge of the contention between the New York and the Chicago teams.

We were not always climbing and often had good long stretches when I would ask questions and get him started on any subject which presented itself to my mind. For instance, I told him of going into the second-hand book stores in London and once asking a big book man what American author had the largest sale in England; and how he had told me Edgar Allan Poe was now and always had been the biggest American seller.

"I am not surprised," said the President. "He is our one supereminent genius. In spite of the persistent effort to belittle him, and I must say it has come largely from New England, he still remains the most eminent literary character we have produced. I do not think that the New England school has tried to belittle him because he was not from New England, but their rules for literature are so adjusted that it will not permit of such an irregular genius as Poe. Even as sane a man as Holmes declared Poe to be one fifth genius and four fifths guff. If any man was ever about five fifths genius, that man was Poe. The next most eminent literary man I think we have produced is Hawthorne, in spite of the fact that I do not care for him and seldom read him."

Somehow we got from Poe to Washington, just how I do not know. I have lost the thread, I remembered his saying suddenly, out of the brush somewhere, that Washington was not a genius, that he could not find anything about him that smacked of anything more than talent, and yet, he said:

"I regard him as the greatest man in our history and one of the very greatest men in the world."

I suggested possibly that his judgment might be regarded as genius.

"Possibly so," he said. "Certainly he possessed something which pitched him on a different plane from other men of his time and on a plane which I do not find any other American occupying since then."

I said that it would be interesting to know what had led up to his [Washington's] declination of a third term, what influences had brought him to that conclusion.

"Of course [the President replied] there are those who believe that he declined a renomination for fear that he would be defeated, or that it was due to momentary irritation, but I find nothing to bear out either of these theories. I believe he was actuated purely by patriotism, his far-reaching vision which pierced the future, and saw the danger to our Republic if such a precedent were not established. It was his judgment—that judgment which never seemed to be at fault. If, when that most imbecile of Congresses, the Continental Congress headed by Horatio Gates and his crowd, was hounding him, and when it drove the army into practical mutiny by cutting down their pay to starvation, and when that army called to Washington to lead it where he might, if then he had had the passions of Cromwell or his lack of judgment, he would have dissolved the Congress and trod the path of Cromwell. There was every justification for him, apparently, to have accepted another term and to continue on in power. But he was always sane, always poised, always patriotic.

"It is so easy for a man to deceive himself into doing what others want him to do when it coincides with his own wishes. In my own case, I could so easily have persuaded myself that I was really needed to carry out my own policies. I sometimes felt that it was weakness which made me adhere to my resolution, taken nearly four years ago now. Nine tenths of my reasoning bade me accept another term, and only one tenth, but that one tenth was the still small voice, kept me firm. But how much harder must it have been for Washington, with no precedents to follow, with a united army and people back of him! When Washington ceases to be an inspiration in this country then the people had better look to themselves."

"Mr. President," I said later, "do you think the time will come when the country will be able to look dispassionately on Jefferson Davis, when there will be an awakening interest in his personality, when the people will demand to know all the good as well as the evil in him; in other words, will we have a Davis revival as we have repeated Napoleonic revivals?"

"Undoubtedly," said the President, "for, after all, his record in the Mexican War, his record as Secretary of War, as Senator, and his record as President of the Confederacy are filled with romance and interest. Who can say how much was due to him that the Confederate Government lasted four years? He was certainly a great soldier; his formation of his army showed that. Of course I was brought up with the belief that he was a second Benedict Arnold. It has taken decades to see differently. Lee and Lincoln are going to be the two great heroic figures of the Civil War, but I am convinced that Davis will be spared the violent and unripe judgment of such persons as myself."

There, my dear mother, that ought to pacify you for all he said on other occasions. You see how broad his own judgment is when he can impale himself as a hasty critic. We talked about Mrs. Roosevelt, and I felt that this was an evidence of how kindly he regarded me, for he feels too deeply about her to mention her casually, or to persons of whom he is not fond. I remarked what a position she had given the White House, how it now led society in Washington, and what a factor it had become in the moral social life of America. He was especially pleased when I added that the people of the United States no longer have to hark back to the days of Harriet Lane Johnson for a First Lady of the Land to be proud of.

"Nor to dear old Dolly Madison," added the President. "I feel that Mrs. Roosevelt has given poise to the White House. She is so gracious and kind, and withal so careful that she has imparted to the White House much of herself. It is my wife who often reminds me," continued the President, "of some new struggling author and suggests that he be invited to visit us or to dine or lunch. She really knows the value of such things more than I do, I fear, and I often get the credit of doing things to which she is entitled. You may not know it, but her education is much broader than mine. She is better read, and her value of literary merit is better than mine. I have a tremendous admiration for her judgment. She is not only cultured but scholarly. I sometimes fear that she has a good-natured contempt for my literary criticisms, and I know she scorns secretly my general knowledge of literature."

There were a hundred subjects he touched on, but while I might be able to follow him bodily, my mind cannot contain a part that he said. We crawled up the embankment of the new bridge and walked back to the White House. He had no carriage to meet him, and it was a good thing it was night, for we were soaking and muddy from head to foot. I confess to being a little tired on reaching Pennsylvania Avenue, and he said he was tired but he did not look it. Every year, he said, he discovered he had some new weakness.

"But I hope to hold together until my African trip. You know I have always admired the astuteness of Alexander," he said after a while, apropos of nothing, "for the diplomatic way he declined to enter the Olympic Games. He said he could only contest with kings. I know just how he felt. Should I be invited to a feat requiring endurance, I fear I would be equally foxy. I should not mind entering the arena with the Czar, Edward, the French President or even William, but I should hesitate to go outside this class."

I could not help thinking of the feats I had just seen him perform and felt that his classification of himself was modest. I told him about Cheney, Captain Cheney of the Engineers, one of his aides at the White House, whom I discovered he knew only as the long tall officer who "usually gets as far away from me as possible." It gave me great pleasure to expound Cheney to him. What a clever fellow he was, how well read, what an infinite humour he possessed and, above all, how he spent most of his pay in buying books. He is one of the most cultured men in the service, and I am so glad to have him associated with me at the White House. I really want the President to appreciate him.

"I am glad to hear about him," he said. "Why not ask him to your lunch Tuesday?"

Seeing me hesitate, he added:

"Never mind, I will have him to lunch with you some day next week at the White House."

He then got to telling some jokes on Phillips, and I then told him in what fear Phillips held him and how he had asked me if I was not afraid to have the President to lunch. The President enjoyed my answer, namely, that "I was afraid, but how could I help it?"

"Good, it is too late to back out now," he laughed.

I am going to have Cheney, nevertheless, and as I had just as well be cooked for a goose as a gander, I am asking McCoy also. In fact, it would hardly do to ask Cheney without McCoy. It means getting more Hong Kong china, for my set only contains six or seven pieces of each size, but I think I can afford to spend a few dollars on a lunch to the President.

I am going to have the table bare with only mats on it.

Is all that I have written tiresome or is it of any interest to you? Good-bye. I will sleep well to-night. I have ordered a Potomac roe herring for breakfast to-morrow, so I have something to look forward to on waking up.

Good-bye again, dear little mother.

Your affectionate and tired son,

ARCHIBALD.

In view of the opinions of Poe and Hawthorne which are ascribed to Roosevelt in the foregoing letter, it is worth while to turn to the written record of his literary inclinations.

In the jungles of Africa Roosevelt with an indelible pencil wrote an article on what he calls his Pigskin Library which is really an essay on books and reading. The original manuscript in his characteristically illegible handwriting lies before me as I write. Of poetry he took with him bound in pigskin Shakespeare, Spencer, Homer, Shelley, Lowell, Emerson, Longfellow, Tennyson, Poe, Keats, Milton, Dante, Bret Harte, and Browning. Among novels and romances he carried Poe's short stories. It does not appear that he had anything of Hawthorne's with him. He says, in speaking not only of the Pigskin Library but of the books he carried on other hunting trips: "I doubt if I ever took anything of Hawthorne's, but this was certainly not because I failed to recognize his genius."

The Bible was in the library, and as a Borrovian I am glad to say that he included the four great books of George Borrow. Politics was represented by the Federalist, and history by Macaulay and Carlyle's "Frederick the Great." In the original library there appears to have been no science, although he had sent out to him while he was in Africa Darwin's "Origin of Species" and "Voyage of the Beagle," and Huxley's "Essays."

Those who are interested in the catholicity of Roosevelt's literary tastes, which embraced detective stories at one end and the Greek plays of Euripides, Æschylus, and Sophocles at the other, will find the essay on the Pigskin Library worth reading. It appears in an appendix to "African Game Trails."

XXXVI

Washington, D. C.,
October 14th [1908].

MY DARLING MOTHER:

Luncheon was at 1:30, but the others came a little early. At 1:15 the house was surrounded literally by detectives, one even coming into the yard where he could keep a lookout on the dining room. I never felt quite so important before.

Promptly at 1:30 the President, Mrs. Roosevelt, and Miss Ethel drove up with two more detectives following on bicycles. Of course, the President does not want any detectives, but it is now a law and he has no say-so and is not even permitted to dictate what they shall or shall not do. They distributed themselves about so as not to appear conspicuous, and they might have been mistaken for ordinary citizens sunning themselves on I Street.

We had luncheon as soon as the presidential party arrived. There were eight of us in all: the President, Mrs. Roosevelt, Miss Roosevelt, Miss Hagner, Capt. McCoy, Capt. Cheney, and Mr. Phillips. The menu was simple as I was determined it should be—cantaloupe, asparagus soup, chops surrounding rice, and spinach and green peas with the chops. The salad was nothing more than tomatoes and lettuce, but I made a delicious dressing with roquefort cheese mixed in it. Nearly everyone was helped twice to it. I had Demonet's peach ice cream with an extra dish of fresh peaches and one of McGruder's homemade cakes. The lunch ended with cream cheese and guava jelly and coffee. I served sherry with the soup and sauterne with the rest of the lunch. I know these details will interest you.

After dinner the President wandered about the rooms and inspected everything of interest. He admired your miniature tremendously and was much interested in my library. Mrs. Roosevelt admires the Spanish furniture very much and enjoyed looking at the fans and other junk in the cabinet. When I saw the President that morning he asked if we could not get up some joke on Phillips about wearing spurs in the water. You remember, when I was at Oyster Bay and I cut myself on barnacles, the President asked me how it happened and I told him that Phillips had not manicured himself before coming in the water. Whereupon the President said:

"Billy, Archie says that if you were a gentleman you would not wear your spurs in the water."

Well, ever since then this has been a constant joke at the White House. The only reason there is anything funny to it is due to the sensitively refined nature which Phillips seems to possess. In telling the French Ambassador of the incident on the tennis court the other day, the President added: "Of course, Phillips thinks this is a joke that could only come from two vulgar-minded Georgians."

At any rate, now that you may recall the incident of which I wrote you last summer from Oyster Bay, you will understand the joke of yesterday. When the soup was served I had placed in front of Phillips a pair of spurs in a plate of water and with a scroll of paper tied with red tape on top of it. Everybody at the table knew its significance and had a good laugh at the expense of Phillips, which was continued when he opened what purported to be a commission, reading as follows:

GEORGIA

Recognizes New England's right to set a new fashion in warfare, and in token of such recognition Mr. William Phillips of Massachusetts is hereby created

KNIGHT of the

WATER SPURS

by direction of the President with the consent and advice of his Aides.

It proved to be a pleasant incident. Logan loaned me his man James, and he and Joseph served the luncheon rapidly and smoothly. The President spoke this morning of how much they all enjoyed themselves and how appreciative Mrs. Roosevelt was of it. I am glad it is over, for it does give one the frights to entertain the President; for after all nothing can be simple where he is. There is bound to be a certain amount of form and everybody is keyed up.

He did not leave the house until after three and then only when he remembered that he had an informal conference at 3:00 with Hatzfeldt of the German Embassy. There were a lot of people standing about when he came out, and the house has been an object of interest in the neighbourhood ever since. Nothing has been in the papers as yet and I sincerely hope it will not be noticed.

McCoy told me yesterday that the President had not dined or lunched out of cabinet circles more than three times since he has been President, and that it was a most extraordinary thing his coming to me as he did. I think he had two reasons: one being that he wanted to get away from routine for a few minutes, and the other to emphasize the fact that he liked me. There is certainly nothing to be gained anywhere by his showing such marked favours to me, and the man is so whole souled and honest that he would never think of such a thing, anyhow. Good-bye, darling mother, with lots of love. I am as ever,

Your devoted son,

ARCHIBALD.

XXXVII

Washington, D. C.,
Oct. 19th [1908].

MY DEAREST MOTHER:

We are having such a hot spell that I resent the arrival of each Minister or Ambassador as he makes his appearance. Really some of them are the queerest specimens I have ever chanced to see. The fact that they come decked in so much gold as to look tawdry makes them all the more insignificant looking. This ill humour may be the result of the last hour. I have been standing like a statue in full-dress uniform while the President has accepted the adieux of the retiring Minister from Honduras and welcomed the Minister from the Netherlands "near unto this Government."

For the last two or three days the weather has been intolerable. It is very unseasonable, and in consequence there is much sickness. They have been very busy days for me. The President turned over the White House grounds to the Ben Greet Players Friday afternoon and Saturday morning. The proceeds went to play-grounds for children—a most laudable charity in which Mrs. Roosevelt is deeply interested. I have never seen a more beautiful spectacle than the stage, the actors, the audience, and the fall colouring presented. The stage was simply the extension of one of the slopes in the White House grounds, very near the fountain, and the fall of the water was audible through it all.

The sky was spotless both on Friday and Saturday, and whatever was best in Washington socially was there. Whenever the White House opens its doors smart society turns out en masse, even when it has to pay to come. Nothing shows the position of the White House socially as this, for in years gone by the alleged smart element was wont to sneer at entertainments at the Executive Mansion, and would have it appear that it only attended functions there as a matter of duty. Now there is a scramble for tickets where there is nothing more to see than a set of inferior actors in childish rôles on the White House lawn. The women all wore their light summer gowns, and many who could not secure seats stood under the trees or wandered about the grounds. I wish you could have seen it. It was like a wonderful stage setting, except on a grand scale, but the grass was greener and the sky bluer and the trees more varied in colour than one could have put on canvas. The company gave two short plays, the first being "Pandora" and the second "Midas, or the Golden Touch." When Pandora opened the box and envy, hatred, and malice sprang out, followed by smoke and fumes, the audience broke into uproarious applause, the scenic effect was so good. There were boxes in a semi-circle about the stage and the seats back of them were arranged as they would be in a theatre.

The morning before the performance Mrs. Roosevelt sent for me to come to the White House. She was visibly nervous, as the President had decided that it was his duty to attend the show. She asked me to caution the aides to keep their eyes open and watch the audience carefully.

She said, and what was perfectly true, too, that the secret service men always kept near the President and kept their eyes fixed on him, and that while they would be able to prevent any one rushing upon the President with a knife, they would be of little use against any one rising to fire at him from a crowd. I told her I would use every precaution and later I got the aides together, instructing them to station themselves about the audience. Only two of them had pistols and I have asked them in the future to provide themselves with small revolvers, for if anything should happen we would all be severely condemned if it became known that military men who were supposed to be a guard to the President should be found unarmed at such a crisis.

At 4:30 Commander Sims and I went to the south portico and escorted the President and Mrs. Roosevelt to the box reserved for them.

The President, all unmindful of the anxiety which those of his household felt for him, sat perfectly unconscious of any danger and laughed and applauded the performance like any schoolboy. After the performance he held sort of informal reception of the foreigners present, the Japanese Ambassador and his wife coming up first to pay their respects. Baroness Takahira is a quaint little woman and would doubtless be extremely pretty in a kimono squatting near a tea tray. She is not pretty in her European dress and she looks very uncomfortable in her stays and tight-fitting clothes. She is very much at her ease, however, and her manner is quite charming when talking.

The Austrian Ambassador is beginning to look very old and is growing too fat for his court dress. He looks like a big, full-blooded Englishman rather than the trim, smart-looking Austrian he was a few years ago. The Baroness is fast losing her figure, but she dresses most stylishly, and as her face is literally covered with cosmetics it is impossible to detect her age.

The next performance, Saturday morning, the White House people did not attend, but at 11:00 I went to the office for the President, as he had promised to enter his box for a few minutes at least. It is surprising how eager even a Washington audience is to get a glimpse of Mr. Roosevelt. If it is advertised that he will be present anywhere, that alone will guarantee a large crowd. As the papers had stated he would be present at both performances he felt that he ought not to disappoint the crowd, but as we passed into the sun I told him that his box was unendurable, that I had sat there during the first part of the show and had simply melted. He conceived the happy idea of going behind the trees and meeting the actors and then appearing on the stage just long enough to make an address of welcome.

The audience was made up almost entirely of children and it was very pretty to see them all stand and wave their handkerchiefs to him as he stepped on the platform. I stood about three feet back of him and I could not help thinking that it would be an easy thing for an anarchist to reach him with a bomb or pistol ball. However, I never seem to think that anything is ever going to happen to him. Possibly I get this from his perfect indifference to environment.

After the performance I made a hasty shift of uniform and got into walking togs, for the Glovers had invited Mrs. Roosevelt, Miss Ethel and her guest, Miss Parker, and myself to lunch, and Mrs. Roosevelt had decided to walk. It was hot, but the tramp was enjoyable. We started at 12:30 and reached the house about 1:30. We had a delicious luncheon. The others drove home, but Mrs.

Roosevelt and I tramped it back. We had a most delightful time. It had grown cooler and the woods were lovely. . . .

Mr. Taft was in the city yesterday. I saw him for a minute. He had just come from the Southern tour and said that he did not expect to carry any of the Southern States, but that he did not think he had the right to ignore that section of the country any more than he had to ignore those states which seemed certain to give him the electoral vote. He feels very national, and if he is elected he will give the South every show along with the rest of the country. He is opposed to treating the Southern States in the vassalage class. He looks fine and campaigning seems to agree with him. He says he believes confidently that he will be elected. He was full of enthusiasm over his reception at Richmond, where the best people all turned out to give him a welcome. He is most anxious to break the solid South, but says he is not sanguine of doing it this time, but believes that the next presidential election will see three or four Southern States in the doubtful column.

This afternoon I donned the full-dress uniform and received Señor Ugarte, the retiring Minister of Honduras, who is going to Mexico; also the Secretary of State, who came to present the new Minister from Holland, M. Jonkheer Loudon, who succeeds Swinderin. As I went on the south portico to tell the President that the Honduras Minister had arrived, he said he would like a breathing spell from them for a short period and was inclined to be jocular.

But here is something which I have watched with the keenest interest in him. He intended merely to accept the letters of recall and say a few words and then bid Ugarte good-bye. But after he got into the Green Room something the Minister said struck a sympathetic chord in the

President and he made one of the most impressive addresses to this man that I have yet heard him make. He was deeply interested and spoke with such knowledge of the affairs and resources of Honduras that he even awakened interest in the wooden figure before him.

We then went into the East Room, where he received the survivors of the Thirteenth Vermont Regiment, their sons, wives, and daughters, about sixty in all. He made them a most happy address, and as he left the room he turned to me and said:

"What a nice lot of old boys they are, and now for the Double Dutch."

The Secretary of State looked horribly bored as we entered, for he was late and the President had kept him waiting while he spoke to the Vermonters.

Jonkheer Loudon was literally covered with gold, and is a splendid looking man. By the way, his wife is an American and very charming, so I am told. He read his address, and the Secretary handed the President the response which had been prepared for him to say parrot-like in the State Department. When they had finished, both looking very foolish, the President took him by the hand and said what he really wanted to say, that he knew the Dutch, that he could even sing some baby Dutch songs which had been handed down for generations in the Roosevelt family and which he had heard had passed out of the knowledge of the present generation of Dutchmen. He repeated some of them to the new Minister, who seemed absolutely delighted and almost danced with enjoyment over the President's pronunciation of them.

After they had had quite a little chit-chat, they all got up and began bowing most formally until we finally got them bowed out. The President turned to me and said:

"Archie, that is the most imbecile thing I have to do.

This is not a fair sample, however. What is especially asinine is when some South American reads a lengthy address, none of which I understand, and I in turn read expressions of approval back to him, which Adee has prepared for me, and when we have finished we smile one at the other, shake hands as if we had really settled something of importance. The *entente cordiale* goes on unimpaired for another four years, or else breaks up the next day as it sometimes happens. I feel like the Roman augurs who would cut open a chicken, look wise, and utter prophecies." Good-night.

Affectionately,
ARCHIBALD.

XXXVIII

Washington, D. C.,
October 20th [1908].

MY DEAREST MOTHER:

This morning when I got to the office I found a message from the White House for me to come to the breakfast room, as the President wanted to see me there. I found him posing for his portrait to De Camp, an artist of some note. He is always willing to pose for artists who can paint, but it makes him furious for societies to send sign painters to him, as he calls them. De Camp had merely sketched in the President, but I could see he knew his business. Quite different from the last portrait he allowed painted. The —— Club of New York wanted an oil portrait and petitioned the President to sit for it until finally he consented. I forget the name of the unfortunate artist, but from the moment he entered the room of the office it was clearly discernible that he was a pot-boiler artist.

He had a photograph, but he placed his easel in front of the desk where he continued to stare at the President while he worked. You can imagine that this would get on his nerves. The President got so he would simply glare at the artist every time he looked up from his work. The artist at best was a poor portrait painter, but, of course, it was somewhat disconcerting to find his subject glaring at him when he was frightened to death as it was. The more he painted, the worse the portrait looked, but he got in the face and it was a travesty. I advised the President to cut it up, but he said he could not do so without offending his faithful friends in the —— Club.

The next day after he had got the face in I went into the office, and there I found McKenna, one of the messengers, a stocky and heavy chap, posing as the President, and the artist painting literally with a brush of fire, with only one idea in his mind—to get through with it as quickly as possible. You can imagine what the portrait looked like when finished. But it was finished and that was what the poor artist wanted, and I hope the club accepted and paid him for it. I don't think he will ever be as ambitious again.

Mr. Morgan will arrive to-night and will spend the time in Washington with me. I mentioned the fact to the President, but he was very sharp about Morgan. He said:

"Captain Butt, if a man disappoints me the first time it is his fault; if he disappoints me the second time it is mine. I never blame a man who fails from accident, but I cannot get over the fact that Mr. Morgan did not know that there was a revolution stewing in Cuba. That was possible, however, but when I cabled him to return to his post at once he did not sail from Europe for a week, on the ground that he could not get a steamer. He ought to have come by steerage rather than not have started the same day.

"But I like Morgan personally, and, contrary to my own convictions, I gave him another chance. He is kindly, courteous, and succeeds in all the small things, but he fell down in the one big thing that came his way. I wish you would tell him what I say and just how I feel about him, for it may do him good, and I don't want him to make another failure if I can help it, even if I have to be cross and disagreeable to him. It is hard for me to take this attitude toward him, for my family all like him, and yet I will not let these things weigh with me when a man's real worth is at stake."

I took up the cudgels for Morgan and told the President that he had at least conducted himself with wonderful credit and in a most trying condition since the establishment of the provisional Government, and I cited how he had subscribed to magazines and periodicals for the soldiers and in numberless ways made the lives of the Americans pleasanter in Cuba. All this he agreed to.

"But, after all, they are the small things; the big thing was that Cuba was in a state of revolution, and he did not know it and took a leave just when he was most needed. He may be most useful to his Government yet, and I hope that he may be, and you may depend on my giving him another chance if it comes in my way. But, nevertheless, you tell him how I feel, and it may be the kindest act you will ever do him."

I am going to talk very freely on the subject with Mr. Morgan, but I shall tone down the language of the President to more diplomatic form.

One thing I did, and I don't know whether it was entirely acceptable or not, but if it were not he did not show his displeasure. I told the President that I felt one of the most unfortunate results of the political divorcement of the South from the party in power was the fact that the

South was not properly represented in the diplomatic service; that the suavity combined with the force of the Southern character well fitted the Southern man to represent his country abroad, that it was such a fine American type that it was a pity that it was not seen oftener at the foreign courts. He extolled the Southern man in like manner and added that he and Mr. Root had often discussed that very matter and that one idea of having competitive examinations for the consular service was to have the offices filled more equally from the various sections.

Of course, Senator Lodge of Massachusetts, being so long at the head of the Foreign Affairs Committee, has simply packed our foreign service with New England types, and as a rule with a class that is anything but representative of the manhood and strength of our country. He seems to run to advancing the decadent type in our foreign service. The dilettante who has a smattering of French is the candidate most likely to succeed in securing his influence. I think that both the Secretary of State and the President begin to see that Senator Lodge is using the foreign service as a political asset, and are trying to circumvent him without giving offense. . . . Good-bye, with love to all.

Affectionately,

ARCHIBALD.

Edwin Vernon Morgan, an accomplished and experienced diplomatist, was American Minister to Cuba at the time of the conversation reported in the above letter. Whether or not Captain Butt told him of the President's feeling the record does not say; but he has certainly made good, for he now holds with success, and has held for more than ten years, the important post of American Ambassador to Brazil. Captain Butt's suspicion sixteen years ago that Senator Lodge is sometimes swayed by motives of mere political expediency cannot, in the light of present events, be ascribed wholly to the sectional prejudices of a Southerner!

XXXIX

Washington, D. C.,
Oct. 21 [1908].

DEAR MOTHER:

We had tea in the office, Madame Jusserand and Mrs. Winthrop coming in about 6:00. I had a dinner at the Garlingtons' at 7:30, but did not get there until 8:15, for when the President gets to talking it is not for us to break up his party, and so we sit on only anxiously looking at the clock. It is a barbarous custom to eat at 7:30, and invariably someone is always late at a 7:30 dinner, for 8:00 is the regular time, and one gets in the habit of dressing and making all plans to fit into that hour in Washington.

The President gave it as his judgment that Mr. Taft would win in the election. I have never heard him make this prediction before, but he said that he would win, he thought, with about the same majority that he himself had in the Electoral College four years ago. He did not think the popular majority would be anything like the same, but that it would be about the same in the college.

He was too funny when he described the making of Taft into a popular campaigner.

"I told him he simply had to stop saying what he had said in this or that decision; for the moment you begin to cite decisions people at once think it is impossible for them to understand and they cease trying to comprehend and promptly begin to nod. I told him that he must treat the political audience as one coming, not to see an etching, but a poster. He must, therefore, have streaks of blue, yellow, and red to catch the eye, and eliminate all fine lines and soft colours. I think Mr. Taft thought I was a barbarian and a mountebank at first, but I am pleased to say that he is at last catching the attention of the crowd and I think he is holding it."

He then got discussing his forthcoming Romanes lecture with the Ambassador, and I never heard him more interesting or more profound.

I really think he was practising on us. He said that he had already prepared his lecture for the Sorbonne and that while De Camp was painting his portrait he was dictating his Romanes lecture, for he was anxious to have both completed before he started on his African trip. He is going to lecture on some paleontological subject and is going into a discussion of the continuance and disappearance of species on the American continent. That is what I judged from his remarks. As he came out the Ambassador[1] said:

"Was there ever such a man before? How he knew all the facts or where he gathered them I cannot imagine. I have been studying almost for a lifetime on the very subject on which he was talking, and yet he seems to have gone deeper in three weeks' preparation than I almost in a lifetime."

The subject was one of which I knew nothing, but yet, when he finished with his narrative of the continuance, disappearance, and reappearance of species, I felt that the fauna of South America was a subject on which I could at least listen in the future with some degree of under-

[1]It is not clear from the letter whether this was Mr. Bryce or Mr. Jusserand—probably Ambassador Bryce, as the Romanes lecture was given at Oxford and Bryce was an Oxford man.

standing. The last time we had played tennis it was "Alice in Wonderland"; this time it was paleontology. Such is the man's scope in reading.

This morning I went to the White House at 9:00 and, as I had overslept myself, I had to go without breakfast. He was walking in the south garden with Mrs. Roosevelt. He always breakfasts early, at 8:00 sharp, and invariably spends the time from that hour until 9:45 either walking with Mrs. Roosevelt in the garden or among the greens on the terrace. But that is her time and she does not like to have it broken into. However, this morning, he wanted to have a final discussion as to his needs for the African trip.

He is going to have the entire outfit made by the army tailors. He said to me:

"My dear fellow, please don't think that I am unmindful of all your goodness to me at this time, but I do not know what I would do without you. This is going to be a trying winter for me, for I have got to attend to all my duties and at the same time keep in shape for the hunt. I do not know what I would do if I did not have you to play with. You do all I like to do, and then your advice is always so clear and direct that I somehow feel that I am imposing on you."

He made me feel really remorseful, for sometimes I have felt that he was taking all my time, but if ever a man gave *quid pro quo* for what he gets he is that man.

We were talking about the time I went to Cuba and how I had been given only from 12:00 until 3:00 to get ready to go; how you were sick, and what I had to face in leaving you.

"Had your mother got worse or had she been so ill that she might have died in your absence, would you still have gone?"

I felt that he was somehow putting me to the test, but I answered truthfully, "Yes, sir."

You did not know it then, but when General Humphrey asked me if I could go at 3:00 my first thought was of you, but when I had said yes I had made up my mind to go and that nothing could stand in the way. I don't believe that you understand this attitude yet, but I was glad to tell the President how you had bucked up, and that of all the women at the station you were the only one who was not blubbering. Of course, it did not turn out to be any great conflict, but it looked serious at the moment. This is only to lead up to what he said:

"I know just how you felt. When the chance came for me to go to Cuba with the Rough Riders Mrs. Roosevelt was very ill and so was Teddy. It was a question if either would ultimately get well. You know what my wife and children mean to me; and yet I made up my mind that I would not allow even a death to stand in my way; that it was my one chance to do something for my country and for my family and my one chance to cut my little notch on the stick that stands as a measuring rod in every family. I know now that I would have turned from my wife's deathbed to have answered that call."

And he worships his wife and children.

These talks with him by himself are always delightful. He simply talks as he thinks; but he nearly always does that.

He wants to jump Roswell and I have asked him not to do much jumping this winter, that there was no use running any risks of starting out on his hunt with a bad leg or a patched-up bone.

"Yes, this is my last fling. I feel it," he said. "If I can only last through this hunt I shall not quarrel with fate when she leads me into old age. I have set my whole mind on this trip and those lectures. No, I will promise you only to take jumps that Roswell would scorn."

He then got to talking about different things and the chances of interruptions to one's plans.

"I often think," he said, "of poor John Pitcher, who had trained and planned for warfare all his life, and when it came, it found him with a broken leg. I should have railed aloud against such fate."

He spoke of Gifford Pinchot of whom he is really very fond.

"Gifford truly has an affection for me," he said. "It is almost fetish worship, and I have figured it out that Pinchot truly believes that in case of certain conditions I am perfectly capable of killing either himself or me. If conditions were such that only one could live he knows that I should possibly kill him as the weaker of the two, and he, therefore, worships this in me. I do not know the man I would sooner choose to send to some danger point than Pinchot. The two men in my regiment whom I loved above all others [Goodrich was one, I have forgotten the name of the other he mentioned] I put in direct line to be killed. I have the feeling, Archie, that I could trust you and Fitz Lee in mighty dangerous places, and it is that which makes me like to be with you two."

I wonder if I am deserving all his good, generous thoughts of me. Sometimes his friendship almost frightens me. I have tried to do right and be honourable without thinking about it very much, but when I am with him I become stampeded for fear that I may do something that if he knew he would not approve. From all this you will see that I am growing, if I have not already grown, fond of him. I always admired him, but I never thought I should grow fond of him. I find that I am getting in the Pinchot class. I sometimes fear that I may give you a wrong impression of him; that you may not see his splendid qualities of mind and heart. I want you to know him some day. You will be inclined to see the side of him at first that the cartoonists have caricatured, but later he will completely carry you off your feet. By the way, as you predicted, Mrs. Roosevelt has had her way. He has said nothing more of late about wearing uniforms abroad. I think she has squelched the plan. Good-bye.

As ever your affectionate son,

ARCHIBALD.

XL

Washington, D. C.,
October 21 [1908].

MY DEAR MOTHER:

Mr. Morgan got in late last night and is now comfortably ensconced in your room. He thinks the house charming and is pleased as possible with his apartments. This morning he has gone to see the Baroness Speck von Sternberg, who has lost her husband since she was in Cuba. She, poor lady, is here trying to close up her house and dispose of her household goods. Her case is pathetic.

It was always said that Speck Sternberg was only trying to live longer than his father, who opposed his marriage, in order that his young widow might be provided for properly after his death. It seems that he feared that should he die before his father, the old Baron, things would be made very uncomfortable for his widow. This is exactly what has happened. He was operated on in Heidelberg this fall, and while the operation was successful the patient caught pneumonia and died in a few days.

The German Government permitted the Baroness to

The last picture of the Roosevelt Tennis Cabinet. Taken on the White House lawn after the presentation of the bronze cougar to President Roosevelt

occupy the Embassy until the 1st of December, and she is here now trying to dispose of whatever is valuable in the house. We heard her pension was something like three hundred a month, but the President thinks it is not more than sixty or seventy dollars. Mrs. Roosevelt, who has seen her several times, says the poor little thing is simply heartbroken.

The Baron left his collection of chinaware, which covers the wall in the great drawing room, to the Baroness, but it seems that under the German law a father has a right to put in a claim for a part of the personal estate of a son who dies. This the old villain has done, and while it seems absolutely disgraceful, yet he insists upon his rights in the matter.

From being the wife of the most powerful Ambassador in Washington she has become an impoverished woman, who has not only herself to care for, but who has assumed the support of her mother and sister. Her lameness makes her position all the more pitiful. Mrs. Roosevelt says she is even more beautiful than when happy, but that she weeps as if broken-hearted all the time.

What brutes the Germans are in matters of money! J. Pierpont Morgan has written to the Baroness asking for the valuation of the Sternberg collection, but it is doubtful whether it has the value which has been placed upon it. I am interested in her because I have known her ever since she was a child visiting the Castlemans in Louisville, and her uncle, practically her foster father, is one of the best friends I have ever had. I have left my card on her, but have not attempted to see her. Mrs. Roosevelt has been much with her and is keenly interested in her affairs. Of course, any one as beautiful will certainly have opportunities to marry, and to marry well, but it is rather hard to think of this solution as being necessary. In spite of poor Speck's infirmities, she simply adored him and I never saw any one more gentle or considerate than she was with him last year in Cuba. . . .

Your affectionate son,

ARCHIE.

In his Autobiography Roosevelt speaks of his friendship with Baron Speck von Sternberg:

> I never did much with the shotgun, but I practised a good deal with the rifle. I had a rifle range at Sagamore Hill, where I often took friends to shoot. . . . The best man with both pistol and rifle who ever shot there was Stewart Edward White. Among many other good men was a stanch friend, Baron Speck von Sternberg, afterwards German Ambassador at Washington during my Presidency. . . . It was he who first talked over with me the raising of a regiment [The Rough Riders of the Spanish War] of horse riflemen from among the ranchmen and cowboys of the plains. When Ambassador, the poor, gallant, tender-hearted fellow was dying of a slow and painful disease, so that he could not play with the rest of us, but the agony of his mortal illness never in the slightest degree interfered with his work.

The break of nearly two weeks which now occurs in Captain Butt's epistolary narrative was occasioned by the sudden but not wholly unexpected death of his mother. Writing of Captain Butt in the spring of 1912, after the *Titanic* disaster, President Taft said:

> Later, Major Butt brought his mother to Washington, and I had the pleasure of meeting her and hearing her crisp sentences on everything that happened there, and on much of what happened in Augusta. He loved her devotedly—it always seemed to me he never married because he loved her so—and the greatest sorrow of his life was when she left him.

Fortunately, the warmest affection existed between Archie and his sister-in-law Clara (Mrs. Lewis F. Butt), and on his return from his mother's funeral he resumed his correspondence, addressing the letters to his sister-in-law. On the occasion of her marriage to his brother in 1904 Archie had written her: "The most hideous expression in the English language is the term 'in-law.' Please, Clara, do not ever let it intrude itself between us!"

XLI

Washington, D. C.,
November 2 [1908].

My dear Clara:

I arrived from Augusta last night and was met at the train by friends. I was very glad to see them, for I was very low in my mind by the time I reached Washington.

I am so glad, however, that I went South. As distressing as it was it gave me a chance to pull myself together. Each day I seem to miss Mother the more, and the awful fact that I will not see her again almost paralyzes my brain if I allow myself to think of it. . . .

When I reached the house yesterday afternoon I found a box of flowers from the President and Mrs. Roosevelt.

I took up my routine duty this morning, and at 9:30 called as usual on the President. He was really as affected as I was, and after a few minutes' conversation told me that Mrs. Roosevelt expected me to go down the river with her on the presidential yacht, the *Sylph*, and that if there were any other duties to be performed for the day to turn them over to one of the assistant aides.

I think they got up the trip merely to break my first day in Washington. My own people could not be kinder or more considerate than they have been. We steamed down the river about six miles below Mount Vernon, where we took the little naphtha launch and went up Pohick Creek and walked then about five miles to the old Colonial church which was built by George Washington, John

Mason, and some others of that time. It has been restored by the Colonial Dames and is a most interesting old structure. It was built in 1758 and it has been restored exactly as it was. The walls and windows and carvings are just as they were, though they were considerably defaced by the Federal troops who camped there during the war. The rector is Doctor Meade, a grandson of Bishop Meade.[1] We did not get back until nearly 6 o'clock and I had dinner alone.

At 10:30 I have to put on my uniform and go to the Union Station to see the President off as he leaves at 11:00 for Oyster Bay to vote to-morrow. Unless he decides to take me with him at the last moment I will have the day to myself.

He will return at 6:00 to-morrow evening, and at 8:00 I am to be at the White House to hear the returns. Mrs. Roosevelt told me not to come if I did not feel equal to it, but it is just as well to take up my duties at once. You know that they will not hear of my retiring from my work there.

Mr. Morgan told both the President and Mrs. Roosevelt just what I had said, that it might be pleasanter for them not to have an aide who was in mourning.

I realize that they ought to have an aide who is going out and who can look after Miss Ethel at the cotillion and other private affairs. I told them that while I could not go out anywhere else, my duties at the White House would be my highest duty to perform and that, while I thought it best to retire and let McCoy or someone else take up the detail, if they wanted me I should not intrude my grief into the White House. Mr. Morgan wrote me

[1]Rt. Rev. William Meade, Bishop of Virginia from 1841 until his death in 1862. He opposed the secession of Virginia, but when his state decided to leave the Union, like Robert E. Lee, he followed her.

that they would not hear of my leaving, and they so told me this morning. . . .

Mother's last letter to me from England was a dissertation upon the politics of this country. She freely admitted that she thought Taft the better equipped man, but that she felt it would be more beneficial to have a change of parties in power than to elect him. Her mind was clear and vigorous within a week of her death, at any rate. There is some consolation in that thought. It would have been worse than death for her to have had her faculties paralyzed. Good night, my dear sister. Give my love to Lewis and believe me always,

Your affectionate brother,

ARCHIBALD W. BUTT.

XLII

Washington, D. C.,
November 5 [1908].

MY DEAR CLARA:

The President was simply radiant over Taft's victory, and made no attempt to disguise it. After all, it was largely his victory. Certainly he looks at the result as an indorsement of his own policy.

"We have them beaten to a frazzle," he would say from time to time, "and if any one does not know what this term signifies let him ask Captain Butt, who comes from that section which coined the word."

He had quite a joke on Mrs. Roosevelt when he faked a telegram announcing that Pine Knot had gone for Bryan. Pine Knot is the home of Mrs. Roosevelt in Virginia, consisting of about ten acres somewhere in the Virginia woods.[1]

The President sneaked off from his party—for it was

[1]Pine Knot: see comment on Letter I.

nothing more than that—at an early hour, and Mrs. Roosevelt asked me to find him, and if he would not return, for me to tell him that the Commissioner of Labour and his wife had arrived, and if he did not come to welcome them it would look as if he did not care to be polite now that the labour vote had been delivered. I found him, but he would not come for a long time. He was in his library comfortably ensconced and reading, the election already almost a thing of the past to him. He finally came down, greeted the Commissioner of Labour and his wife, and as quickly disappeared again. The guests seemed in no hurry to leave, although by 10:00 the results were known except as to details. Mrs. Roosevelt was worn out, having travelled to Oyster Bay the night before and having returned only that evening. But it is hard to get persons to leave the White House. Commander Sims at 10:30 announced to a lot of women gossiping on the sofa:

"It seems that this party is about to break up. I wonder if it is time for me to go?"

This announcement made not the slightest effect, for not a woman budged. Finally one couple, who looked tired, said they had to go, and I asked them to bid good night to every one in an audible voice, which they did, but still no one took the hint.

At last a telegram came announcing that Mr. Taft was satisfied with the result and was going to bed and Mrs. Roosevelt exclaimed:

"Well, I should think it was time for him to go to bed." And instead of its being taken as she meant it the party about her took it for a witticism and went into roars of laughter, in which we all had to join, as the laugh seemed to be on us who were behind the scenes as it were. Secretary and Mrs. Wright said good-bye, which ought to have been the signal for any party to break up, as they were the most exalted guests there, but no. I heard one woman say, "What a pity Mrs. Wright is not strong and has to take such care of herself!"

By 12:30, long after everybody who had any real interests in the election was abed and asleep, the party broke up, and Mrs. Roosevelt, turning to us, said with graceful gesture and tired smile:

"My real friends will not stand upon the order of their going but will go at once."

We took the hint and each sought a tired couch that night.

The next morning I was at the office early, and, as is usually the case, the President was late. Secretary Garfield, Mr. Loeb, and I were discussing the returns when the President came in. Going over to Loeb, he took his hand and looking at us said:

"You army officers and politicians who still have futures before you may continue the struggle, but Mr. Loeb and I will sing 'Nunc Dimittis.'"

He was in a splendid humour, and I thought it a good time to spring a matter of which General Barry had written to me only several days ago. It was that the occupation in Cuba should be regarded as a campaign and that a service medal should be ordered struck off and worn in commemoration of it. The suggestion caught his attention at once, and I did not have to present all the arguments which General Barry had given me and others which I had thought of myself.

"As you go out, Archie, just dictate a letter to the Secretary of War for me to sign, directing that such a campaign medal be issued in accordance with the wishes of General Barry."

As I went out I dictated the letter and added on my

own account that the medal be ready for distribution by the time the troops were ready to leave Cuba.

We had a splendid horseback ride this afternoon, he riding Audrey and I Georgia. I found out one thing, that Georgia is the fastest horse in the President's stables, and I nearly pulled my arms out of joint holding her in.

As we went on we spoke of Secretary Taft's efforts at horsemanship, and I found that the President agreed with me that he should not attempt to ride, that it was dangerous for him and cruelty to the horse.

"If I were Taft," said the President, "I would not attempt to take much exercise. I would content myself with the record I was able to make in the next four years or the next eight and then be content to die. The life in the White House will be sufficiently strenuous for him without fretting about exercise, and I do not think exercise does Taft any good. It does not do to try to live too long. Many people are urging me not to go to Africa, as I may get killed or catch the sleeping sickness or die in a thousand and one ways. I am ready to go at any time. Certainly the fear of dying would not deter me from doing what I wanted to do. I do not know what the future has in store for me, but I am ready to rest my case here, or," he added with a keen laugh, showing his teeth by way of emphasis, "after I have had a little fling in Africa."

Friday Evening, Nov. 6 [1908].

I left my letter uncompleted yesterday, it seemed to me, so I will finish it to-night. It is cold and crisp outside, but with the furnace going and a large fire in the open fireplace, and with no desire in my heart to go out, the inside looks very attractive. There is little to record, though there is an air of uneasiness about the executive office to-day, due to Governor Haskell of Oklahoma, the man whom the President gave such a body blow to during the campaign just ended.

Ever since then he has not failed to send a menacing telegram each day, and now he threatens to bring a suit for slander against Mr. Roosevelt and have him extradited after the 4th of March to answer in the courts of his own state.

The President sees in it only a ruse to prevent him from taking his African trip and is aroused accordingly. So he is out to fight.

"The only way to put the fear of God into that man is to let him understand that you will fight him to the end, and I think I have the weapons," he said.

He was very angry, and I should hate to stand in the shoes of Haskell.

This afternoon I was at the White House when the British Ambassador, Mr. Bryce, came by appointment to present Doctor Shackford, an Oxford pedant. The latter was so like Rockefeller in his personal appearance that the President actually started when he first saw him. He told the President that he had come just at this time to see the elections in America and had been greatly disappointed at the orderly behaviour he had seen everywhere.

He said: "Your people are not nearly as disorderly as the British on an ordinary election."

"Of course not," agreed the President, "and, moreover, what is tolerated in England would not be countenanced here for a minute. During a campaign in England your orators are prepared for interruptions of every character, but here if one man interrupts with questions he is shouted down as a brute. Some Yale students were classified as a lot of hoodlums during the last campaign because they made frequent interruptions during one of Mr. Bryan's speeches, and the entire country denounced their conduct as most extraordinary and vulgar. Such a thing as an egg episode, which I understand is quite common in your campaigns" ("Quite so, quite so," from the Britisher) "would create such a furor in this country as to endanger the election of the party in whose favour the demonstration was made."

Doctor Shackford kept repeating, "Remarkable, extraordinary," but seemed to become appeased when the President added:

"Yet I fear we sometimes have episodes the effects of which are more serious; for instance, we have been known to lose ballot boxes and otherwise to resort to tricks which I do not think would enter the mind of the British politician."

Doctor Shackford was almost as great an interrogator as Li Hung Chang. He asked the President if much money had been spent in this country on the election. The President told him that he thought a million dollars would cover both parties; that it would certainly not go over twelve hundred thousand.

Doctor Shackford said that any one of their general elections would cost this much and was greatly surprised at the information, which the President assured him was correct.

He [the President] then paid one of the best tributes to Taft I have ever heard him pay any one. He said in answer to some question:

"Taft has pitched this campaign on a higher plane than any campaign in the history of this country. He has not made one demagogic appeal. Every statement has been based on some principle he believed to be right and honest, and the other candidate has appealed to every prejudice or passion he could think of. It was a wonderfully intelligent vote. Even the fact that Taft was a Unitarian did not influence many voters, and Gompers was not able to handle the labour vote at all. It shows a very healthful condition of the public mind when the people can separate the issues as they have done in this campaign." . . .

During the interview an incident occurred which amused Mrs. Roosevelt very much when I repeated it this morning. The President has a great way of asking me to be seated when I enter with him at these Ambassadorial conferences, which requests I simply ignore. Yesterday he forgot to go through this formality until he had been talking for five minutes or more, and then, suddenly remembering himself, he turned round deliberately and said:

"Captain, please take a seat and join us."

It was so marked that I had to do something, so I crossed the room and shut down the window back of Doctor Shackford and resumed my military position. The room was frightfully warm, and I think these two cold-blooded Britishers nearly expired before the interview was closed.

Mrs. R. laughed very heartily over the discomfiture of the British visitors, but agreed with me that I had to do something and that was all there was left for me to do.

She then said that she would tell the President to cut this little piece of politeness out of his interviews in the future. She said that there were some things he could never get accustomed to, and one was his objection to ladies rising whenever he entered a room.

"I have told him that it is only respect for the office; that there is nothing personal in it, but he always answers the same:

"'Even if I am President, I am a gentleman, and no gentleman would allow a woman to rise to him.'"

I made the contract for the state dinners to-day, awarding them to Rauscher at seven dollars and seventy-five cents a plate, he to furnish everything, dishes, glasses, linen, all except the plates and the champagne and the cigars. . . .

We were talking about the expenses of the White House to-day and Mrs. Roosevelt said that she thought Congress ought to grant a pension to ex-Presidents and ex-Presidents' wives. She said that so many had really to economize in the White House to save something to live on later; that such was not the case with them, so that there was nothing personal in her attitude. . . .

She also said that they had not saved any of the President's pay; that it had all gone in the effort to keep up the White House as they thought it should be kept up.

But others who were less fortunate would have to try to save something out of their pay, and in consequence the entertainments at the White House must necessarily suffer. I was glad to learn the true state of the case, for Bromwell had told me, and I had written it to Mother on one occasion, that the Roosevelts spent at least thirty thousand dollars more than their pay amounted to.

Your affectionate brother,

ARCHIBALD.

XLIII

Washington, D. C.,
November 8 [1908].

DEAR CLARA:

The diplomatic tea yesterday afternoon was not the trying ordeal that I feared it would be, yet it is the only occasion on which I have felt nervous, but when I confessed to a certain degree of stage fright to Mrs. Roosevelt she said that I did not show it and, in fact, had carried off the occasion with a considerable degree of aplomb. . . .

Mrs. Roosevelt wore a black velvet gown with silver passementerie work down the front, and it must have been a new one, for I never remember having seen it before. We get quite accustomed to the gowns in the White House, and usually before an entertainment begins someone starts a discussion over them and usually ends with Mrs. Roosevelt saying that she knows how to dress, and while she does not object to opinions being expressed, yet it does not have any weight with her.

The President, if he is present, usually starts the discussion with an announcement pro or con.

Each child, from Mrs. Longworth down, has the greatest affection for the mother, and it shows itself in a hundred ways, but in no way more than the desire of each to have Mrs. Roosevelt look young and pretty. Each has his or her favourite gown, and always there is a fight as to which gown she is to wear before one of the state functions. I know so much about this because Mrs. Roosevelt has told me, and once when I expressed my admiration for a gown she had on, a heavy black silk, ribbed and slashed with white, she said it was the gown Kermit and the President loved to see her wear, and that if they could have their way she would have to wear it all the time.

She has a queer steel-blue which she likes for luncheon and which is very soft and becoming to her, and I always will think of her mostly in this gown. She has a rich plum-coloured one this winter which I have seen her wear only once, but I think it will do yeoman's service later on.

I watched every old dame yesterday, and I saw none that I thought more beautifully gowned than the hostess. I was so nervous at first that I hardly noticed anything, but after the first lull Mrs. Roosevelt put me quite at my ease by laughing at some of my mistakes, especially when I got awfully flustered and introduced the Argentine Minister as the American Minister. But I could not get his name, nor could I catch it as he mumbled it through his moth-eaten moustache.

Since I was one of the beaux about the diplomatic set, many have changed and new faces have appeared. Two years makes a great difference in Washington, especially in the diplomatic set, and there has been a remarkably large number of changes within the last two seasons.

I knew all the Ambassadors and their wives, but it is the South American continent which caught, twisted and threw me down. I am going to try to have the custom established, making it obligatory for the Minister or attaché to precede his wife and daughters. They rank their wives and families and should precede them, but yesterday most of them stepped back and waved the women ahead.

The women are usually flustered and often don't give their names, and if they do they mumble them so low as to mislead you if you try to pronounce them. I mumbled over those I did not know, and my mistakes were not as conspicuous as those McCoy used to make, who was wont to shout out what he thought their names ought to be and thereby emphasized his errors.

I frequently announced the Second Secretary of mum mum Legation, bringing out the legation good and loud and passing on glibly to some name I did know. I was conscious of making so many mistakes that I really felt anxious to compare my mistakes to my predecessors', but I found out that I was supposed to have got through very well. . . .

As a rule the diplomatic corps is made up of more ordinary looking men and homely women this year than for many years past. The best equipped women in the corps by all odds are the Americans who have married foreigners. Madame Jusserand, Madame Loudon, wife of the Minister from the Netherlands, and Countess Moltke of Denmark, Madame de Porter of the Spanish Legation, are not only the most finished but the last three named are the most beautiful in the corps.

Loudon is very handsome, looking like some splendid, well-groomed Englishman, and his wife is lovely and gracious to every one. Countess Moltke was a Miss Thayer of Boston and reminds one of Flavia, chiefly for the reason that the Count Moltke is so purely of the Prisoner of Zenda type that his wife simply has to remind you of someone to go with him. They are well mated and were quite the cynosure of all eyes yesterday.

I started out to tell you merely how I got on in this first diplomatic function, and here I have run into a long letter, which must bore you unless you have a weakness for memoirs of court gossip or scandal. I am sorry that there is not a large size piece of gossip as yet developed in the diplomatic corps. One or two hang over from the last season, but they never had much vitality in them. . . .

One hears that Washington is an awfully wicked place, but it is those on the outside who think it, for after all there is very little going on which one could not mention at the breakfast table on Sunday morning. . . . Good-bye.

ARCHIBALD.

XLIV

Washington, D. C.,
November 12 [1908].

DEAR CLARA:

The days have seemed long, yet there has been enough to keep me busy. But while I try to appear interested in what interests others, yet my thoughts are constantly turned inward. But as long as one is outwardly interested in doing his duty, it takes a keen eye, such as Mrs. Roosevelt has, to see the heartaches underneath.

It has rarely been my good fortune to meet any one with such kindly feelings. It is right difficult for her to ask me to do things which she feels grate on one's sensibilities, yet in handling the affairs of the White House she has to sacrifice all other considerations to those which make for good order and proper standards, which she has established and maintained there.

For instance, yesterday, when she was having a large luncheon party she sent me word that, while she felt it might be objectionable to me, still she wanted me to come. It was official for them and equally so for me. In fact, the luncheon was largely official in its character. It was given ostensibly to bring together the leading factors in the recent Republican success. The personnel was all interesting.

In the first place there was Mr. Sherman, the Vice-President elect. He looks unusually well and does not appear to be the invalid which it was feared he would be after his attack in the summer. He had no official rank, and therefore was seated on the left of Mrs. Roosevelt.

After the 4th of March, as Mrs. Roosevelt says, he will be promoted from the left to the right hand of the hostess. On her right was the British Ambassador, Mr. Bryce. His hair and beard are snow-white, and yet his face is youthful. He is very small and wiry and most energetic in his conversation.

Hitchcock,[1] the young man who was made chairman of

---

[1]Frank H. Hitchcock, who successfully managed the presidential campaign of Mr. Taft in 1908 and became Postmaster-General in his cabinet. Postal savings banks and the parcel post were established during Mr. Hitchcock's administration of the Postal Department.

the campaign committee against the advice of Senator Scott and a number of the old-time politicians, was also there. He has not red but pink hair and eyebrows and pink skin and light blue eyes. The marvel to me is how he was ever discovered to be what he is, for he possesses great force of character and integrity of purpose. He looks like one of the conventional characters in up-to-date plays usually described on the bills as "Reggie—whom there is nothing in." He has a good many more seams about the eyes and mouth since I last saw him. He will very likely be made Postmaster-General or Secretary of the Treasury.

This is not purely guesswork, for I have heard him mentioned by those higher up as destined for one of these posts. Seth Low was there also, grown gray and fat. He has all the appearance of a prosperous reformer.

Mr. and Mrs. John R. McLean were there, and while a Democrat he did much for the success of Taft. A Mr. [Howard] Pyle, a distinguished illustrator, and his wife were guests also. The former spent most of his time making sketches of those at the table and presenting them to Mrs. Longworth. Dave Barry of the Library Bureau and Jimmie Williams,[1] the young newspaper man of North Carolina whom Taft takes with him everywhere, were present. Williams is a nephew of Silas McBee of Sewanee, who now edits the *Churchman.* Lewis knows them both well, I think. Williams is wearing himself thin trying to make up his mind what billet he wants under the next administration. He hitched his wagon to the Taft star early in the game, and I think, too, without motive. He truly loves the big Ohioan.

There were a number of others whom you are destined

[1]James T. Williams, Jr., at the date of this letter Washington correspondent of the Boston *Transcript.* He is now editor of that excellent newspaper.

to hear of within the next four years, but who at present are unknown save to the inner circles of campaign management. . . .

After a while the President and the Ambassador joined the ladies and in a few minutes Mr. Roosevelt called to me to come in.

"I only want you to hear what the wife of the President and the wife of the world's most distinguished diplomat are saying to your chief. They dare to criticize my letter on religious tolerance."

This letter, as you know, was published a few days ago and was intended to be very broad-minded in its scope.

Mrs. Bryce, who is much younger-looking than her husband and with a good deal of the British argumentative side to her, I imagine, said:

"Yes, sir, I dare to criticize your letter, and especially so as your wife agrees with me. I do not object to your advocacy of a Jew for President, but I most certainly do not want to see a Catholic ever the President of this country or over an Anglo-Saxon people."

"A fine Christian spirit you ladies have—a Jew rather than a Catholic!"

"Most assuredly," said Mrs. Bryce, "for a Jew is loyal to whatever country he adopts, while a Catholic is loyal first to another power, and a temporal one at that."

"Do you really think," asked the President seriously, "that Catholics would subordinate their own country to the interests of Rome?"

"Not only to the interests of Rome, but to Catholic countries as well. I have known it done in my own country, as Mr. Bryce would testify to if he dared."

The President rather avoids religious discussions save when he introduces them for some purpose, and so stopped the conversation with the remark:

"Oh, you hidebound aristocratic Episcopalians!"

"But I am not one," said Mrs. Bryce. "Just a plain Protestant like yourself."

"Then we cannot differ," said the President, reaching across and shaking her by the hand.

While they stood thus, Mrs. Roosevelt held out her hand to me and said: "Then we will stand for the established church, Captain."

The Ambassador added, holding up his hands in benediction: "Bless this Protestant reunion. You look like Roundheads, all of you, taking the oath against popery."

"If we have impressed the President with the fact that we do not approve of his sentiments we will have accomplished all we started out to do," said Mrs. Roosevelt.

"My mail is burdened each day now with similar protests, but I hardly expected the revolution to enter my own household."

After the Bryces left, the new Danish Minister was presented. He is extremely handsome and will be a great favourite socially. He has all the earmarks of popularity about him. I was struck by his uniform or court dress, quite the most elaborate which has appeared this season. Blue and crimson is the general effect, and his cape, which covers his entire body, is dark blue lined with crimson silk. He is a Count Moltke. He said he was a relative of the German Von Moltke, and that the German Von Moltke had gone from Denmark to Germany, whereas he had come from Germany to Denmark.

I suppose you saw the account of the walk in Rock Creek Park of the General Staff and the President. The papers have made a good deal of fun of it, but they have not had the fun which I had watching the performance. I had been over the same ground several times before and I know it is very difficult to take. General Bell suggested to the President to ask the War College and General Staff —more, I fear, to advertise himself as being strenuous than for any good to be got out of it. He had General Duvall invited, and I think had hopes, from what I hear, to see Duvall fall by the wayside or in the creek, as he himself once did.

However, General Duvall was the only general who kept side by side with the President the entire way and made every cliff and precipice without assistance, while General Bell was considerably blown and had to stop several times to rest. He hid this fact under the excuse of remaining in the rear to give advice to others how to make some of the difficult places. But the officers soon caught on to the ruse and passed the winks one to another.

Just before we came to the last steep cliff I went to the President and asked if he was going to take the creek.

He said he ought not, but looked quizzically at me as much as to ask: "Shall we do it?"

I said: "I think they would like to go with you, Mr. President, and I think they will remember this walk longer if they have to do a little swimming."

"Just as you say, Archie," and I dropped behind to watch the fun.

He scaled the last wall, about sixty feet high, and while most of the officers followed I saw quite a number make a détour and gain the ledge without the dangerous climb. I had posted Sloan the detective what I had done, and so, when the President reached the bottom on the bank of the creek, Sloan, fearing he would fail at the last moment, said:

"I think this is a good place to go off, Mr. President."

No sooner said than done, and the President stepped off the bank about four or five feet high, up to his chest in about as cold water as I ever felt.

Colonel Sturgis, who was near me when the President

went in, turned to me and said: "I wonder what fool suggested that."

"I cannot imagine," I said, "but I told you to wear your oldest clothes," glancing at Colonel Sturgis, for he had a good cutaway on.

He confessed to me yesterday, however, that he would not have missed swimming the creek now for anything, that it was the feature of the walk. . . .

Your affectionate brother,

ARCHIBALD.

President Roosevelt's open letter on the subject of religious tolerance, which was the occasion of the conversation between Mrs. Roosevelt, Ambassador and Mrs. Bryce, and himself, as reported in the foregoing instalment of Captain Butt's correspondence, was written to one J. C. Martin of Dayton, Ohio. Ex-Ambassador Oscar Straus describes the incident, which was considered one of serious importance by Roosevelt's Cabinet, in his volume of reminiscences entitled: "Under Four Administrations." The letter is reproduced by Mr. Straus from the original draft in his possession, as follows:

The White House,
Washington, November 4th, 1908.

MY DEAR SIR:

I have received your letter running in part as follows:

"While it is claimed almost universally that religion should not enter into politics, yet there is no denying that it does, and the mass of the voters that are not Catholics will not support a man for any office, especially for President of the United States, who is a Roman Catholic.

"Since Taft has been nominated for President by the Republican party, it is being circulated and is constantly urged as a reason for not voting for Taft that he is an infidel (Unitarian) and his wife and brother Roman Catholics. . . . If his feelings are in sympathy with the Roman Catholic Church on account of his wife and brother being Catholics, that would be objectionable to a sufficient number of voters to defeat him. On the other hand if he is an infidel, that would be sure to mean defeat. . . . I am writing this letter for the sole purpose of giving Mr. Taft an opportunity to let the world know what his religious belief is."

I received many such letters as yours during the campaign, expressing dissatisfaction with Mr. Taft on religious grounds; some of them on the ground that he was a Unitarian, and others on the ground that he was suspected to be in sympathy with Catholics. I did not answer any of these letters during the campaign because I regarded it as an outrage even to agitate such a question as a man's religious convictions, with the purpose of influencing a political election. But now that the campaign is over, when there is opportunity for men calmly to consider whither such propositions as those you make in your letter would lead, I wish to invite them to consider them, and I have selected your letter to answer because you advance both the objections commonly urged against Mr. Taft, namely: that he is a Unitarian, and also that he is suspected of improper sympathy with the Catholics.

You ask that Mr. Taft shall "let the world know what his religious belief is." This is purely his own private concern; it is a matter between him and his Maker, a matter for his own conscience; and to require it to be made public under penalty of political discrimination is to negative the first principles of our Government, which guarantee complete religious liberty, and the right to each man to act in religious [affairs] as his own conscience dictates. Mr. Taft never asked my advice in the matter, but if he had asked it, I should have emphatically advised him against thus stating publicly his religious belief. The demand for a statement of a candidate's religious belief can have no meaning except that there may be discrimination for or against him because of that belief. Discrimination against the holder of one faith means retaliatory discrimination against men of other faiths. The inevitable result of entering upon such a practice would be an abandonment of our real freedom of conscience and a reversion to the dreadful conditions of religious dissensions which in so many lands have proved fatal to true liberty, to true religion and to all advance in civilization.

To discriminate against a thoroughly upright citizen because he belongs to some particular church, or because, like Abraham Lincoln, he has not avowed his allegiance to any church, is an outrage against that liberty of conscience which is one of the foundations of American life. You are entitled to know whether a man seeking your suffrages is a man of clean and upright life, honourable in all his dealings with his fellows, and fit by qualification and purpose to do well in the great office for which he is a candidate; but you are not entitled to know matters which lie purely between himself and his Maker. If it is proper or legitimate to oppose a man for being a Unitarian, as was John Quincy Adams, for instance, as is the Rev. Edward Everett Hale, at the present moment Chaplain of the Senate, and an American of whose life all good Americans are proud—then it would be equally proper to support or oppose a man because of his views on justification by faith, or the method of administering the sacrament, or the gospel of salvation by works. If you once enter on such a career there is absolutely no limit at which you can legitimately stop.

So much for your objections to Mr. Taft because he is a Unitarian. Now for your objections to him because you think his wife and brother to be Roman Catholics. As it happens they are not; but if they were, or if he were a Roman Catholic himself, it ought not to affect in the slightest degree any man's supporting him for the position of President. You say that "the mass of the voters that are not Catholics will not support a man for any office, especially for President of the United States, who is a Roman Catholic." I believe that when you say this you foully slander your fellow countrymen. I do not for one moment believe that the mass of our fellow citizens or that any considerable number of our fellow citizens can be influenced by such narrow bigotry as to refuse to vote for any thoroughly upright and fit man because he happens to have a particular religious creed. Such a consideration should never be treated as a reason for either supporting or opposing a candidate for political office. Are you aware that there are several states in this Union where the majority of the people are now Catholics? I should reprobate in the severest terms the Catholics who in those states (or in any other states) refused to vote for the most fit man because he happened to be a Protestant; and my condemnation would be exactly as severe for Protestants who, under reversed circumstances, refused to vote for a Catholic. In public life I am happy to say I have known many men who were elected, and constantly reëlected, to office in districts where the great majority of their constituents were of a different religious belief. I know Catholics who have for many years represented constituencies mainly Protestant, and Protestants who have for many years represented constituencies mainly Catholic; and among the Congressmen whom I knew particularly well was one man of Jewish faith who represented a district in which there were hardly any Jews at all. All of these men by their very existence in political life refute the slander you have uttered against your fellow Americans.

I believe that this Republic will endure for many centuries. If so there will doubtless be among its Presidents Protestants and Catholics, and very probably at some time Jews. I have consistently tried while President to act in relation to my fellow Americans of Catholic faith as I hope that any future President who happens to be a Catholic will act towards his fellow Americans of Protestant faith. Had I followed any other course I should have felt that I was unfit to represent the American people.

In my cabinet at the present moment there sit side by side Catholic and Protestant, Christian and Jew, each man chosen because in my belief he is peculiarly fit to exercise on behalf of all our people the duties of the office to which I have appointed him. In no case does the man's religious belief in any way influence his discharge of his duties, save as it makes him more eager to act justly and uprightly in his relations to all men. The same principles that have obtained in appointing the members of my cabinet, the highest officials under me, the officials to whom is entrusted the work of carrying on all the important policies of my administration, are the principles upon which all good Americans should act in choosing, whether by election or appointment, the man to fill any office from the highest to the lowest in the land.

Yours truly,
THEODORE ROOSEVELT.

XLV

Washington, D. C.,
November 16 (1908).

MY DEAR CLARA:

I am asked a dozen times a day if I expect to remain with the Taft Administration. My answer to all is the same: "I don't know." If I said I thought not it would involve a discussion: if by chance I should say yes it would sound ridiculous. I will tell you that I am absolutely indifferent.

Should he want to retain me as his aide, it would be pleasant to see his policy unroll itself from the inside, yet Mrs. Taft might not prove to be as considerate as Mrs. Roosevelt, nor President Taft near as interesting [as President Roosevelt]. I like and admire him extremely, and I have always found her to be true and loyal. I shall never forget the fact that she called on my mother the day after she arrived from Cuba in 1906, merely to tell her of conditions there and to assure her as to my health and surroundings. Three women on that trip each volunteered to call on Mother on their return, and Mrs. Taft, who was the busiest of the three, was the only one to call.

She is an intellectual woman and a woman of wonderful executive ability. I have no doubt but she will make some startling changes. It has been suggested that she will put the servants and attachés of the White House in uniform, but I hardly think so, though it would be a most agreeable change.

Mr. Roosevelt doubtless sees how incongruous it is for men in white ties and long black frock coats to meet callers, especially foreign ones. The whole thing looks sloppy, yet it is un-American to have it otherwise.

Moreover, most of the attachés at the White House are gentlemen and secured their appointments through influence. Mrs. Roosevelt has done so much that she hardly dares to do more. And Mr. Taft is not apt to permit anything which would offend the good grangers of the country.

I see the papers this afternoon have a story to the effect that Mr. Roosevelt had thirteen persons at dinner the other evening. He would not have objected to having them, but for fear of offending the wives of some of the men present he asked Nick Longworth at the last moment to make the fourteenth. . . .

When the President gives a bachelor dinner Mrs. Roosevelt usually dines with her secretary, Miss Hagner. Miss Hagner has a tiny apartment at the Don Carlos. Her front room serves as both parlour and dining room, and in spite of the inconveniences and lack of form or ceremony people love to be asked there, and those who are admitted feel especially honoured. She and her brother Charley live together, and as he is a fine-looking fellow her friends fear he will soon be getting married and leaving Belle alone. She does not seem to care to marry. I presume the life she has led makes the average social flippant who comes her way seem insignificant. Her friends are very anxious for Mrs. Taft to retain her, but fear that she will not do so. Of course, she has made enemies in her position, and these will do all in their power to undermine her to Mrs. Taft; in fact, they have already done so. There is no one like a well-trained society dame of Washington to know the places to insert the knife. . . .

The news of the death of the Empress of China as well as the Emperor was confirmed by our Minister, Mr. Rockhill, this morning. As soon as I saw it I went to the State Department and sought out old Adee the diplomatic guide book for the past five or six administrations, to ask what the President was supposed to do besides cabling his sympathy. I found that there was no fixed policy in such matters; that once when a sovereign had been assassinated the President had sent his card. I thought this the proper thing to do in this and all similar cases, but Adee was at sea, and the Secretary could not be found, so we got hold of Assistant Secretary Bacon and discussed the pros and cons and finally came to the conclusion that it was the proper thing for the President to send his card to the Legation by a uniformed aide.

I then went to the President and laid the matter of our decision before him and told him that the State Department thought on "certain occasions" that it was eminently fit for him to send his card as I have indicated.

He looked up, smiled, and said:

"And this seems to be a double-barrel occasion, for I suspect that they have permitted the Emperor to die for want of nourishment and poisoned the Dowager. So leave my card with incense and as many joss sticks as you think befit the occasion."

I think I succeeded in getting this precedent fixed as a policy. To-morrow I shall make a long note of the incident in the record book, so that when the death of a sovereign occurs again all who are interested can refer to this case as a precedent. Thus are social customs established. . . .

While talking with Miss Hagner I told her of the report in the paper of the thirteen dinner. She corroborated what I knew to be the facts, that Longworth had been called in to make the fourteenth. But she also told me that many of their luncheons were composed of thirteen persons only, and that she knew of several at which I was present. She then told me the matter was settled shortly after the Roosevelts came to the White House. It was on one occasion when a fourteenth guest declined and the question was brought up then as to the advisability of having thirteen. The President was enraged when he heard that such a discussion was taking place and ordered that whenever it was not convenient to have more than thirteen to have only that number, and since then luncheons of thirteen have been, she said, frequent occurrences. . . .

Your affectionate brother,

ARCHIBALD.

XLVI

Washington, D. C.,
November 17th [1908].

MY DEAR CLARA:

I played tennis with the President yesterday afternoon, but noticed that he was very silent all during the game, nor did he play as good a game as usual. This was for the reason that his mind was preoccupied on his message or some move in Congress. He took the time this morning to say that he wanted me to lunch to-morrow, that he was going to have the editor of *Scribner's Magazine* and one or two other literary men there, and that it might be to my interest to know them in the future.

"Some day when you have something which you may want to publish, to be able to say to these men that you met them at lunch at the White House when you were aide there, will get you a reading at least. I do not think a position such as you occupy would get your matter published if it did not have merit, but the important thing in this day, when every magazine is flooded with manuscripts, is to secure a reading, and I want to put you in touch with the men who will always be big figures in the magazine world. I hope some day that you will take up your writing again."

I merely give you this incident to illustrate his thoughtfulness for those around him. . . .

The more I see of the President the more surprised I am at the way he reaches conclusions and the method he adopts in putting them into effect. I realize, I know, only one side of him. The big political side, the presidential side, I hardly ever see, only getting glimpses of it occasionally. It is the general impression that everybody around him knows his business and has his say so. Nothing is further from the truth. If he thinks I know something which he ought to know, he will ask me about it, as he did the other day regarding General Bell. I do not know what is stewing there. Whatever plan he has up his sleeve, he gave me no intimation. . . .

I find the same thing is true with his cabinet. He deals with each member separately, and often one cabinet member has no idea what is going on in another department until some important change is announced through the press. Yet in matters of minor importance there is no one I have ever met who is freer in conversation than he.

After all, it is the unimportant things which have the more interest as far as his personality is concerned. The big things become a part of the history of the country. It is the little things which give the side lights to his character. But it always makes me angry when I hear people say that he goes off half cocked or does things without consideration. The fact of the matter is, every one of his big official acts is the result of clear, keen-cut, rapid thinking, a lot of hard thought condensed into a small period of space.

To-night he is having his dinner to the labour leaders, but there will be no aide there.

"As much as I would like your company, I fear that all your gold braid would jar upon the liberty-loving labour leaders," he said this morning, when I told him that no aide was put down on the official list, and I thought he might want one.

General Wood and his wife are guests of the White House. . . . He is a wonderfully able man, and the army, which once was of one opinion against his promotion, almost concede to a man now that he is the ablest soldier in it. The President thinks he is one of the most remarkable men of this period and resents most bitterly the suggestion that he stands by him merely because he was Colonel of the Rough Riders. Mrs. Wood is gracious and charming and always well poised.

Your affectionate brother,

ARCHIBALD.

XLVII

Washington, D. C.,
November 18, 1908.

DEAR CLARA:

The luncheon at the White House to-day was very stupid, but the remainder of the afternoon proved to be very pleasant. In the first place there were four Abbotts at the table. I went into the dining room while Miss Hagner was placing the cards at the plates and read off the names of the guests on the chart, and when the last Abbott was read out I asked:

"Why all the Abbotts?"

"They are the owners of the *Outlook* and the family are getting acquainted with them *en masse*," she said, laughing.

The Abbotts own the *Outlook* and the President has chosen that magazine as the purveyor of his thoughts in the coming years. Incidentally, he reaps a rich harvest from it, but he has got to do something and, as he says, writing seems to be about the most harmless thing he can do. He said it is no longer "Oh, that mine enemy would write a book," but "Oh, that mine enemy would write for the magazines!"

However, all the Abbotts have characters and fairly sizzle with convictions. They are great social purists and so their magazine makes a good medium for the President.[1] He has chosen *Scribner's* for all his hunting and African stories, although he was offered much more money by some of the other magazines. Mr. [Robert] Bridges, its editor, was the publisher the President wanted

---

[1]Captain Butt was mistaken as to one or two details, although they are of no special importance. There were only three Abbotts connected with the *Outlook*. So that, at most, there could have been not more than three at this luncheon. The salary which Roosevelt received from the *Outlook* could hardly have been called "a rich harvest." It was less than he was offered by more than one other periodical. In self-defense I may, perhaps, be permitted to add that in the following summer I played a game of golf with Captain Butt in Washington. Unfortunately my game did not sizzle with good shots and my recollection is that I was beaten. I hope it was something more than pity for the vanquished that led Archie to write to his sister-in-law on August 3, 1909: "Yesterday we played golf; the President and Senator Bourne in a twosome, and Mr. Lawrence Abbott of the *Outlook* and I. I got to know the Abbotts in the last administration and to have great respect for both the father and the son."

me to meet. I had little chance to talk to him, but the little I saw of him impressed me most favourably.

General and Mrs. Wood were there and they are always pleasant to meet. The ranking lady was an ancient dowager from New York, of a distinguished family, but obviously hopeless as an intellectual member of modern society. Colonel Lyon of Texas gave a zest to the conversation, but as a rule it was an ill-assorted luncheon and everybody seemed hungry and anxious to eat and get away, especially the President.

As he came from the office I met him and showed him the lady's name he was to take out. He threw up his hands in horror and exclaimed:

"See here, Archie, if you see me commit murder before the third course be prepared to go on the witness stand and swear it to be justifiable homicide."

He really suffered, through the entire meal, for he simply cannot talk to any one who lacks understanding or appreciation. He made conversation around the table with a sort of look of "help, help." During the luncheon he asked me if I could play tennis, and I looked at Mrs. Roosevelt, who answered for me:

"No, Captain Butt cannot. He has promised to walk with me and you must find someone else."

Turning to the rest of the table he said:

"That is how I am henpecked. She steals all my aides and I am forced to associate with old men like Root, Wood, and Garfield."

I think this caused the only laugh that went around the table.

Miss Ethel, who had come back, sat next to me and I found her very entertaining. She was telling me that she had only decided one thing: that she would never marry a man who would not promise in advance to buy back the old Bulloch home in Roswell, Georgia. She is going to have a very brilliant but necessarily short season. I feared that this being the last winter of the Roosevelts she would not have as many entertainments given her as she might otherwise have had, but I think that she will have more.

Already almost every evening from December 15th to January 15th is taken. I know that Mrs. Townsend wants to give her a ball, and Saturday the 26th of December is the only evening left open, so she will have to be content with having a dinner in her honour. She looks very much grown up since she has put on her young lady clothes and when she went out in her furs this afternoon she looked lovely. I never thought her pretty before. She was always dainty and sweet looking, but she will develop into a splendid looking woman. She has a tremendous amount of dignity which she gets from her mother, and yet there is nothing snippy about her.

Mrs. Roosevelt drove by for me about 3:30. I took Duke along with us. We drove to the edge of the park and walked steadily until 6 o'clock. We talked about everything and even got to making up cabinets for Mr. Taft. She does not seem to know anything more about it than any of the rest of us. I gave her all the gossip of the Metropolitan Club on the subject, and she enjoyed hugely the reasons given for eliminating certain of the present Cabinet. She agreed with the opinion of those who think that Mr. Wright would remain in the Cabinet, at least for a while.

I said how disappointed I was that Mr. Wright had gone on the stump for Taft; that his position in the South had been greatly weakened, and to keep him now was no special compliment to the South. I further said that what the South wanted, and all she wanted, was to feel that there was a gentleman from the South in the Cabinet, who, when occasion demanded, could state the position of the South on national issues. She told me that the President felt the same way and had tried to persuade the Secretary from taking the stump at all. This much is interesting, I think.

When I went into the cabinet room this morning I found them removing the chair of the Secretary of the Navy, Mr. Metcalf, recently resigned on account of ill health. . . . Following the custom of some, he asked permission to purchase the chair assigned to him at the cabinet table, and he will replace it with another of the same uniform pattern.

I never knew until this morning—and I must have been in the cabinet room several hundred times—that at the back of each chair is a brass plate bearing the official rank of each member. They sit from right to left of the President in order of the creation of the department. For instance, the Secretary of State sits to the right and then the Secretary of War, and after that the Postmaster-General. I was quite interested in looking them over and learning of the order in which they came.

If Secretary Wilson of the Agricultural Department is permitted to serve in the new Cabinet until the 12th of next March he will have served longer as a cabinet officer than any other member in the history of the Government. I do not think the new President will have the heart to drop him before that date, especially as I understand that the Secretary has not hesitated to make this ambition known.

I brought home [Willard] Straight and [George] Marvin to dinner this evening. It gets so lonesome eating alone. I have had many urgent requests to come to family dinners and dine with friends alone, but I have only gone to the Townsends, where Mrs. Townsend and Mathilde and I dined together, and to General Edwards's, where there were only his wife and myself and the General. Straight, you may remember, is the young consul at Mukden who became an international issue at one time and who is regarded as the best authority in our foreign service on China and Eastern questions.[1] Marvin was with the legation in Pekin, but left our foreign service to enter the service of China and is now here to prepare the way for the great embassy which China is sending to this country to thank the United States for waiving the indemnity imposed upon her by the Allied Powers.

I suppose China is going to spend more than the indemnity would have amounted to, but she regards the rejection of the indemnity as an unprecedented honour and she takes this way to show her appreciation of it.

Both Marvin and Straight are most interesting men, and the evening was as pleasant as it could be with the shadow which still continues to hang over the home. I came across a lot of letters in Spanish written by Mother for practice. Wasn't it wonderful, her ability really to master a foreign language as she did in two years, when over seventy years of age? What would I do with these long evenings if I could not write to you as I do?

Good-night,

ARCHIBALD.

The story of the waiving of the Chinese indemnity has an element of romance in it. The waiver was conceived and its details planned by a veteran American missionary

[1]Willard Straight later joined the firm of Messrs. J. P. Morgan & Company. He entered the army during the World War with the rank of colonel and died, still a young man, of influenza in Paris.

living in China, Dr. Arthur Smith, who made a special journey to the United States to enlist the interest of President Roosevelt. The full story is told in my "Impressions of Theodore Roosevelt."

XLVIII

Washington, D. C.,
Nov. 19, 1908.

DEAR CLARA:

The day has been filled with funny little incidents, but nothing of importance. I went to the President's office early, looked over the books and saw no engagements which would interest me in any way, and therefore thought to have the day to myself and personal work or play, as the case might be. While waiting for the President the Secretary of State came in and we talked on conventional topics for a few minutes. At 10:00 the President came in, evidently in a good humour.

"Elihu, I am glad to see you, and as soon as I have said a word to my fellow Georgian I will be ready to discuss international politics from Greenland to the Balkans."

Turning to me, he said:

"Wood has persuaded me that the new yellow underwear which the army is getting out will prevent the actinic rays from eating up my spinal cord. Will you look into the matter and tell me what he means, and if you think I can afford to wear yellow order me some of it? It is awful to put these things on you, but what is a man to do when he knows nothing about actinic rays and never knew he had a nerve?"

As he left the room I heard him say, "Root, I think we must come to some understanding about——" and closed the door, and I went to the White House. There I found nothing waiting for my attention, and so went to Sloan's auction rooms, where a very interesting sale was going on in old mahogany and rugs. Needless to say, I bought neither. I asked Lieutenant Commander Crank to lunch with me, and later we were going to walk, but before the meal was half over I got a message from the White House that the Austro-Hungarian Ambassador had asked for a conference at 2:30, which caused me to leave Crank alone and hastily to don my full-dress uniform, for ambassadors always rank gold lace and patent-leather boots.

Promptly at 2:30 the President and Mrs. Roosevelt, who had been dining alone, came into the corridors, laughing like two children. Mrs. Roosevelt left us in a few minutes, and the President asked me to sit with him in the Red Room. He spoke of the humiliation[1] the German Emperor must be feeling and added:

"But he has been riding for a fall for some time. It does not make it any the less pathetic, however, but I fear that it is going to have a serious effect on monarchical Germany."

Then he referred to his recent order taking the marines from the battleships.

"I do not hesitate to say that their downfall, as the German Emperor's, is due largely to themselves. They have augmented to themselves such importance, and their influence, which they have gained by pandering to every political influence, has given them such an abnormal position for the size of their corps that they have simply invited their own destruction. I do not hesitate to say that they should be absorbed into the army and no vestige of their organization should be allowed to remain. They cannot get along with the navy, and as a separate com-

[1]On the 10th of November the Reichstag had admonished the Kaiser for indiscreet talk upon foreign affairs and on the 17th the Kaiser promised to be more discreet in the future.

mand with the army the conditions would be intolerable."

The Austrian Ambassador arrived, and, bowing to the President, I led the way into the Blue Room. Knowing the conference to be one of importance and seeing secrecy written all over Hengelmüller's face, I retired to the corridor and stood at attention at the door. The conference lasted nearly an hour, and when the Ambassador came out there was a decided scowl on his face. As I turned to enter the room I caught a glimpse of the President dancing what appeared to be a jig. His face was beaming and he said, poised like a bird in midair:

"I have just had a splendid fencing match, and if I don't get some of these international complications off my chest I will expire. I feel as if I could whip an elephant, so the next best thing is to take a good ride, and Roswell has not been out for some time. I think I would like to try his mettle. This has been one of the most trying days to me in many a month, but I feel just as happy as if I had been lying in a bed of sweet peas dreaming of the millennium."

He then told me that he got a lot of entertainment out of Sir Harry Johnston; that he was constantly surprised at the viewpoint of foreigners.

"For instance, it has never occurred to me that New York could be considered beautiful. Yet Johnston tells me that it is one of the most beautiful places he has ever seen and that coming into it late in the evening he thought he was approaching fairyland. He was not quite as flattering about our women, but his description of a certain type was very funny. He said that some of the women he had met had a marvellous way of screeching like a peacock, and when their voices were at the highest notes they had a way of putting their heads sideways and mewing like a cat. While I was tempted to argue the question with him, I had only recently noticed this peculiarity in some of my own friends and I simply had not the heart to other than laugh."

I saw Mrs. Charley McCauley on the street to-day, and it seems to me the older she gets the more beautiful she grows. I leave to-morrow afternoon at 1 o'clock for a shoot at quail at Mount Vernon with Mr. Dodge, the superintendent, and after spending the night there we are going Saturday morning over into Maryland for wild turkey. Mr. Dodge says he knows where there are some turkeys, but if we miss these there will be plenty of quail.

Good-night,
ARCHIBALD.

Sir Harry Johnston, a distinguished African explorer and an authority on the zoölogy, ethnology, and geography of the "Dark Continent," came over from England in the autumn of 1908 at the invitation of Roosevelt to discuss various aspects of the latter's proposed visit to Africa. In his recently published "Story of My Life" Sir Harry gives the following pleasant picture of the White House and its occupants:

The chief object in coming to Washington was to see Roosevelt, both before and after other excursions. The White House is, of course, a palace. Every room and the furniture of every room at the time I first saw it was something to be admired in architecture, design, and decoration; and the extreme comfort and aptness of its appointments must have impressed most visitors. But in 1908 it gave me the impression—perhaps a mistaken one—of not offering an excessive amount of accommodation for the President's Staff. I was honoured by the allotment of an historical bedroom, the room in which President Lincoln had signed the edict enfranchising over four million slaves in 1865. Greaves [Sir Harry's photographer] had a bedroom at no great distance, and what I thought showed such a sense of hospitality was that the President, after bursting into my room to greet me and see that I was comfortable, passed along the passage to ascertain the same fact as to my companion.

Some of the meals were banquets, with the numbers of guests, the forms and ceremonies of reception and withdrawal, the menus and the wines (it was before the days of Prohibition) one would have expected in the royal palaces of a first-class power. But the breakfasts, the teas in the afternoon, and occasionally a luncheon or a Sunday dinner were *en famille*, and Mrs. Roosevelt, whose bonhomie and kindly informality "rested" her guests, played the part of a hostess in private life. In fact, I thought the breakfasts particularly homely in a pleasant way. The children took their places with curt greetings, exclaimed, chuckled, pouted over their correspondence, or over the eggs being either hard-boiled or not boiled enough. Roosevelt divided his attentions between his trays of correspondence and his breakfast dishes or cups of coffee; and Mrs. Roosevelt showed me the patterns from which she was invited to select materials for winter garments.

After the stately dinners (at each of which one met exceedingly interesting people—Governors of States, of West Indian Islands, or the Philippines, heads of Oxford Colleges, ambassadors, inventors, soldiers and sailors) Roosevelt would take me away, when he had bidden his formal farewell at ten-thirty, to some upper room furnished more like a studio, with natural history specimens or examples of modern inventions. Here, Chinese tea or Mocha coffee would be served to us, but here alone we would talk and argue until midnight or even one o'clock. I think I have never spent my time with any man more interesting. He knew the things on which he spoke, yet by no means monopolized the conversation, either at banquets, at cosy meals, or in these retired duologues.

He would lead out the head of Oriel College to discourse on the Latin and the literature of the fifth century after Christ; and then he himself would give a wonderful and arresting account of the Tartar occupation of Russia, between 1200 and 1400 A.D. Or one of his guests might be a German oölogist. He would see that he told us enough about rare birds' eggs, without becoming a bore. He would ascertain that the Governor of the Philippines was competent to describe the Negroid population of the jungles, before he gave vent to any opinion which might be detected as inaccurate by the Dutch ethnologist seated next him.

I have never known such a house for universality and detail; for kind and practical anxiety as to my footgear's adaptability to the appalling snowfall which began in the middle of this visit, the suitability of my outfit for the West Indies, or the extent of my worry over Liberian affairs, or lecture engagements.

XLIX

Washington, D. C.,
November 24, 1908.

DEAR CLARA:

Since writing last I have been much amused by the newspapers, which have been making much over the conference of Mr. Hearst of the New York *American* and the President, and of all the wild guesses not one of them has hit within a mile of the truth. Such a conference was certain to mystify everyone, for no two men have been as far apart in every way as these two, and for them now to make common cause against Haskell of Oklahoma[1] is certainly disconcerting. But the President really believes that Haskell is going to make an effort to stop his African trip, and he cannot make an official move until Haskell opens the way.

I think myself that Haskell would do anything to even up the score between Mr. Roosevelt and himself. But he has entered suit against Hearst and the President intimated that he would be willing to meet Mr. Hearst halfway on the subject of Haskell. The President has all sorts of evidence, so he thinks, against Haskell, and he will turn it over to Hearst if the latter can by the 4th of next March use it to squelch this troublesome Governor of Oklahoma. This is the bottom of the conference which has caused so much speculation for the last few days.

We have had quite an accident over at the White House

[1]The story of Roosevelt's attacks on Governor Charles N. Haskell of Oklahoma is fully related in the first chapter of "Impressions of Theodore Roosevelt." Haskell's threats were merely a bluff, and he did not attempt to stop the African trip. He has recently had some further unflattering newspaper notoriety as an oil promoter.

and one which has more general interest than appears at first. In cleaning the White House rooms two or three days ago the shades were all raised high and for the first time in several months everything in the Red Room was visible. Much to the consternation of everyone, it was discovered that the portrait of Washington by Stuart was in such wretched condition that the canvas was separating. This is the portrait that Dolly Madison cut or caused to be cut from its frame when the English were reported to have reached Washington city in the War of 1812. It was afterward framed and placed in the Red Room over the fireplace and has hung there ever since. Mrs. Roosevelt ordered it sent to Veerhorf to be restored. I think it will have to be glued in some way to another piece of canvas, and the greatest caution has to be taken, as too much heat would cause the paint to peel off. Mrs. Roosevelt regards it as the most valuable possession of the White House and is greatly distressed over its condition.

Everybody is wondering why the Corbins subscribed $10,000 for the Taft campaign fund, Mrs. Corbin, who was Edythe Patten, is rich, but not wealthy enough to throw away $10,000 without adequate return. Of course General Corbin[1] has always played for high stakes and has usually won. The general supposition is that Mrs. Corbin wants the Court of St. James's for the General, or even Berlin, and that $10,000 is a cheap price to pay for it, but it would not be cheap if the General has to resign from the army to accept it or any other post of honour under the Taft Administration. He is drawing the pay of a Lieuten-

---

[1]General Henry C. Corbin who entered the army as a lieutenant in the Civil War. In 1894 he was made Adjutant-General and in this office was the active head of the army during the Spanish War. He died in 1909 soon after President Taft was inaugurated.

ant-General retired, and there is a law that prevents him from holding two offices at the same time. . . .

As I was walking up the avenue this afternoon I saw the Corbin automobile in front of the Post Building, and I am inclined to think that he will take the public into his confidence or partial confidence to-morrow. Whatever he says can be discounted, for the "Ministers of Darkness tell us partial truths to betray us in the deepest consequences."

However, General Corbin is not as dark as he is painted. His chief offence is that he has succeeded in methods which, since his days of promotion, have become far more common and which no longer take the army by surprise. He was the first to secure preferment in the army by political pull, but since then the system is one which has to be taken into consideration whenever an officer figures on his future.

Many seem to think that all the Pattens subscribed to the amount, as they are very ambitious socially, and having reached everything in Washington worth having socially they now sigh for other worlds to conquer. . . . They were so bitter with the General at the time of his marriage to Edythe that none of them would speak to him. They have learned to like him very much since and star him on all occasions. If he can make the Cabinet or be sent to England, France, or Germany, they will never cease to refer with affection to their "brother-in-law the Ambassador," etc.

I see nothing incongruous in putting him in the Cabinet, for he is a very brainy man, and I have never seen anything but what was honourable and upright in his character. He conducted the whole of the Spanish-American War, and if it had gone badly for us he would have been given all the blame, yet there has always been an effort to rob him of the credit due him. But whatever opinions there may be about him, there is but one regarding her—that she would adorn any post she would find herself in. She is especially fitted for the rôle of "Madame l'Ambassadrice." It will be interesting to watch the cards fall, and the publication of this ten-thousand-dollar subscription of the Corbins will cause the pack to be scanned even more eagerly than otherwise here in Washington. . . .

To-morrow the statue of Sheridan is to be unveiled, and Bromwell and I will have to escort the President and Mrs. Roosevelt to the ceremonies. Richie Simpkins and Oden Hoerstman were here to dinner to-night, and when the birds which I had brought home from my trip down the river were brought on the table they each said they could not eat more and, asking for a piece of paper, they wrapped up their quail and took them home for their breakfasts. It is what I have often wanted to do myself, but this is the first time I have actually seen this mannish wish put into execution. As there were lying in my ice-box a wild goose and two redheads, a gift from Simpkins, I had no cause to object. He is certainly one of the kindest hearted persons in the world and goes out of his way to take me out of the house and away from my sad thoughts these days. . . .

Well, good-night. As ever,
Your affectionate brother,
ARCHIBALD.

L

Washington, D. C.,
November 25, 1908.

DEAR CLARA:

I have just come from the unveiling of the Sheridan statue, having been there since half-past two. I lunched at the White House, only a Professor Jordan, Mr. Malcolm Donald, and Mr. Gutzon Borglum and myself being guests.

Mr. Borglum is the sculptor of the statue, and a good deal of his fame will rest on it, though of course his group of wild horses at the Metropolitan Museum of Art in New York is his best known piece as yet. His head of Lincoln, which is going to be placed in the rotunda of the Capitol, is greatly admired, and while it is a wonderful piece of sculpture, yet it is absurd to call it Lincoln. It is true he calls it the "Ideal Lincoln," but it is softened to such a point as to eliminate all the roughness and coarseness out of him and leaves an angelic face of a gentleman. It seems to be the first sign of a growing tendency to be ashamed of his roughness. We have gradually made over so many of our older types that their own generations would hardly recognize them, but when an artist makes Lincoln into a gentleman and the Senate accepts it and puts its approval upon it, it is getting a little bit absurd. A wonderful man, a great man, we all admit, but why try to change history and flatter the physiognomy of one of our best known men out of all resemblance to the original?

However, this statue of Sheridan is fine and I hope it ushers in a period of art for our equestrian figures in Washington, for most of them are wooden and inartistic.

Before we had finished lunch Colonel Bromwell and Commander Sims of the navy came to accompany the President, and he was in an ugly humour at having to leave lunch, for General Corbin had told him if he got there by three o'clock he would be in ample time, whereas, as I told him before he sat down, the exercises begin at two-thirty. The President, Mrs. Roosevelt, and Colonel Bromwell went in one carriage, and Sims, Borglum, and I in the other. We met the party at the entrance and while waiting must have been photographed a dozen times, for they snapped us with big cameras every time an Ambassador came by.

The exercises were very long and for the most part very tiresome. Immediately back of me was the Austro-Hungarian Ambassador and his wife and other members of the diplomatic corps. During General Horace Porter's speech I was much amused at the Baroness, who was dressed in velvets and furs and who was evidently very warm. She kept murmuring from time to time:

"*Ô mon Dieu, mon Dieu, failes moi mourir ce soir!*"

The speech was unnecessarily long, and the President was getting frightfully impatient when it finally came to a close. General Corbin had to eliminate his speech altogether.

It was a fine gathering of social lights of Washington, who sat in the stands, while beneath them in what was shaped into a sort of arena or circus ring sat the old comrades of Sheridan. Bromwell, who has charge of Public Buildings and Grounds, is well known socially, so that when he has to get up these formal functions he arranges it so that the well-known society people have the front seats and really makes what would otherwise be a promiscuous gathering quite a social event. It looks well from the diplomatic seats and in the photographs, even if it does not tickle the palates of the proletariat.

Mrs. Sheridan, who looked young and pretty enough to be the daughter instead of the widow of the man they were unveiling, was there dressed in a garnet cloth gown and a hat to match. Lieutenant Sheridan pulled the string that caused the flags to fall and there was quite a cheer from his father's old comrades when he stepped on the platform. He looks very much like his father, which is a matter of great delight to his family. Mary Sheridan, the oldest daughter, and the twin girls sat with their mother also, and were becomingly gowned in colours. Just why I thought they would be in dark colours I do not exactly know. Mrs. Sheridan does not look a day older than the twins and is quite as fascinating as she is pretty and piquant.

Mrs. Herbert Wadsworth came late with a new attaché of some embassy and the Patten sisters were also in evidence. While the President was reviewing the troops Mrs. Fairbanks sat with Mrs. Roosevelt and seemed quite as chatty as if it were a common thing for them to sit tête-à-tête. Mrs. Ellis's entrance created some extra attention as she is known to be a great friend of the Tafts and calls the President-elect "Will," and will be one of the kitchen cabinet in the next administration. It is interesting to see the additional importance certain persons take on when some intimate friend or relative comes into power. It is natural, of course. Mrs. Ellis is a sweet, charming woman, and made her way very rapidly into what was best socially almost immediately upon her arrival here from Cincinnati. She now becomes one of the "Ins," and some who have been very important for the last four years become the "Outs." As Gibbons often said, it takes a special mind to follow the shifting changes of the "isms" and the "wasms" in Washington.

This administration has developed two factors heretofore unclassified in former administrations. The kitchen cabinets have given place to the Tennis Cabinet and to the Incense Swingers. Every now and then I hear jokes passed about the Incense Swingers, and the other day I made inquiry of General Clarence Edwards of just what was meant by the Incense Swingers. He said that as yet I had not been put among them, but he feared from signs he saw in me that I would be soon somewhere in the second or third row, anyhow. The Incense Swingers are made up largely of the New England element, possibly more the Harvard type, who are supposed to stand around the President as acolytes do about a priest and swing incense at him and about him, while the centre figure stands with his skirts outspread to receive the laudation. Among the chief Incense Swingers are the Beekman Winthrops, the Pinchots, my good friend Billy Phillips, Secretary Garfield, Assistant Secretary of State Bacon, and in fact, that small coterie who think the President never makes a mistake, and who believe, moreover, that he cannot make a mistake. It is the type of New Englander who murmurs always when you are telling anything to one of them:

"Perfectly wonderful. Isn't it marvellous? How extraordinary!"

When the President came into his office this morning there were several Incense Swingers waiting for him, I being one among them, and I fear I am getting to be "of them," too. He was in a good humour, but he usually is in the morning. He says that the normal time for a normal man to be in a good humour is the morning, and if he is not it is a sign that he is a heavy drinker or else possesses an abnormally bad temper if not a perverse one. He looked over his list of engagements and read them aloud. As he came to "12:30—Dr. Booker T. Washington," he looked up and, with that quizzical smile of his, said:

"How fortunate for you, Archie, that it is not 1:30. I might add that it is equally fortunate for me. The last time this distinguished citizen was here it was nearer 1:30, and I did not know for some time after whether I would be quartered or hung."

Is this enough gossip for to-day? If so, I will proceed

to more important things, namely, a wire this afternoon tells me that Aunt Kitty and Kate, with Lewis, will be here at 8:50 to-morrow morning. . . .

Adios. As ever,
Your affectionate brother,
ARCHIBALD.

There was undoubtedly a good deal of "incense swinging" about President Roosevelt. Indeed, I am not sure but that I may have been one of the guilty ones myself. The incense, however, was the perfume of a very genuine sentiment of confidence and admiration. But Roosevelt was rarely if ever anæsthetized by it. This is perhaps an appropriate place to tell a heretofore unpublished story of Roosevelt's reaction when one of his important associates refused to "swing incense." It was told me by a distinguished lawyer of New York, Judge Hiram R. Steele, who was an old and intimate friend of the late Chief Justice White. Judge Steele had been a close legal associate of Mr. White when they were both young men in New Orleans years ago. Not long before the death of the Chief Justice they spent an evening together in Mr. White's study in Washington. In discussing the personality of Roosevelt, whose death had only recently occurred, the Chief Justice said that one of his most remarkable traits was his willingness to take advice, and related the following story as an illustration of this quality. My friend was unwilling that the story should be published during Justice White's lifetime but has now given me permission to print it.

Not long after Roosevelt's election to the Presidency in 1904 he invited a party of gentlemen, most of them of high official position, to dine with him. After dinner he told them that he had called them together in order to read to them the draft of his first Message to Congress as an elected President. When the reading was finished they all "swung incense" save Justice White, who kept silence. The President asked for his comment. The Justice demurred on the ground that he was neither a Republican nor a member of the Executive or Legislative branches of the Government, and so his opinion could be of little value. The President persisted. The Justice, aware of his own reputation for brusqueness, still declined on the ground that if he expressed an opinion it must be a perfectly frank one. But as the President would not take "no" for an answer the Justice said: "Well, in some respects I think it is the worst state paper I have ever heard."

The incense swingers were aghast, and even the President looked a little shocked. But when he asked for a bill of particulars the Justice went into details and pointed out half-a-dozen passages which he thought Mr. Bryan would seize upon as material for effective Democratic criticism. The party broke up in gloom. Justice White went home and said to his wife, "We shall never be invited to the White House again."

"What in the world has happened?" was her surprised query.

"Why, I've upset the apple-cart. The President read us his Message and I severely criticized it."

"Oh, my dear, what could have induced you to do such a thing as that!"

"I didn't want to," complained the Justice, "but he dragooned me into doing it!"

For some time they felt perturbed about the incident, believing that their pleasant and friendly relations with Roosevelt had been interrupted if not destroyed. Two or three days later Mrs. White attended a state reception at the White House although another engagement prevented the Chief Justice from accompanying her. As she approached the President in the formal line he stepped out of his place and literally "grabbed both her hands"—as the Chief Justice expressed it—exclaiming: "Mrs. White, do you know your husband gave me the worst abuse the other evening that I have received since I've been President!" And then, just as she was wishing that the floor would open and swallow her up, he quickly added with his magnetic smile: "And the worst of it was he was absolutely right, *absolutely right!*"

Of course, Mrs. White reported this to her husband as soon as she got home and with relieved feelings they watched for the publication of the Message with some curiosity. When it appeared they found to their satisfaction that the criticized passages in the original draft had been completely modified in accordance with the suggestions of the Chief Justice.

"Where," said the Chief Justice to my friend in commenting on this incident, "will you find a more striking instance of open-mindedness in a great political leader than this?"

LI

Washington, D. C.,
November 26 [1908].
Thanksgiving Day.

DEAR CLARA:

While I had not thought it necessary to go to the White House to-day, it being a holiday and one the President generally spends in the country, yet it was fortunate that I did go, for I found much to do. In the first place when I got home last night I found a message from Mrs. Roosevelt asking me to take dinner with them this evening.

Acting on my usual custom never to make excuses to the White House, I telephoned the usher that I would be there. The first thing the President said to me on seeing me this morning:

"You are coming to dinner to-night with us?"

"Yes, sir," I said, and he continued:

"You are sure you have no other engagement?" and I answered promptly:

"I have no other engagement, sir," for I did not regard the presence of my relatives as an engagement, though I wanted very much to take this dinner with them.

"Now see here, Archie, unless you are perfectly frank with us and do not come to us when you have other things you want to do, we will never know whether we are kind in asking you or not. In other words, don't let us be nasty when our only desire is to be nice."

Like unto Peter I denied it almost with an oath, although had I known last night that it was only a family dinner I was invited to I should have felt no hesitancy in declining. But you can never tell how important dinners and luncheons are going to be there. At any rate, this shows the kindness of heart which prompts these people in most of their private acts.

As I passed through the office I looked at the list of the day's engagements which is always kept in Mr. Loeb's office and there learned that the President was to make a speech at the laying of a cornerstone of the Young Coloured Men's Christian Association Building, 'way out on Twelfth Street. I called Mr. Forster's[1] attention to it and asked him to find out from the President what time he wanted Colonel Bromwell or myself to come for him. He sent me word that he would not take an aide with him.

---

[1]Rudolph Forster, for many years and still the efficient and indispensable Executive Clerk at the White House.

It seemed to me that this would be a mistake, and I so told Forster and he agreed with me, but said he could not take it up with him again. I took it upon myself, in spite of Bromwell's oft-repeated advice to me never to make a suggestion after the President had expressed an opinion, to go into the office again and to say what was in my mind. I thought it my duty as an aide. So entering, I said, as if I had not received his message:

"Mr. President, you have an engagement for this afternoon."

"Yes," said he, "but I sent you word that I would not need an aide; didn't Mr. Forster tell you?"

I felt cornered, but I said:

"Yes, Mr. President, but I think you should take one, for these coloured men know that you usually are accompanied by an aide on such occasions, and if you do not have one now I fear they will think there is some discrimination against them."

He had begun by frowning, but ended with a smile.

"That is true, and I had not thought of it in that light, so I will ask you to accompany me and let us look our best."

I repeat this, for it gives a new light on his character. I left his office feeling that if he had had more subordinates around him that would not mind making suggestions to him, even though they were counter to his preconceived notion, he might have made even fewer mistakes than he has made. I refer now to his memorandum on phonetic spelling and his order to leave off "In God We Trust" from the coinage of the country.

I had a nice Thanksgiving's lunch at home, eating a large mince pie which Mrs. Roosevelt sent me yesterday, one made out of her own mincemeat. It was a pleasant treat for little Lewis to eat a pie made at the White House.

I think Aunt Kitty thought it a specially good pie also.

Going out to the ceremonies Mr. Loeb said to the President that he had looked over his speech and he and Mr. Forster thought he ought to insert a little more ginger into it. I saw what Loeb meant when I heard the speech, but I did not think it lacked ginger. It was a very cleverly worded lecture to the Negroes to live properly and a word to the whites to help them. It did not mince matters, yet there was nothing in it to incite the Negroes to hail him as a second Saviour, and nothing in it to offend the white sentiment of the South or of any portion of the country.

Coming back in the carriage I told him this. . . .

Loeb confessed it sounded better than he thought it would sound and quite receded from his former position. The President then said this, which I think the only thing of importance I am quoting to-day:

"They wanted me to say something about the fourteenth and fifteenth amendments, but I refused most emphatically to do so or to advocate standing the Pyramid on its apex or inverting the Washington monument."

It was evidently Booker Washington who made this suggestion yesterday and I am glad to know that it went unheeded.

I spent the rest of the afternoon with Aunt Kitty and Kate and at 8:00 was at the White House. It was truly a family dinner, only Straight of the State Department and I being outsiders. The Longworths were there, Miss Ethel, Mr. Wallingford, an in-law of the Longworths, and the President and Mrs. Roosevelt and Quentin. It was a simple dinner, but oh! such a good one. The only thing needed was snow on the ground and wind whistling on the outside.

When the waiter began to serve the sherry, Mrs.

Roosevelt said to him that it being Thanksgiving he could serve champagne. It is the only time I have ever seen anything stronger than sherry or Rhine wine on the White House table, except at formal dinners.

I know you are interested to know what we had to eat and I will satisfy your curiosity.

We had creamed pea soup, no fish of any kind, and then was brought in the largest turkey I have ever seen in my life. I had often read about the turkeys which some old fellow, a Mr. Vose in New Jersey, always sent the White House at Thanksgiving time, but I had not expected ever actually to participate in the mastication of one. The President asked how much it weighed, and said unless it weighed up to the standard that he refused to touch it. The head waiter told him it weighed a little over twenty-five pounds dressed.

Following the first waiter was a second carrying a large silver platter containing a roast pig with an apple in its mouth. Mrs. Roosevelt said that they would not get much else, so to take both kinds of meat. Quentin caused a laugh by asking:

"Mother, aren't we going to have vegetables?"

He was soon satisfied, for there followed spinach, sweet potatoes, sugared Southern style, and boiled rice. After this we had salad of lettuce and alligator pears. Then came apple and mince pies and ice cream moulded in the shape of quail with melted brown sugar poured over each to resemble gravy.

Mrs. Roosevelt said the President and Ethel never ate mincemeat, and that whenever she had mince pies she had to have apple or lemon pies for them.

The President was in a splendid humour all through dinner and told anecdote after anecdote with as much zeal as if he had had a large and carefully selected audience to listen to him. In fact, I think he is more charming when only surrounded by his household. After dinner, while smoking in his library—while the rest of us were smoking, I should say, for the President never touches tobacco in any form—he spoke with some concern over the prospect of being followed into Africa by tourists or, worse still, by a horde of reporters. He said that before going he would issue a statement saying that he would not open his mouth to a reporter while in Africa and that whatever was printed would be without authority and foundation.

"I feel absolutely ferocious at times when I am not allowed to have a moment to myself. I do not think any English newspaper men will attempt to follow me, for the English are rather decent in such matters, and if our own people pursue me as they did when I hunted in the West I might be able to get the authorities to intervene until I elude them in the wilds. They will never catch up with me if I get ahead of them once, and if they do in the jungle you may see my expense report to the National Museum read something after this order: 'One hundred dollars for buying the means to rid myself of one *World* reporter; three hundred dollars expended in dispatching a reporter of the *American;* five hundred dollars for furnishing wine to cannibal chiefs with which to wash down a reporter of the New York *Evening Post.*'"

We did not linger long over the cigars and we soon went into Mrs. Roosevelt's sitting room and library, which is over the Blue Room and which is largely furnished with her own personal belongings, where we sat down and tried to help Miss Ethel and Mrs. Longworth work out one of these new-fangled puzzles, which are now all the rage. Mrs. Roosevelt sat on the sofa knitting, and the President excused himself to work on his Message. Everybody showed signs of being sleepy early, and the family were left to their own devices a little after 10:30.

These little incidents will form pleasant memories as the shadows lengthen in life. Inseparable with them was the ever recurring thought that she who was wont always to be thankful for any little blessings which might come into our lives was not here and would not be here any more. . . .

Good-night and God bless you both,

Affectionately,

ARCHIBALD.

LII

Washington, D. C.,
November 30th, 1908.

DEAR CLARA:

I have just received my first word from the incoming Administration. It is to the effect that both the President-elect and Mrs. Taft want me to remain on at the White House after March the fourth. General Edwards, who is the personal friend of the President-elect and his wife, returned yesterday from the Hot Springs and at once sent word he wanted to see me. I met him near his own house as I was coming from the White House, where the President and Mrs. Roosevelt had been receiving informally some delegation from New York. He had already sent me word through his wife that I was to be kept on, but it was a matter of such supreme indifference to me that I had not thought about it one way or another.

Of course, everyone thinks I am anxious to remain, whereas the contrary is correct. It would be a matter of more personal distinction to serve out with the Roosevelts and then retire. But I am not in a position where I can say one thing or another. I did tell [General] Edwards yesterday, and tried to hammer it in, that it was a matter of indifference to me and that it would not be the act of a friend to mention my name in connection with the White House to the Tafts. But he said that both were decided that I was to remain, and that there would probably be some other officer chosen to divide the duties with me, such a person as Tibby Mott[1] for instance.

Mott is a splendid officer, a Virginian, has been military attaché in Paris, speaks French beautifully, is a gentleman, and in every way capable of running the whole thing just as I have had to do, but if he has any other duties to perform than I have in the White House, it is too much for one man to undertake.

Edwards's suggestion was, though he said it was Taft's suggestion, that I have supervision of the White House and all functions as I have now, and that Mott take the outside work, stables, and as he ranks me, naturally he would assume the duties which Bromwell performs now, which is largely to represent the President on more formal occasions.

As I thought would be the case, Mrs. Taft contemplates some sweeping changes in her régime, the most important being to do away with the frock-coated ushers at the White House and substitute them with liveried servants. As I have pointed out before, it would certainly look much better, but these ushers have been at the White House always and are often men of importance, politically, and to change them I fear will run counter to a very deep-seated prejudice in this country.

I told General Edwards yesterday, when he took up the matter with me, that while I thought it would improve the appearance of the White House entrance, yet the

[1]Col. Bentley Mott, who, in 1910, was Roosevelt's personal aide in London when the latter was filling the office of international social importance, of special Ambassador at the funeral of King Edward. See comment on Letter XXVIII.

change would be so radical that Mrs. Taft must be prepared for criticism of a severe character. I told Mrs. Roosevelt of the proposed change while we were out walking this morning and it almost broke her heart. I knew that it would strike pretty deeply, for she has a great affection for all these men, but I did not know that she would take it as hard as she did.

She had telephoned to me to bring my dog and walk with her early to-day, as her engagements would keep her in the house the rest of the day. We started out at 9:00 and while I had not intended to tell her of my conversation with General Edwards at this time, still the conversation turned on the Tafts and what changes they would make. I told her first that Mrs. Taft had decided not to retain Miss Hagner, and then about the ushers. She had no criticism to make about Miss Hagner and thought it a matter entirely to be arranged by the incoming lady, and she felt it was just as well, as Miss Hagner had held such an intimate place with Mrs. Roosevelt that to serve under any one else would be hard for both. Besides she thought Mrs. Taft really would need a stenographer, which of course Miss Hagner is not.

We were walking down the old road in front of the Garner Hubbard place when she asked me the straight-out question:

"Are they going to change the ushers?"

I told her yes.

"All of them?" she asked, her voice quivering.

"All of them," I said, "and will substitute them with coloured liveried servants."

"Oh, it will hurt them so," and her voice broke and she stopped, raised her veil, and for a few minutes could not speak.

To me it was the woman I saw only, not the President's

wife, not the mother; simply the woman who felt keenly the humiliation which those who had served her so faithfully would be called upon to suffer.

"Captain Butt," she said finally, when able to control her voice, "don't think me foolish, but if you knew how those men had served us and how kind and thoughtful they have been in times of illness and trouble, you would understand me now."

I did understand her and I tried to comfort her by telling her that I had made a suggestion that I hoped would set the matter right with the ushers. It was to retire Major Loeffler, now in the office of the President, and to put in his place Mr. Stone, the head usher at the White House, and to replace McKenna with Hoover, who is now Stone's assistant and who would occupy the same place in the office instead of the house. I am to see Mrs. Taft next Monday and talk over the matter. I asked Mrs. Roosevelt not to tell the President for two reasons, that it might unnecessarily distress him and then he might take it on himself to read the riot act to Mr. Taft on the subject and thereby have the whole programme changed. Mrs. Roosevelt would not like this, either, for she does not want to make any suggestions to Mrs. Taft at all, naturally feeling that she should not be hampered in any way in making changes she might have in mind.

I am afraid I spoiled Mrs. Roosevelt's walk, but I thought it much better for her to hear of these changes from me rather than from others. Then, too, my loyalty certainly at the present time is to the Roosevelts, and if I am continued by the Tafts I hope to serve them as faithfully, but whether with the same interest and enthusiasm as I do the President and his wife I have my doubts.

The personal compliment in appointing me aide came from the Roosevelts. If I am continued under the Tafts it will be largely in the capacity of an officer who knows the routine and who is needed for some special duty. Then, too, I could never hope to occupy the place under them as I do now. While I have a great deal too much to do, yet it gives me a prestige and influence that I could not retain were the duties more divided.

I have finally succeeded in selling Audrey, the President's mare. I heard that Mrs. Straus was looking for a riding horse and so offered her to the Secretary for six hundred dollars, and he was very glad to get her. He said she would be kept as an heirloom in the family. As Audrey is now about ten years old, I fear as an heirloom she will not descend to many generations of little Strauses.

Yesterday the Assistant Secretary of State, Colonel Bromwell, Commander Sims, and I went to the station to meet the Special Ambassador from China, who has been sent to thank this Government for remitting the indemnity imposed upon her by the Allied Powers. The Ambassador, Tang Chao Li, is accompanied by Prince Tsai Fu, a prince of the imperial blood, a small, retiring, but quite a handsome man for a Chinaman. The Ambassador is a large, distinguished-looking man and takes precedence over the Prince, as he is the direct representative of the Emperor on this occasion. The Prince had not heard of the death of his cousins, the Emperor and the Empress Dowager, until he had got to San Francisco and yesterday showed the signs of the grief which he is said really to feel. They were accompanied by about twenty-five, and we all drove in state to the home of the Percy Morgans on Scott Circle, one of the most palatial houses in the city.

It was too funny to see the Orientals burrowing themselves into the Morgan comforts. They simply purred and revelled in the luxury presented. The Minister,

Mr. Wu, told the Ambassador that he had been unable to get a Chinese cook, and the interpreter told me that his excellency said:

"Don't get one. I like French cooking better than any other kind and I want to teach my suite to eat as the Westerners do."

To-morrow we receive them in state at the White House.

Good-bye.
ARCHIBALD.

LIII

Washington, D. C.,
December 2, 1908.

DEAR CLARA:

It has been a busy day. I have changed my clothes five times, and if I had done as I should have done to-night and put on a dinner jacket, I would have changed six times. The President is starred to-night in the bulletins as having had an unusually busy day, but I have not only had to keep pace with him, but shift from citizen's clothes to uniforms and back again with a rapidity that has astonished my good relatives from home, who have looked aghast at the lightning changes.

The President had to attend the High Mass celebration at St. Patrick's Church in honour of the Diamond Jubilee of the Austrian Emperor, visit the Corcoran Art Gallery, have a luncheon, and at 2:30 receive with all the ceremony we could muster the Special Embassy from China. Either of these celebrations would have been a day's work in itself. When, added to this, I had to call at the Chinese Legation and leave the cards and the congratulations of the President on the assumption to the throne of the New Emperor of China and make a luncheon at the White House at 1:30, you will get some idea of the rapidity with which I had to carry out the day's programme.

The President dearly loves a day in which he has a difficult time making his engagements, and in consequence he has been in a good humour every time I have seen him.

We drove to St. Patrick's Church in the open landau, passing through great crowds who had been attracted to the neighbourhood by the published statement that the diplomatic corps would attend the services in uniform and that the President would be in attendance likewise. St. Patrick's Church is the most imposing Roman Catholic church in the district and is located on Tenth Street, between F and G, in the thickest shopping settlement of the city.

By the time we reached the church the edifice was already filled to overflowing with all the diplomatic corps and members of fashionable society which the Austrian Embassy had invited to be present. Everybody was in his best, the women vying with each other in their gowns and hats and the Ambassadors, Ministers, and attachés in full court uniforms. The two front seats on the left side of the aisle were reserved for the President and his aides, so he occupied the first and I the second, sitting just behind him. The Austrian Ambassador was across the aisle, and his wife looked like a gorgeous bird of paradise in electric, glittering colours. The dean of the diplomatic corps and his wife, Baron and Baroness des Planches, sat with them, and back of them came the rest of the corps according to rank, while social Washington sat back of us.

The procession of clergy and choristers up the aisle was a grand pageant. Signor Falcon, the papal delegate, was present in gray and purple, with a long train held up by boys in red. . . .

As we sat down a priest brought the President the

printed programme. After looking over it he turned to me and whispered:

"When I see the length of this programme I regret my letter on the liberty of religious observances."

A few minutes later he caught a glimpse of Baroness von Hengelmüller, and with a twinkle in his eye he leaned back and said:

"Archie, I hope you will not be so ungallant as to remind the Baroness of the coronation and to ask her if the last sixty years has not passed like a dream to her."

These long waits sitting by himself, knowing himself observed by every one, really get on his nerves, and he simply has to talk. He thinks of the most ridiculous things and, he says, the more solemn the occasion the more ridiculous the things are which suggest themselves to his mind.

The procession stopped further conversation and we had to centre all our attention on the programme to keep up with the good Catholics who were supposed to know when to kneel and when to sit and when again to stand. The President kept his eye on the Austrian Ambassador, whom I soon found to be entirely misleading in the observances of church etiquette. At one part of the service the Ambassador, the President, and myself were the only persons standing and I had to touch the President to make him sit down. In commenting afterward on this he said:

"If you had not touched my elbow I should have gone on following the Ambassador, although realizing that he was leading me at times into blind alleys. When I see him again I shall denounce him as a heretic in disguise."

I saw that Madame Jusserand was the best posted Catholic present, and I followed her lead, and when it was time to kneel I would do so, at the same time giving the

President a slight touch on the arm, which very soon he learned to respond to with such agility as to deceive any one who might be watching him. At one part of the service when the censer was brought to the Cardinal to fill, one of the priests attending him coughed and then sneezed. I knew the President was dying to laugh. On leaving the church the first thing he said after getting into the carriage, while bowing to the applauding populace on the streets:

"Archie, a priest who can't stand incense must be about as useless as a naval officer who gets sick when he goes to sea."

A little later he said:

"If my dear old grandfather could have seen me there to-day he would have met me at the door and offered me poison and a pistol to choose my own form of death. It would never have occurred to him that I should not have been killed instantly for the salvation of my soul."

As a pageant it was a gorgeous spectacle. However, I am no judge, for I fear I am prejudiced, belonging as I do to the low church wing of the Episcopal Church.

The reception of the Chinese was as solemn as the mass was diverting. At the express request of the President we had all the aides present, and formed a line from the entrance into the Blue Room. Bromwell called for the Special Ambassador and the Prince, in the President's carriage, and as they drove up to the White House, followed by his suite, Commander Sims and I and Second Assistant Secretary of State Adee went to the portico to meet them. There were about twenty in all, and they were dressed in wonderful Chinese garments, elaborately embroidered and brilliant in design and colouring. I have been to the East a good deal, but never saw any garments so rich or beautiful. Leaving them in the far

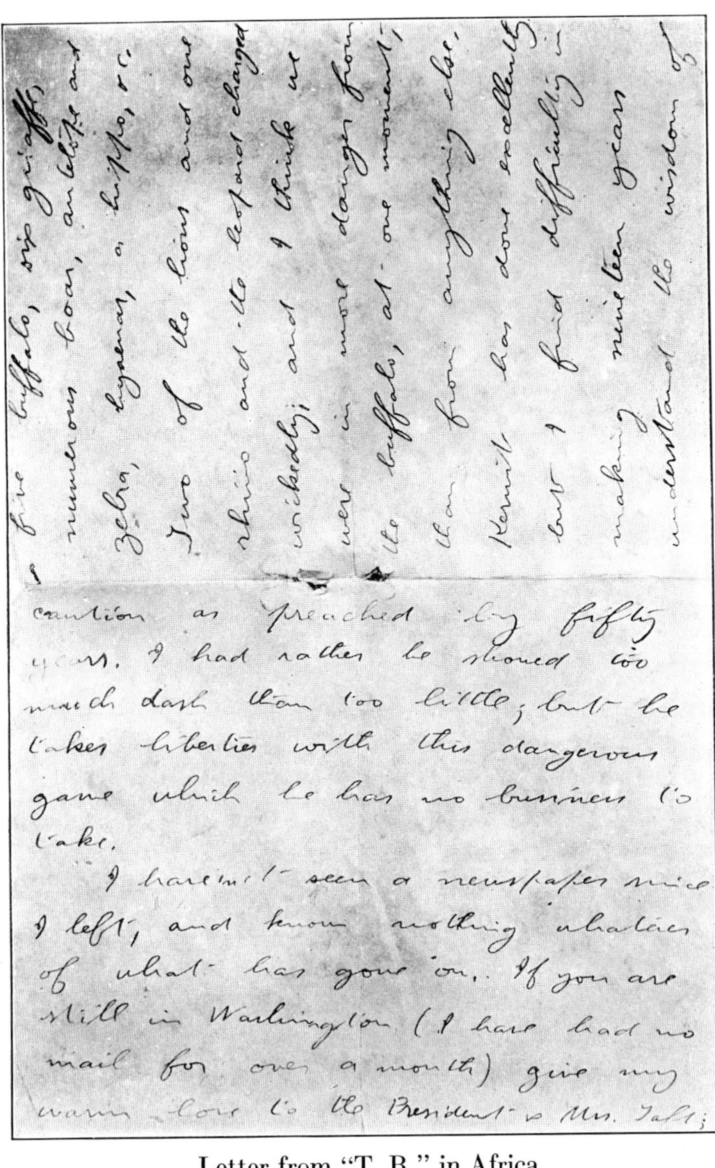

five buffalo, six giraffe,
numerous boar, antelope and
zebra, hyenas, a hippo, a rhino.
Two of the lions and one
rhino and the leopard charged
wickedly; and I think we
were in more danger from
the buffalo, at one moment,
than from anything else.
Kermit has done excellently
but I find difficulty in
making nineteen years
understand the wisdom of
caution as preached by fifty
years. I had rather he showed too
much dash than too little; but he
takes liberties with this dangerous
game which he has no business to
take.

I haven't seen a newspaper since
I left, and know nothing whatever
of what has gone on. If you are
still in Washington (I have had no
mail for over a month) give my
warm love to the President and Mrs. Taft;

Letter from "T. R." in Africa

This was found in Major Butt's scrapbook, and is of a date, of course, several months after Roosevelt's departure from the White House

end of the Blue Room, Bromwell, Sims, and I went for the President and Secretary Adee.

The Special Ambassador read his address in English, after which the President read similar complimentary remarks prepared by Adee. After this formality the President made an extemporary address of welcome which really meant something.

I am sorry that there is no way these remarks can be preserved, but there are never any stenographers present at these presentations and no one can reproduce them from memory. What he said was thoroughly understood both by the Ambassador and the Official Interpreter, who was one of the suite, so I presume it will be made a matter of record as far as it can be remembered. The Prince Imperial Ysai Fu acted as Secretary to the Ambassador and carried off his part in a modest manner. He took no part beyond acknowledging the presentation to the President, although as an Imperial Highness he is far beyond the Ambassador in point of rank. The President shook hands with the entire suite.

I am more impressed every time I see Chinese officials on such occasions with their dignity and splendid manner. Their wooden countenances lend themselves admirably to the seriousness of such occasions, and when they appear in a body they are most impressive and distinguished.

The President was very much pleased with the manner with which the aides carried out their part of the programme, but he did not seem quite as well pleased with Adee's part of it. As he left the room he stopped in the corridor and sent word he wanted to see the Secretary. While Adee is deaf, still we did not hear what the President said to him, but those aides who had taken their stations again in the corridor had the full advantage of it.

"Adee," said the President, "I have ordered the State

Department to look over these foreign addresses on a former occasion and I now want it done without another word from me. I will not be referred to as 'Excellency' by them. It is not democratic, and it is not proper and seemly, and I don't like it."

I noticed the Secretary looked somewhat crestfallen as we escorted the Chinese to their carriages, but I did not know the reason until Captain Lay told me what the President had said.

Your affectionate brother,

ARCHIBALD.

LIV

Washington, D. C.,
December 4th, 1908.

DEAR CLARA:

When we got through tennis the President asked those who played with him to return to the White House at 9:00 at night, and to see some kinetoscope or vitascope pictures showing Mr. Abernathy, Marshal of Oklahoma, catching wolves alive by forcing his hands into their mouths. This last act was most interesting. The President had seen Abernathy do this very thing several years ago, and as no one seemed to believe it, he suggested to Abernathy to have some of these scenes photographed, with the result that Abernathy had it done in the most vivid manner.

One scene showed Abernathy in the water fighting with a wolf weighing more than one hundred and twenty-five pounds, and finally controlling him by seizing him by the upper jaw as the wolf made a spring for the Marshal's face. I had expected to be bored, but on the contrary, it was most interesting.

After the performance was over, the President asked Beekman Winthrop and myself to go upstairs and to let

Mrs. Roosevelt know what she had missed. We went, but we did not succeed in our diplomatic mission, for Mrs. Roosevelt said that catching wolves had no interest for her at all, and that she feared the President would introduce this kinetoscope in the White House as a feature some evening when they had dinner guests: that in fact he had already suggested it. I did not, and neither did Beekman, let her know that he had only just a few moments before suggested to Abernathy to bring his pictures to the White House next Tuesday evening for the entertainment of some guests who were coming to dinner. When he first suggested it to Mrs. Roosevelt she said:

"How would you like to be asked to sit through a kinetoscope performance of a lady showing antique fans?"

"Why, Edith, I cannot understand being so tortured."

"It would not be worse than your wolf pictures to the average dinner guest in Washington."

How he is going to break it to her I do not know, but as she usually has her way in matters of this kind I still have my doubts whether the pictures will be a dinner feature or not.

At the request of Mrs. Taft I am getting up a list of the assistants about the White House and what their duties are. I took the opportunity yesterday to talk over some of the matters pertaining to the White House with Mrs. Roosevelt, which led to a discussion of the expenses of the White House. She said it would be very difficult to curtail the expenses of the White House; that she herself was regarded as a careful manager, and that while she had kept a careful set of books and that every cent spent was accounted for, yet there were so many little things which one would scrutinize in their own homes that you simply let pass by in the White House as being unworthy of notice.

To attempt to stop waste or profligacy in cooking, either for the White House proper or for the servants, would result only in demoralizing the force, and the saving would not be even noticeable. She keeps bills and receipts for everything, and tries to keep down the list of servants, yet to live as they have lived in the White House, they must make up their minds to spend practically every cent of the President's pay. . . .

They had not attempted to save anything, for neither the President nor herself, she said, cared for money, or to have any great amount, and she did think the White House should be kept up as well as the amount alloted to the President would allow.

"But once begin to worry about the expenses of the White House, the life of the President's wife becomes one of misery and drudgery," she said. "My experience is that if one can see that the place is run orderly and with dignity it is as much as can be expected in the way of housekeeping. You must trust the stewards for the management of the culinary department and the supplies. What is needed badly is a competent housekeeper, but I never engaged one, for I feared the trouble which I felt would ensue with the coloured servants."

. . . .

The most interesting occurrence yesterday, and one which I failed to mention, was the presentation of a present to Mrs. Longworth from the deceased Empress Dowager of China through the Special Ambassador. While in China Mrs. Longworth spent the night before her presentation at the home of Prince Tsai Fu's father, and she and her friends were beautifully entertained. Remembering this visit, the old Empress sent Alice a pair of beautiful gold bracelets with jade settings.

The Special Ambassador, whom I presented as His Excellency the Chinese Ambassador, told Mrs. Roosevelt that he had brought to her from His August Majesty some silks and silver pieces, but that they were not unpacked as yet, and then begged to present Mrs. Longworth the bracelets. What I think happened is that they only brought the bracelets, but on arrival they were told by the Minister and the Chinese agents that it would be a breach of etiquette to present a gift to the President's daughter and not to his wife, and so they are waiting to secure suitable gifts for Mrs. Roosevelt. This is mere conjecture, however, and I may be doing an injustice to the Ambassador. Mrs. Roosevelt received the Special Ambassador and four of his suite in the Blue Room and wore a splendid black satin gown, while Mrs. Longworth wore cream satin with a lot of gold over it. They both wore trains and looked lovely.

Good-bye. Hastily,
ARCHIBALD.

LV

Washington, D. C.,
December 4th [1908].

DEAR CLARA:

While I have dated this letter the fourth, it should properly be dated the fifth for the reason that it is now two o'clock in the morning. . . . Colonel and Mrs. Bromwell and Mrs. Timmons left me at my door on their way to the Herbert Wadsworths. Mrs. Wadsworth has a beautiful home on Dupont Circle. . . . Mrs. Timmons, to go back where I began, is the daughter of Vice-President Fairbanks and is attractive. Her first marriage was unfortunate, but her second to a poor naval officer has proved, I believe, to be a most happy event. She looks like her mother, in a way, but as she has always had money and never has known the days of poverty and struggle which her mother knew, she is more at ease in the fashionable world, and has not that uncertain look which characterizes so many women who have achieved position late in life.

Both the Vice-President and Mrs. Fairbanks have always desired political popularity, and one cannot have that and cachet in the fashionable set at the same time. The President does not understand the type of man of the Vice-President, nor does he get along very well with Mrs. Fairbanks, but Mrs. Roosevelt likes both and has a good deal of affection for Mrs. Fairbanks. I said this morning that I always thought of Mrs. Fairbanks as a modern type, desirous of managing every one in her sphere and rather inclined to advocate the principles of woman's rights at the polls. Mrs. Roosevelt told me that I had a wrong idea of her altogether, as she was in reality a kindly, motherly woman, not too sure of herself, but anxious to be agreeable and thoughtful at all times. She is a handsome woman and dresses well. I have been busy to-day at the White House and will be busy again to-morrow. I much prefer to play with the President than to hang about the White House arranging tables and seating guests according to rank. But since it is not beneath the President to do this sort of thing I presume I should not resent having to do it.

To-night was the Congressional reception, which, by the way, is the worst of all the receptions. More than eighteen hundred persons passed the Blue Room, and that is more than the number of invitations which had been issued. Mrs. Roosevelt, however, always keeps her guests in the Blue Room at a certain social stratum, and the suppers after the receptions are invariably charming affairs. To-night she had more than seventy persons invited to remain for supper; they were seated at eight tables in the upper corridor. We had to seat them this morning. Mrs. Roosevelt was not feeling very fit, so we did not begin the work until nearly 12:00. She always attends to these matters herself, and after she seats the tables the chart has to be taken to the Executive Office and the President looks over it, and if it meets with his approval he O.K.'s it and it is then settled.

No matter how busy he is, he always attends to matters of this kind, and it is marvellous how he keeps his interest up sufficiently to do it. Before we begin to seat the table I take the list of guests over to the office, and he designates the men and women he wishes to honour by placing them at his table. He has discovered that one of the surest ways to make a friend is to pay him some social attention. To find one's self or one's wife at the President's table superinduces at once a great admiration for the Chief Executive. I do not think it is all a matter of policy, however, for he usually chooses agreeable men as well as women, and he cannot be got to have a bore at his table, no matter how much he may desire his support or friendship.

When I took the list over to him this morning he chose Mrs. Scribner, wife of the publisher; Mrs. Lawrence, wife of the Bishop of Massachusetts; Mrs. Meyer, who is always agreeable to him, and Mrs. Bacon, the wife of the new Secretary of State. After we complete the tables the chart has to be taken to him again, and though it often bores him horribly, he always takes the time to look it over and as often makes certain suggestions and changes in the arrangements.

I sat at the table to-night with his two sisters, Mrs. Cowles and Mrs. Robinson. We had also Mrs. Bonaparte, wife of the Attorney-General. Mrs. Cowles and Mrs. Robinson are witty and very quick at repartee.

Mrs. Robinson told me of the last election time four years ago, and the great anxiety they all felt for her brother. His whole life seemed to hinge on this election, and on his way from Oyster Bay he was very much excited, and, as he described it to her, every nerve was strained to the bursting point. He said that when he was so nerve centred that he felt he could not stand it much longer he suddenly reflected that after all he had already the greatest gift which life could hold out to him, namely, the relationship with his wife and children. He became quiet, he said, and really felt at peace and almost indifferent as to the results. As he drove up to the White House, he was met at the door by Mrs. Roosevelt, who asked him what he had learned. His answer was:

"I do not know anything as yet, but it makes no difference how it goes. I have had a vision on the train, and it was of you and the children. Nothing matters as long as we are well and content with each other."

I remained to lunch and came back for dinner to-night. Bishop Lawrence of Massachusetts and his wife had arrived as White House guests, and also a Mrs. Sage, and the dinner was extremely pleasant. The President kept reverting to the trouble which might result from the incautious action on the part of the West toward Japan. After dinner he told Bishop Lawrence that he was extremely anxious over the situation.

"Such troubles as I have had with Congress do not affect me at all, but to prevent war with Japan I would make any sacrifice."

"Yet, Mr. President, I remember it was urged against you that you would be a war President if elected, and that you would involve the United States in a war a year."

"Instead of which," said the President, "I have only waged war on the enemies within our own borders, and now at this late day my sole care is to establish peace permanently with the East. I am thankful that our squadron left Japanese waters before California and other Western States began this idiotic procedure, for if it had not left nothing could have convinced the Japanese that it was not all a prearranged plan."[1]

He told us at the table also that he had had a call that day from the head of the Associated Press, who wanted permission to send a representative along with him on his African trip, and when the President refused he urged it something after this fashion:

"Now, see here, Mr. President, if you do not permit a representative of the press to go with you, the yellow journals will follow and track you every foot of the way and will print all sorts of stories about you, and, moreover, if anything should happen we could not afford to be scooped by the yellow press."

"What do you mean by anything happening?" asked the President.

"Well, I don't like to anticipate evil, but should a lion really do his duty as a lion, you must realize that it will be the one great news item of the year and we could not afford to get left."

The President and his guests laughed over the recital of this story, but I glanced at Mrs. Roosevelt and she not only did not laugh, but it seemed to me that she was a trifle paler.

To-morrow evening is the last of the dances, and it will be the most brilliant of the year, as the majority of those invited are among the best of the various sets in the city. After all, the best society here is composed of the best of the political crowd, the best of the old cave dwellers, as the Georgetown and Washington families are called, the

[1]See comment on Letter XXV.

smartest and the most cultured and the smart set, which includes the diplomatic corps, and the persons in the literary and artistic set who have really accomplished something. All these sets will be represented to-morrow night, and there will be a small coterie of the nicest among the army and navy to add colour and brightness by their uniforms.

Well, I am off to dreamland. Good-night.

ARCHIBALD.

LVI

Washington, D. C.,
December 7 [1908].

DEAR CLARA:

Everybody has been in a bad humour to-day, and there is a general ruffling of official feathers all along the line. I started with the President at half-past nine. He made an effort to be cheerful, but it was a pretty poor effort. He looked out of sorts, but whether it was due to his effort to chastise the New York *Sun* and the Indianapolis *News*, or the answer of Laffan, which came out in the press along with his attack on these editors, or whether it was simply a Monday morning humour which all men, be they Presidents or army officers, have in common, I do not know.

Doctor Lambert[1] came to the office with him. He and his wife are house guests and both seem to be most charming people. Doctor Lambert is a great huntsman and has accompanied the President several times on expeditions. When he saw me he told Doctor Lambert how he had asked me to be his partner at tennis the other day and how he had found out later that I had already arranged with his nephew, Monroe Robinson, to play

[1]Dr. Alexander Lambert of New York, for many years the personal physician and intimate friend of Roosevelt.

against Beekman Winthrop and himself. He described his chagrin upon learning that "his favourite aide" preferred another partner than himself, and finally the satisfaction he had when he and Winthrop had beaten us every set. He did not put quite as much life in the recital as is his wont when he gets a joke on one of us, and his humour was a little forced.

I knew that something was worrying him. He said he had no programme for the day other than the regular engagements, but did ask me as I was leaving to suggest to Mrs. Roosevelt the names of any men who I thought would enjoy his wolf scenes, which he insisted upon having after dinner to-night in spite of Mrs. Roosevelt's objections.

I hate to see the President get into controversies with the newspapers, for after all there are so few which criticize him that he ought to take it as a matter of course. One has to have the bitter with the sweet in this world and if the *Sun* abuses him and charges him with things he does not do, there are fifty others which promptly take up the cudgel in his defence. To me that is his one weakness. He cannot brook criticism, yet he will tell you that he does not mind it at all and rather invites it. Possibly he is right, for as intimately as I am thrown with him, sometimes I feel that I know but a very small side of him. If I continue to record the actual humours he seems to have and to note his personal remarks and watch his varying and changing characteristics I may at the end come to some definite conclusion about his character, but I am startled at times by the wonderful bigness of the man. When with him, if I stopped to think of him as I sometimes think of him when away from him, I would possibly get stage fright, as Bromwell does, and never be able to say anything to him at all. But when I am with him everything he does seems so natural and so logical that I forget the side which the public sees through the press and through his official acts.

I don't know what he has on his mind to-day, but I am inclined to think that he is meditating saying something or doing something which will be startling when it comes to the surface. A casual observer would not have seen anything different in his manner this morning from any other morning, for, after all, what I saw in him to-day was indefinable, and even to you I cannot make myself clear possibly.

At the White House I went upstairs to Mrs. Roosevelt's secretary and there I found everything in a whirl. Several house guests were arriving to-day. Mr. and Mrs. Lawrence Lowell and Professor and Mrs. Ferrero[1] of Italy, besides Doctor and Mrs. Lambert, who have already come. There are only six guest chambers in the White House, which limits always the number of guests to be invited. I think Mrs. Roosevelt is very glad that there are not more, for while she is hospitable he is profligate in his invitations.

Mrs. Roosevelt says that it is innate with him, that as soon as he meets anybody he likes he at once thinks the only way he can evince this liking is to invite him or her to visit him. She calls it his predominating Southern trait. But sometimes he invites more persons than there are rooms, and then there is a great scurrying about for available beds in consequence.

I found a note there of a luncheon to-day and a dinner to-night, and another larger luncheon to-morrow, and

---

[1]Guglielmo Ferrero, an Italian historian whose bold and controversial work created considerable discussion among European scholars. His wife, the daughter of Lombroso, the eminent criminologist, is also a student of criminal psychology. Lombroso was one of the originators of the modern science of psychiatry.

a larger dinner to-morrow night, with the Abernathy wolf vitascopic performance after dinner. I was expected to both luncheons, but I suggested that it would be nice to have some one of the junior aides to these luncheons occasionally and suggested that Captain Lay come to lunch to-day.

"In other words, you do not care for my invitation to-day," laughed Mrs. Roosevelt.

"On the contrary," I said, "I love to come to lunch here, but I was only thinking that it might be nice to have someone else occasionally, as these youngsters do a lot of work at the large things and I know they would appreciate lunching sometimes at the White House."

While Mrs. Roosevelt sat at her desk to answer a note I got Lay on the 'phone and began: "Harry, Mrs. Roosevelt would like for you to lunch at the White House to-day——"

At this point Mrs. Roosevelt stopped long enough to say: "You mean you would like Captain Lay to lunch at the White House to-day."

That ended that incident, but I made up my mind to make no more suggestions when asked again to luncheon, be it for every day in the week, for while she laughed and the banter appeared good-humoured, I felt that there might be a little feeling about it underneath.

Miss Hagner was rushing out invitations to dinner, and when I asked her what should be done about extra guests for the wolf pictures, she snapped:

"Don't ask me; I am buried in troubles of my own; better ask Mrs. Roosevelt."

I then asked Mrs. Roosevelt what I should do and how those who I thought would enjoy the scenic views of a wolf hunt should be invited.

"Don't ask me," said Mrs. Roosevelt. "It is yours

and the President's party: I won't have anything to do with it."

She really chuckled over the predicament.

"But the President told me to see you," I said.

"Then you and the President must fix it up. I do not want dogs and wolves introduced to my dinner guests. These pictures may make my guests sick, especially after eating a big dinner. You can't tell what will happen. He thought the young members of the diplomatic corps would enjoy it, but I positively refuse to invite foreigners to witness this strangling of wolves."

"But, Mrs. Roosevelt," I insisted, "I did not have——"

"Oh, yes, you did. You encouraged him in this idea and even told me it was a most enjoyable affair."

"Only by his order," I said.

"Well, then, you arrange the guests by his orders," she laughed, and went into her room.

There was I, between two stools, Miss Hagner got to laughing, and a minute later Miss Ethel came out of her mother's room laughing and they all enjoyed getting me in a pickle over this unfortunate performance which the President insisted upon intruding on his dinner guests. Finally, when she came out again, I read her a list of those I thought should be asked, and she agreed to having the aides, General and Mrs. Duvall, Colonel and Mrs. Treat, Straight and Marvin; the others she eliminated along with the President's suggestion of the attachés.

When I got home to lunch I found Straight of the State Department, who had besought me to tell him of the incident at the White House when the Chinese Ambassador addressed the President as "Your Excellency" and the President had scolded poor old Adee in public for permitting the Ambassador so to address him. It seems that, not satisfied with scolding Adee, the President had ripped up the entire State Department and each Secretary was in an awful flunk over it. His letter was pretty stiff, from what Straight said, and he came in the interest of the Third Assistant Secretary of State, Wilson, who had handled the matter and who felt that the President was hitting him personally and was possibly trying to force him to resign. Nothing was farther from the facts, for the President had not even known Wilson in the matter at all and really held Adee responsible for the mistake, for he had spoken to Adee about the matter in times gone by and seeing Adee at the presentation had presumed that Adee was the author of the reply he read to the Ambassador and also that it was Secretary Adee who had overlooked the remarks of the Ambassador.

I could not speak with any authority, but I gave this version to Straight, who felt greatly relieved and said that Wilson would see it in the same way, for, after all, poor Adee had been the one to decide upon the matter, as all papers had been submitted to him for his approval. It was unfortunate simply for Adee that both Mr. Root and Mr. Bacon were absent from the city on that day and that he had to be the representative of the State Department. Wilson[1] is very young and very sensitive and takes things very seriously. He handles the Eastern matters of the Department and to have his one big act, which he was so anxious should go smoothly, bring about such a reprimand was almost more than he could stand.

Of course, mistakes should not occur where the President is concerned, and after his orders not to permit foreigners to address him as "Excellency" someone should have seen to it that these orders were carried out. The big stick is no joke, be it known, for I have seen it wielded

[1] Huntington Wilson entered the diplomatic service in 1900, was Assistant Secretary of State, 1909–13, Ambassador on special mission to Turkey, 1910, resigned, 1913.

in more cases than in this one case and I hope I will not see it turned in my direction. He told me about the letter and said:

"I am willing to have things done lightly when there is nothing at stake, but serious things must be treated seriously, and that response which the State Department prepared for me to read to the Chinese Ambassador was puerile and inane, and that made me as angry as did the Ambassador's addressing me as 'Your Excellency.' Every little South African is addressed as 'Excellency,' for he thinks it surrounds him with some royal prerogatives of some kind. I want to see the usages of our country pitched on more individual and higher lines and the term 'Mr. President' is all that should be used ever when the Chief Executive of this nation is addressed officially."

The Tafts arrived to-day and I am to call on Mrs. Taft at 5:00 this afternoon. She wants to talk about the personnel of the White House, and I hope I will not offend her by speaking the truth, but I shall certainly advise against any radical changes, and if Mr. Taft gets a tip from me I feel that things will remain very much as they are. However, if she wants the ushers removed and liveried servants put at the doors I will do what I can to carry out her ideas and to let down the poor ushers as gently as possible.

Dropping all this and reverting to something more humorous, I must tell you of an incident which the President related in connection with the swimming of the Potomac by himself, the French Ambassador, and General Wood, some time ago. I have referred once before to this swim, but it was my impression that they had swum the river with their clothes on. But the President said they did not, that they stripped, and just as they were going into the water, he noticed M. Jusserand had kept on his hands his black kid gloves. The Ambassador was waist deep when the President saw him.

"Heavens, Mr. Ambassador," the President called to him, "what on earth are you wearing your gloves for?"

The President says that he thinks the Ambassador simply forgot to take them off, for he looked at them as if he did not know he had them on, but with a shrug of his shoulders he simply said, naïvely:

"Oh, I feared we might meet some ladies, Mr. President."

Colonel Bromwell is coming to dinner with me and at 9:00 we go for the President, Mrs. Roosevelt, and their house guests and accompany them to the Corcoran Art Gallery, which is thrown open to-night to invited guests to view the St. Gaudens collection. To-morrow it is to be open to the public, but to-night admission is only by invitation. I shall now dress for my first interview with the future mistress of the White House. I wish I were not so fond of the President and his family, for I cannot help feeling a bit jealous toward the Tafts.

Hasta la vista.

ARCHIBALD.

LVII

Washington, D. C.,
December 8th, 1908.

DEAR CLARA:

. . . Last night we went to the Art Gallery and our party was of more interest to those who were there than was the exhibit itself. The President was in good form and was keen in his enjoyment of the evening. While there was a great crowd there, yet not in one instance was there anything bordering on bad manners such as pushing or crowding near the presidential party. The

Washington people are well drilled in the way they should act to the President, and while they dearly love to watch Mr. Roosevelt they do it without seeming to intrude on him in any way. The exhibit was entirely a loan one, but really very creditable to America. There were a number of Sargent's there, and his portrait of Mathilde Townsend was greatly admired.

Mr. Ferrero, the Italian historian, who was present, expressed himself as greatly pleased with the exhibit. His wife is such a quaint little person, the smallest woman I ever saw outside of a show, yet very graceful and charming. I had a chance to chat for a moment with Mrs. George Eustis, which repaid me for the trouble of going. So many of my friends were present and each had a kind, sympathetic word for me. I felt very much broken up when dear old Mrs. Wallack came over to press my hand. She does not know why I have always liked her so much, but she reminds me—and always has—of Mother—not in appearance but in manner and gentleness. She looks very feeble, too, and I fear she may go at any time. Mrs. Elkins quite divided attention with the President. As the possible mother-in-law of Abruzzi she is of special interest to those who have heard so much of this possible alliance, although I fear it is fated not to come off. [*Unfinished letter—not signed.*]

LVIII

Washington, D. C.,
December 10th [1908].

Dear Clara:

I lunched yesterday at the White House and sat next to Madame Ferrero. She is the daughter of the great Italian writer, Lombroso. I should hardly say great writer, for the subjects he handles are weird and decadent.

She must have some of his queer characteristics. Her conversation is startling at times.

"I like your American men," she said. "They have such broad shoulders and are so normal. I expected to find them inferior to the women and to see brutal and bad-looking men."

The husband is very hard to "get at," to use a provincialism. He is a remarkable man, but most uninteresting in appearance and conversation. The President says he can get little out of him.

It was an interesting lot of people. Governor Magoon[1] was there and sat to the left of Mrs. Roosevelt. He has grown very heavy, and the tropics have told on him. It is possible he will go into the Cabinet, though I hardly think so, as he does not represent enough politically. I am inclined to think that the President-elect will watch for an opportunity to put him on the bench or send him as Governor to the Philippines.

Governor Montague[2] of Virginia was there also, looking more like a Wall Street broker than a Virginian governor. I am glad to see that our public men in the South are laying aside the long coat and long hair. There is no reason in hanging on to styles of dress which have gone out of fashion. General Castleman was in the city yesterday, and though he is more than seventy years of age, he is punctilious in his dress and at the same time has the old courtliness of the South prior to the war. He is about the handsomest man I know of his age. He does not look his age. Mrs. Edwards and Miss Carroll of

---

[1]Charles E. Magoon, general counsel of the Isthmian Canal Commission, governor of the Panama Canal Zone, and, at the date of this letter, military governor of Cuba.

[2]Andrew J. Montague, Governor of Virginia, 1902–06. At the date of this letter dean of Richmond College Law School and later member of Congress. Known as the "educational" governor.

Maryland, who were here at the same time, thought he was a man about fifty.

I was glad to have an opportunity to meet Frederick Palmer.[1] He is direct and interesting. The President has done so much to recognize this type of man. Any man who has done anything worth notice, whether it be in literature, art, or sport, is certain to receive recognition at the White House. This means a great deal more than one would think. An artist who has not been invited to the White House feels it, and sooner or later will try to do something which he hopes to be worthy of the attention of the President.

Mr. and Mrs. Andrew Carnegie were present and also came to dinner that day. The President likes Carnegie, though he does not relish his conversation save on special lines. I really think the old Scotchman bores him, but he consults the President a great deal about his big charities and the President feels that Carnegie, whatever may be his motive, is doing a tremendous work in the world. Not so much by what he gives but in the way he gives. The conditions which he places on his gifts, such as requiring the various cities to contribute their share, have, so the President thinks, a splendid effect upon the communities which meet these conditions.

This afternoon I accompanied the President to the meeting of the governors at the Belasco Theatre, where he and Secretary Taft met for the first time since the election and had much enjoyment. When I spoke of his speech afterward and said how much everyone seemed to like it, he said:

"But wasn't Taft fine? You know, Archie, that I think he has the most lovable personality I have ever

[1]One of the best-equipped of American war correspondents. He served in France during the World War in the Signal Corps with rank of Lieutenant-Colonel.

come in contact with. He is going to be greatly beloved as President. I almost envy a man possessing a personality like Taft's. People are always prepossessed by it. One loves him at first sight. He has nothing to overcome when he meets people. I realize that I have always got to overcome a little something before I get to the heart of people." And here he gave that characteristic leer that always precedes something humorous and followed it with this remark: "No one could accuse *me* of having a charming personality."

And yet that is exactly what he has got—not in the way Mr. Taft has it—it does not deluge you like a huge pan of sweet milk poured over one as does Mr. Taft's smile, but one never gets away from Mr. Roosevelt's personality. It sticks by one, so when he comes into a room and stands as he always does for one second before doing something characteristic, he electrifies the company and gives one just that sensation which a pointer does when he first quivers and takes a stand on quail. No matter how worn out and tired one might be, suddenly to see a pointer wheel and come to stand electrifies one instantly as nothing else will do unless it be to see the President enter a room.

I had such an agreeable interview with the President-elect and Mrs. Taft this morning. I went to the Boardman house at 9:10 and was told to come to the third floor, where Mr. Taft had been given two bedrooms and an office. The door was open and as I neared the top flight I heard the heartiest laugh imaginable from Mr. Taft. Mrs. Taft was not looking quite as cheerful as he was looking as I entered. He did not stop laughing and Mrs. Taft said:

"Well, I don't see anything to laugh at. Now we must get to business while Captain Butt is here."

He grabbed me by the hand and when he could control himself, said:

"Nothing to laugh at! I think it is the funniest thing I ever heard. I confess it would not be anything for him to laugh at if he knew for one minute how near he was to the Cabinet and how far away he is at this minute." Then turning to me he said: "I was Cabinet-making early this morning, and I had thought that I had settled one place at least, and just as you were announced I had told my wife. She simply wiped him off the face of the earth and I have got to begin all over again. The personal side of politics has always been funny to me, but nothing has been quite as funny as to have a man's career wrecked by a jealous wife."

"Not jealous at all," said Mrs. Taft, "but I could not believe you to be serious when you mentioned that man's name. He is perfectly awful and his family are even worse. I won't even talk about it."

That is how we got down to the question as to whether the ushers should be retained or not. We went into the whole personnel of the White House very carefully and by the utmost use of diplomacy saved the heads of those men of whom Mrs. Roosevelt is the fondest, without feeling that I had sacrificed the Taft interests at all. We will keep two of the ushers as head men and they will have charge of the coloured footmen. The other ushers will be "promoted" to the Executive Office. Mrs. Roosevelt was tremendously relieved and says I have handled the matter with the greatest delicacy. I have not completed the job yet and I may fall down hopelessly before the negotiations are carried successfully through.

Matters are getting complicated as it is. Since I began this letter Mrs. Roosevelt called me up on the 'phone and asked me to let Mrs. Taft know that she will be very glad to discuss the matter with her and give her any assistance in her power. She also asked me to let Mrs. Taft know also that if she did not want to take up these matters with her she would not feel the least offended. I got Mrs. Taft on the telephone on some excuse—in fact, as to how small a number of automobiles the White House could get along with next year—and suggested that she talk over the matter of servants with Mrs. Roosevelt, but she said she did not wish to do it, and then I suggested that she thank Mrs. R. for her kind offer at least, which she agreed to do next Saturday when she lunches there.

I am getting too deep into the "twilight zones" of these two administrations to suit me, but if I am perfectly frank with both I do not see how I can offend either.

Evidently Mrs. Roosevelt feels that she has been a little unjust possibly toward Mrs. Taft in resenting the changes she proposes making and wishes to show the friendliness which she really feels for everyone. I believe Mrs. Roosevelt is the fairest-minded woman I ever met. I have seen her rather intimately during the past seven months and I have never seen her do a petty thing or appear even to think a spiteful one. She never talks about people, though she sometimes has her little laugh, but she hates gossip and will not permit any one to tell her any. Her humour is sufficiently keen not to be dependent upon sarcasm, and while her wit sparkles it never wounds.

Good-bye.

ARCHIE.

LIX

Washington, D. C.,
December 11th, 1908.

DEAR CLARA:

I am not entirely by myself now, for Gen. Alfred E. Bates has come to live with me. He has closed his handsome apartment in the Connecticut and prefers the simplicity of my way of living with company to the luxury of his own home alone. Mrs. Bates is in bad health and has gone South, and the old fellow, who by the way is the youngest old fellow you ever saw, has begged me to take him in, which I have done, giving him the top floor. He voluntarily went above for the reason that he snores horribly and wanted to be where he would not disturb any one. A Mr. Marvin,[1] whom you don't know, wanted to come also but as he is connected with the Chinese Embassy here as a sort of manager, I thought it would not do to have him in the house. . . . He is exceedingly clever, was once a master at Groton and afterwards a Consul in the East, where he worked up the Chinese to a frenzy over his abilities.

Several of these young men who have been in the East are destined, I think, to play a prominent part in the future. There is Willard Straight, about the best-informed member of the Consular Service, who is here this winter to guide the Secretaries on Eastern questions. He is briary, shrewd, and affable. I took him to be a Southern man, but he really comes from Oswego, N. Y., but no one would ever place him from that town or from any other which is not known and which has no special place. He is college bred and adaptable. I heard the President say to Mr. Taft yesterday:

"Do what you can for Straight. I think it will repay you."

A Mr. Fletcher,[2] secretary at the present time at Pekin, is here also on leave. He is just the opposite from Billy

---

[1]George Marvin; see Letter XLVII.

[2]Henry P. Fletcher, one of Roosevelt's "Rough Riders" in the Spanish War. He has been Minister and Ambassador to Chile, Ambassador to Mexico, Under Secretary of State, Ambassador to Belgium, and is now Ambassador to Italy.

Phillips of Boston, who is playing in on the same game as the others, and of whom I have spoken often to you. If Phillips and Fletcher could be melted into one, the result I imagine would be very much what Straight is. I mention these men at length, first because I think their careers will be interesting to watch and secondly because they happened to be here for dinner last evening, and I have found myself thinking about them much to-day and wondering where they will end.

I had rather an interesting time the last few days looking over the china at the White House with a view to destroying all that is chipped or broken in any way. Mrs. Roosevelt does not want it sold at auction, for she thinks this method cheapens the White House. I took the matter up with Bromwell, who really has it on his papers and is responsible for it, and he thought it ought to be sold but that it should be sold by private bids to cabinet officers and others who are connected with the White House in some way. In former years it was regarded as the property of the mistress of the White House, who would give it away as she desired, but Mrs. R. thinks that it should never be given away—and it should not, in my opinion, for it is government property just the same as the furniture. If it were sold by private bids it would create an awful howl in the press should it become known, and so I convinced all concerned that it should be broken up and scattered in the river, which will be done. When I think how I should value even one piece of it, it hurts to smash it, but I am sure it is the only right thing to do.

Mother was accustomed to say that when one was in doubt what to do, it were well to stop to think how it would look in the newspapers and act accordingly. She said that even a mother would forgive what the public would not condone, and so it was not always safe to measure one's actions by what one's mother would think. It is a test I often put myself to, and it has kept me from doing some questionable things in the service, and I think it was that standard as much as anything else which kept me free from the petty scandals in the Philippines.

I ran across one plate in a pawnshop the other day which, if I am rightly informed, was one of the Grant set. The owner wanted fifty dollars for it. Sloan, the auctioneer, tells me that he would be able to get from ten to fifty dollars for every plate which the White House would sell and badly broken pieces would bring something.

Mrs. Roosevelt has collected nearly all the china of past administrations, which is now in cabinets in the White House. She has had some pieces donated to her, and others she has purchased at very high prices. Of course, she paid for them out of the contingent expenses of the White House and they belong to the Government, but if she had not interested herself in collecting what remained of the china of former administrations it is doubtful if it would ever have been done. In order to insure the continuance of their care she has donated them to the Smithsonian Institution, but to be kept in the White House crypt as long as it is desired to have them there. This means that the Smithsonian Institution is responsible for them and takes stock of the collection at regular intervals.

There is only one piece of furniture in the entire White House which Mrs. Roosevelt desires to carry away with her when she leaves on the fourth of March. It is an antique mahogany settee which she bought in 1901, the year they came into the White House. She took the matter up with me to see how it could be purchased and I looked into the matter and found that there was no way it could be acquired in this way; but with the consent of the Superintendent of the Public Buildings and Grounds another piece exact in every detail can be substituted for it and the old piece shipped to Oyster Bay. It was antique when she bought it, so to have it reproduced will cost considerable. She paid only forty dollars for it when she got it. The White House at that time was in such a dilapidated condition that she said she had to have something cosy on the lower floor, where everything was not only large and cold, but shabby. So she bought this settee and put it in the Red Room. It has long since been relegated to the corridor in the upper hall, for the house is now beautifully furnished.

In order that she may have it, I have hit upon the plan of the aides presenting it to her and replacing it before the fourth of March.

The only other things she is going to take from the White House are the Sèvres figures which the Rochambeau Commission brought from France and which are always used on the table at state dinners. Unless you have seen the figures you can have no idea of their beauty. They have usually been put down as belonging to the Government and when written up in the papers have been so described, but Mrs. Roosevelt says they were given to her personally and that she has the documents to prove it. Of course, there will never be any question of her taking them, though I think it will be a great disappointment to Mrs. Taft when she finds them gone, for I have heard her say that they were the most beautiful things in the White House.

The fight between the President and Congress has opened up in rare style. The House is simply foaming at the mouth and even such a conservative New Englander as Butler Ames says he may never enter the White House again while the President is there. It has all come from the statement in his Message that the Congress denied him the use of secret service men for fear he would use them against members and senators. This was not said by accident, but with intent to bring about just such a discussion that has arisen in the past few days. He said to-day that he fears that corruption has made its last stand just where it was least expected, namely, in Congress. It is easier, he says, to arouse the public conscience than the conscience of Congress which has lain dormant for so long. The fact that he has discovered things there and has sent certain men to the penitentiary, was solely responsible for their refusal to have the secret service used by him.

"How can I hunt out corruption, or even know that it exists unless I have the use of men who know where it is and how to get at the facts? I have pledged myself to wage war on corruption and graft wherever they can be found, and the higher up the criminal may be the more necessary it is to strike him down. I want the people to know that I know and then it makes no matter how lenient a President may want to be, he will have to account to the people if corruption goes unchastised."

I could not help but wonder if he does not, way down in his heart, fear that big, generous, unsuspecting heart of Mr. Taft.

Good-bye.
ARCHIBALD.

LX

Washington, D. C.,
December 12th, 1908.

DEAR CLARA:

I have had a very interesting day besides having a very busy one. How to have a talk with the President about his African outfit, make a special call on the Chinese Ambassador for Mrs. Roosevelt, attend a luncheon in honour of Mr. Taft at the White House, have my photograph taken, and yet find time to go to a sale of carpets at Sloan's, was a difficult thing to do, yet I accomplished each and every one of them and was fairly successful in all.

Instead of waiting for 9:45 to see the President, as I usually do, I made an excuse to go to the White House at 9:00 and to catch the President and Mrs. Roosevelt as they were coming out of the breakfast room. As a rule they do not like to be disturbed at this time, for it is the one hour in the day which Mrs. Roosevelt calls her own, and the President puts aside all official business to spend it with her. If the day is fair they spend it walking in the White House grounds. If it is rainy or blustering they spend it sitting in the Red Room, before the fire. A large wood fire is usually kept going in the Red Room at all times. I only wanted to see the President long enough to find out if there was anything special on his mind for that day, so that I would not have to see him later.

There was nothing, and just as I was turning away, Mrs. Roosevelt said: "Captain, will you be here when we come in?" And of course, I said I would be, but I did want so to get to Sloan's in time for the carpet sale, as General Bates had taken the third floor and I had to give him a rug, so I took the one out of the front room next to mine. I did not feel like spending much money on a new one and the sales at Sloan's always begin at 10 o'clock and the carpets are the first things reached, always. But I was able to be there in time to get the rug I had picked out the day before, and I got it, moreover, for $4. It was a large Brussels rug with a border and the body was light coloured with roses scattered over it. I remained long enough also to get a large red rug for my dining room, and for this one I only paid $2. The carpets and rugs were from the

Shoreham Hotel, which is refitting its rooms this season, and some of the carpets were as good as new.

At 12:30 I donned full uniform and drove to the Morgan mansion, now the home of the special Chinese Ambassador and suite, to thank him for the gift which the Chinese Government sent to Mrs. Roosevelt. You have to put on a great deal of "side," as the English say, on such occasions, and the White House carriage with the footman and livery is a *sine qua non* of the etiquette to be observed. I was received at the door by one attaché and ushered into the main hall, where I was met by another and then conducted to the main salon, where the Ambassador and several other Chinese officials awaited me.

I did not bring a written speech or letter, but expressed the thanks of Mrs. Roosevelt for the gifts sent and expressed her sincere sorrow also over the death of the Emperor and the Empress Dowager. What seemed to touch them most was when I said that it was a personal grief to Mrs. Roosevelt that their deaths made it impossible for her ever to see this wonderful woman and remarkable ruler. He thanked me in turn, and, bowing several times, I finally reached the door and made a dash for the White House, as I had only five minutes to make the luncheon to Mr. Taft.

There is no official record made of these gifts to Mrs. Roosevelt and as yet there has been no notice of their presentation in the press. The President said at first that she could not accept them and she did not seem at all disappointed, but prepared to give them up with good grace, as she never questions the President's judgment in such matters. But after talking over the matter with the Secretary of State, the President said that she could have them, as their refusal would not be understood by the Chinese and would be regarded as a rebuke to the Ambassador. The handsomest one, a large Chinese ship done in silver and embedded in a sea of ebony, will be presented to the Smithsonian Institution. Besides this there were two tiger skins, one leopard skin, and several bolts of wonderful brocade and a very large silver bowl.

The luncheon party was very small, very informal, but very interesting.

The President asked the President-elect most informally, and he and Mrs. Taft broke some other engagement to come. The only other persons there were Mr. Reynolds, the labour expert or leader or something of that sort, who played such a conspicuous part in the campaign; Mrs. Longworth, the mother-in-law of Alice; Mrs. Nicholas Longworth; Colonel Nelson, the editor and owner of the Kansas City *Star;* Secretary Root; Major Wadsworth, who was giving a dinner that night to the Boone and Crocket Club, of which he and the President are members; and the President-elect and his wife. Mr. La Farge, a prominent New York architect, was to have been at the luncheon, but five minutes before luncheon was served he telegraphed from some station that he could not reach Washington in time. He came shortly after luncheon and was successful in his mission, which was to get the President to ask the corporation of Trinity Church, New York, not to sell or tear down the Chapel of St. John. . . . The President said he would make a protest provided those interested would get it signed by the Mayor of the city and the Governor of the state. He agreed to make a plea for the building, but fears the corporation, which is made up largely of millionaires from Wall Street, will tell him in polite terms to go to the devil.

When the luncheon party assembled in the Red Room the President and the President-elect retired to a window recess and at once forgot the presence of everyone else.

Mrs. Roosevelt finally took Mrs. Taft by the arm and went in expressing the hope that hunger would drive the two statesmen to the table before the rest had finished. I waited for them, and as they passed me the President said to Mr. Taft:

"I would certainly go to Panama before the inauguration. The people will like it, and I will send you on any war vessel you may choose. You ought to see that work for yourself, for it is going to be the biggest thing in your Administration, as it has been the biggest thing in mine."

We had a pleasant luncheon, the President and Mr. Taft doing most of the talking and most of the conversation being a kind of good-natured banter. Poor Vice-President Fairbanks came in for considerable comment. . . . The President always calls Mr. Taft "Will," while Mr. Taft speaks to him always as "Mr. President." The two men really seem to have a personal affection for one another. It is beautiful to see them together. . . .

After luncheon Mrs. Roosevelt put her arm in that of Mrs. Taft and asked her to come with her into the Green Room, where I know Mrs. Roosevelt wanted to chat with her for I could see sweetness and kindness written all over her face. Mrs. Longworth joined them very soon and the conversation was then merely on conventional lines. After they had all gone Mrs. Roosevelt asked me to come upstairs to see the presents from the Chinese.

Just before they left I had a talk for a few minutes with Mr. Taft, and he informed me that he was going to give up horses and use automobiles at the White House. He wanted me to take up the matter with Mr. Loeb and ask for what I might think would be necessary, and to get prices and plans and to take the matter up with him when I come to Augusta at Christmas time. I saw Mr. Loeb later in the day, and we thought it best to start modestly with Congress and ask for only $12,000, which ought to buy three large cars and several runabouts, for each factory will sell to us very cheaply for the advertisement which is in it.

Campario, the Italian Naval Attaché, Commander Sims, Bromwell, and Centaro dined with me to-night, and I am now sleepy.

Good-night,
ARCHIBALD.

LXI

Washington, D. C.,
December 15, 1908.

MY DEAR CLARA:

Another busy week ahead of me, although the books at the White House show that there is little on the tape there. But it is all preparation now for the coming season, which opens Thursday evening with the cabinet dinner. Colonel Bromwell will be at the cabinet dinner, though I will help him with the presentations and have two junior aides among the guests to help introduce them to each other and assist the blind old members of the Supreme Court and the Senate to find their partners. At the state dinners the guests assemble in the East Room and a much greater degree of formality is necessary at these dinners than others. What are ranked as state dinners have a prescribed routine which seldom varies.

Most people think that because they are called state dinners the dinners are paid for by the State. I found that Mrs. Taft thought so, too, and it was somewhat of a shock when I told her that the President has to pay for every dinner out of his own pay as President. I grant you it is rather hard, and some President's state dinners have been very meagre in consequence, but the Roosevelts spend more money on their dinners than has ever been spent on them before in any past administration. In the first place, they are served by Rauscher, and we pay him seven fifty a plate. This does not include the champagne, and the President always insists upon buying his own wine, for he wants only the best served at the White House. The same is true as to cigars. While he does not smoke himself, he says that a host can give his guests the finest meal in the world and yet wreck his reputation by offering an indifferent cigar after dinner.

It goes against the grain of both Mrs. Roosevelt and the President to have their state dinners served by any one else than the White House chef, but the fact of the matter is the accommodations of the White House hardly admit of a dinner for a hundred people. They have tried it, and every time something goes badly for the lack of room and the inability to get proper game, etc., in this market. But we have got Rauscher now to furnish a dinner that looks so homelike that it is impossible for any one not knowing the fact to suspect it was prepared elsewhere than in the White House kitchen.

Mrs. Taft says she will have all dinners prepared at the White House and she may get very good results, but one thing is certain, she will be harassed to death for days before each dinner or else her assistants will be.

The cabinet dinner on Thursday calls for pheasants, and to-day Rauscher called me up to say that at best he could not find more than twenty English pheasants in America —and what was he to do? I permitted him to furnish French partridges. Just what a French partridge is I am not sure, and I did not like to inquire, but I strongly suspect it of being a small guinea or squab. There is a large force kept checking up the contracts, making out lists for dances and receptions and seeing that all public men, and their wives especially, are properly recognized.

There are over five hundred persons invited to the dance at the White House on the twenty-eighth. Possibly one hundred of these are to be out-of-town guests, so if the White House attempted to prepare the supper and provide tables, etc., there would be little time for anything else than seeing to feeding that number, for Miss Ethel wants the supper served at small tables.

One thing that took up much time this morning was an attempt to seat four hundred guests at the tables. Mrs. Roosevelt sent for me to see if I could help solve the problem. I telephoned to Rauscher, and he said he could seat two hundred in the state dining room, another hundred in the breakfast or family dining room, and another hundred in the Red Room, adjoining the dining room. I offered every objection to this plan, for I hated to see the Red Room turned into a dining room even for one night, and finally in despair she asked: "Then what can we do, have two sittings?"

I produced the card which I had had up my sleeve all the time and suggested that the supper be served in the basement, which met promptly with jeers of derision simply because it had never been done before.

"Well, let us look over the basement," she said, and when we finished our inspection it was unanimously decided that it was the only place for a supper to be served in the White House, and now the whole family is sorrowing that no one had ever thought of it before and regretting that Alice's wedding luncheon had not been served there.

Rauscher said he could easily seat five hundred in the rooms below and at the same time leave us the entire vestibule in the east corridor for coats and wraps and also a dressing room for the women and another for the men.

I venture to say that never again will there be a supper

served at a public dance or reception in the White House, save on the first floor [basement]. The rooms are very beautiful and the corridors contain the most cherished relics of the White House, yet that entire portion of the building is never seen save as a passageway for people coming and going.

I think the way my letters string out is very funny, don't you? When I sat down to write, it was merely to make a note or two and give some facts which have occurred to-day and which I thought would be of interest to you.

General Bates was not ready for lunch, and while waiting for him I thought to while away the time in this way. After I began I got switched off on an entirely different line from that which I had expected to take and have talked to you about things which are of far greater interest possibly than the mere facts that I had in my head when I started, but which I had not expected to speak about at all.

The above are very domestic and yet must be of some interest, for I find that nine times out of ten persons ask me questions such as the above would answer, instead of questions of political importance or state affairs. . . .

It would be easier, and safer, too, to express opinions about Mr. Roosevelt's political policies than to answer questions about the culinary department, for instance. I sometimes feel like a traitor in writing to you all these letters, yet I am sure it would be considered perfectly proper to keep a diary and I know you well enough to feel that what is written to you is the same as buried.

I am incapable of keeping up a diary. I got in the habit of writing everything to my mother because I wanted to entertain her and to keep up interest in what might be going on around me, and it was she who first put the idea in my head that these letters were of much greater value than any diary could be. I have found in her trunks all my letters written to her from the Philippines before she joined me there and some of them had interesting comments from her on the margins.

Don't think from the above that I am acting in the rôle of housekeeper or even as head clerk. I simply make the contracts and give advice, and Mrs. Roosevelt more and more every day seeks my opinions in matters, which I know helps her out greatly. No one who is not behind the scenes can possibly have the faintest conception of the amount of work which is required to keep the White House going in the social season.

There are hundreds of details which have to be taken up and decided, and matters of precedent and policy sometimes crop up that have to be taken even up to the State Department. I flatter myself that I am fairly sound in the matter of judgment and I think my advice has great weight with Mrs. Roosevelt. I hope so, at least, for I should like to feel that I am doing something to repay her for all the kindness and consideration she shows to me. . . .

Good-bye. With love,

ARCHIBALD.

P. S. We had a fine game of tennis. The President and the Postmaster-General played against the French Ambassador and myself, and defeated us three sets out of four, but in games by only three. After the tennis we came as usual into the office, where Mrs. West Roosevelt and Mrs. Roosevelt were prepared to pour tea. We were soon joined by Mrs. Meyer, Madame Jusserand, and Mr. La Farge, and were prepared to have a characteristic afternoon when Mr. Loeb appeared and announced that the Vice-President-elect and some important man whose name I did not catch, who was interested in the distillation of whisky, were there and simply had to be seen.

The President said that he reserved this time of the afternoon for intimate friends and seriously objected to interruptions of this character.

"But I won't be gone a minute if you will remain just as you are. I agree to drink all the whisky the man wants, kill the Vice-President-elect, and be with you smiling again in five minutes."

He did not come back for nearly an hour. In the meantime, Mrs. Roosevelt had left, which seemed to surprise the President very much, for he said he had not been gone ten minutes. Just as we were all going he said to Mr. Loeb:

"Mr. Loeb, please don't go. I understand from Lodge that Congress is going to make me say things about it which I don't want to say, but I fear they will be responsible for what I will have to dictate to-night if you will be kind enough to stay by me."

This reminds me that I once heard him say about Loeb, relative to retaining him as his secretary:

"When I was Governor of New York I was just as erratic about hours as I am here, and when I was seized with a desire to work Loeb was the only stenographer or secretary whom I could ever find after office hours, and it is the same now. He is always on the spot, and that means everything to me."

Good-bye again.
ARCHIBALD.

LXII

Washington, D. C.,
December 18, 1908.

DEAR CLARA:

Last night was the cabinet dinner, and it went off with a bang. The President always takes the opportunity at cabinet dinners to mix with it friends whom he wishes to compliment yet who would not fit in with the judiciary or the diplomatic dinners.

The President recognizes worth and value, but fortunately leaves it to Mrs. Roosevelt to classify. The Vice-President always appears at the cabinet dinners, and last night the Vice-President-elect and his wife were there. . . .

Senator Knox and his wife were there also. He is spoken of as the next Premier of the Cabinet. He is a splendid-looking man, small, but cultured and keen. His wife is a wee little thing, slightly deaf, but graceful and easy in her manners, and she dresses beautifully.

Frank Munsey, editor of the magazine and the Washington *Times*, was present and is sharp and briary looking and every inch a man of affairs. When making up the table in the morning I suggested that he take out Miss Roosevelt, as I felt he would be interesting to her. She found him charming.

No one looked as lovely as Mrs. Roosevelt. She wore a heavy white brocade and a few flowers in her corsage. No jewels. I have never seen her looking lovelier.

Five minutes before eight I sent the two junior aides upstairs to bring down Miss Ethel and the house guests, Paul Morton and his wife. Mrs. Morton is looking much older than when she was here and he does not seem quite the same. After their arrival Colonel Bromwell and I went for the President and Mrs. Roosevelt.

Bromwell and I enter the East Room ahead of the President and his wife—and take station in the centre of the room nearer the south end. Bromwell stands by the President and I opposite. I then go to the other end of the room, announce to the most ranking guest present which last night, of course, was the Vice-President, that the President would receive them. They are announced as they pass, and the President and Mrs. Roosevelt have some little chatty remark to make to each as he or she passes. I forgot to mention, as we come down the stairs the Marine Band, which is stationed in the corridor, plays the National Air.

At the conclusion of the presentations Colonel Bromwell brings the lady whom the President is to take to dinner up on his arm to him, and I the man who is to take Mrs. Roosevelt, and thus they march out the centre door down the long corridor to the air of "Hail to the Chief." As we start the two other aides take station on either side of the door, which, by the way, is not all for the sake of appearance as was shown last night. After the march to the state dining room is begun there is no way for Bromwell or me to get back, for we head the column. It is necessary to have someone there who will keep things moving.

Secretary Root never thinks to follow, and yet no one will budge until he goes. Last night he remained in the East Room chatting with his partner until one of the aides had to start him forcibly. He cares nothing for the line of march, and it makes no difference to him whether the gap between the second and the third couples is the length of the corridor if he is interested in what he is saying. So these aides are really as useful as they are ornamental.

As we approach the centre door of the dining room Bromwell and I take our places on either side and file in after the last guest passes. The dinners are usually good.

And now you know just what a state dinner means, and when you see that one has been given at the White House you will realize that the President is in a bad humour, for he hates them, as he always has to sit by someone he doesn't like, and Mrs. Roosevelt is equally bored—and only the Climber is happy. They are picturesque always, and with the notable faces one sees at them amid the settings of the White House they never lose their dramatic interest.

To-day there was a luncheon at the White House again, but everyone looked frightened to death, and, as the President said, the men all took cigars but seemed too agitated to light them. . . .

After the guests left I told the President that I intended to go South, and he was very kind about it. He said that he would try to get on with the quibs and quirks and wanton smiles of Bromwell. He said there would be several things he would get me to say to Mr. Taft for him, and I am to call in to get these messages to-morrow before leaving.

He spoke then of the changes the Tafts proposed making after the 4th of March.

"I don't feel any resentment at all; only I hope that he will take care of the men who have served me here. I should hate to feel that the man I had helped all in my power to put here would drop men who had been faithful to me. So tell Taft for me that all his changes will meet with my approval, only say to him what I have just said to you.

"Both Mrs. Roosevelt and I grow fond of those who serve us faithfully, and it cuts us to see them suffer. I don't believe in judging people by the way the White House looks and has looked, or even will look. What a poor showing old Zack Taylor would have made measured by this standard! When he died the Filmores had to have the White House disinfected in order to make it habitable, and yet, Taylor stands out to me as one of the great Presidents and Filmore a pompous old nonentity.

"I can understand Taylor, when he came to the White House, spreading matting over all the carpets so that he could spit where he chose without hunting for cuspidors. That had been his habit, and he did not like to change and thereby divert his thoughts from the real things in life. I can imagine nothing more diverting or disconcerting than to have to look for cuspidors if one has the habit of spitting.

With love,
ARCHIBALD.

LXIII

Washington, D. C.,
Christmas Night, 1908.

MY DEAR CLARA:

I spent most of the morning in the house, but at 2 o'clock I went for Christmas dinner at the White House. I thought there would be only the family and was prepared for a comfortable family dinner such as we had on Thanksgiving night, but to my surprise I was told that at least sixty persons were expected.

All the Roosevelt family was there, and in addition a number of intimate friends and their children. I received them as they arrived in the East Room, and soon it was a merry party of men, women, and children. It was the last Christmas in the White House for the Roosevelts and this was uppermost in everyone's mind. They had determined, evidently, to make it a Christmas which they and their intimate friends should remember so long as each present should live.

It all bore evidence of the good taste and refinement of Mrs. Roosevelt. There was no one there who was not in some way connected closely with the home life of the occupants. Senator Lodge and his wife were the first to come and were followed soon after by their son, Ray

Lodge, and his wife and children. Their own daughter and her husband, Representative Gardner, were there also. Mrs. Gardner looks so ill and there is great fear that she has consumption.

The Nicholas Longworths, Admiral and Mrs. Cowles, Mrs. Lowndes and her boy, and Mr. and Mrs. George Eustis, with their two daughters, about five and six years of age, helped to make up the party. The McIlhennys, some of the Sheffield Cowleses, and some children who seemed to be unattached ran the number to fifty-eight. Ted, Kermit, Archie, and Quentin were all there.

I took out Miss Ethel and sat between her and Kermit. The table was decorated with red leaves and ferns and did look so like old-time Christmas at home. At each plate there were tissue-paper packages which popped when opened, and everyone wore some sort of paper headgear, from fool's cap to crown. Quite a laugh went round when Quentin opened his package and found a tissue paper crown in it.

The dinner was just such a one as you would imagine Mrs. Roosevelt would order for Christmas. Turkeys went round and round and were handed as long as any child would take any. Even the salad was one which a child could eat without fear of cramps, and the plum puddings were ablaze with burning brandy as they came in the room. The ices were miniature Santa Clauses holding each a little Christmas tree with a burning taper in his hand. You have no idea how pretty it all was.

After dinner the men went into the Red Room to smoke, and the women and children into the crypt where all had been darkened and lighted only with lanterns. Mrs. Roosevelt had prepared a Christmas tree with presents on it for all the guests. The children got toys and the other guests mostly books. I drew "The Heretic," made up of a series of essays, which luckily I had not read.[1]

During the distribution of the presents the French Ambassador and the British Ambassador with their wives and the cabinet ministers with their wives and children came in and each had a present from the tree. The President was overflowing with good humour and kissed the youngsters and played with them with the same vim as he talked politics with his other guests. Mrs. Roosevelt moved in and out among her guests, handing presents about herself and making all feel comfortable and content with their Christmas. She thanked me for the two volumes of the Memoirs of the Princesse de Ligne which I sent her last night. . . .

To-morrow the work for Miss Ethel's ball begins in earnest and I am to meet Mrs. Roosevelt at 9:00 to decide upon a number of things which will have to be settled, such as the location of the music, whether we shall have the orchestra divided in two so that there may be no cessation of music, and whether lemonade and punch shall be served from tables in the state dining room or handed by waiters. The florists and the electrician are to meet us there, and also the caterer. There are still 140 persons who have not answered their invitations, so it is difficult to know just how many tables to order. There will be at least four hundred guests. There have not been as many declinations as it was thought there would be, and most of the out-of-town guests are coming.

I told the President that I had spent one evening with the Tafts while I was in Augusta and that the interview had been satisfactory. Mr. Taft said that any changes I made were not to affect the employees now at the White House. It is going to be work to find places for those we

[1]This was, perhaps, G. K. Chesterton's entertaining volume of characteristically paradoxical essays entitled "Heretics."

want to shift, but with the President-elect wanting them found it is safe to predict that they will be found. Next week I will take up the purchase of the automobiles for the next administration. Up to date there has been no serious objection to the appropriation of $12,000 for the motors, but Mrs. Taft wants to get four motors out of this amount. There is only one way to do it; that is, to take the cars at a reduced rate and permit the makers to advertise the fact that their cars are being used for the White House.

With love,

ARCHIBALD.

LXIV

Washington, D. C.,
December 28, 1908.

DEAR CLARA:

Mrs. Roosevelt has left everything practically to me for the dêbut ball of Ethel, which is going to take place this evening. I have directed everything and when I left at 4 o'clock everything was well under way, and when I see it to-night I know that it will look more beautiful than it has ever looked before, far more beautiful than it was even at Alice's wedding.

I had come home rather tired and had lain down to rest with John Fox's story of the "Trail of the Lonesome Pine" to pass the time if I could not sleep. I was just dropping into a slumber when the 'phone rang, and it was a message from the President telling me to come to dinner with the family. They meant it kindly, but I wanted to be with my own thoughts until it was time to dress for the ball. I said I would come, of course, and for a moment felt flattered that they wanted me, for I felt that it was only for that reason that they had asked me to-night. Then I drifted away thinking of my mother, whose picture surrounds me everywhere, and wondered if she knew what an effort I was making to keep her first in my thoughts and how this other life that I am leading does not encroach upon my inner thoughts of her; that she is still enshrined above every one else in my mind. I began to fear that somehow she might fade away from my memory, and I tried to picture her just as she was and the picture was blurred somewhat. That is the awful part of it all. One does forget, and to feel the image fading is as terrible as the first shock of death. . . . The hollowness of it all was borne upon me to-day when Mrs. Longworth and I went through the big White House, and she was unutterably sad. . . .

We went from room to room and each one had some sweet memory for this girl whose career in the White House has been the most dramatic of any in its history. "Princess Alice," she was called, and she ruled over her kingdom as no other woman has ever done there, not excepting Dolly Madison and Nellie Grant. To me she is far more attractive now than she was as a young girl, for she has developed not only physically but mentally and in poise. She was sad this afternoon, for she seemed to realize just what the change would mean to her. She was not complaining, for she has too much of her father in her for that, but she did not hesitate to give voice to the note of sadness.

ARCHIBALD.

LXV

Washington, D. C.,
December 29 [1908].

DEAR CLARA:

Before I was out of bed this morning several persons called me up to say that every one was speaking of the ball, what a success it was, and all my friends were giving me credit for carrying it off with éclat and dignity, too. Among those who 'phoned to me merely to assure me of the success of the evening were Ritchie Simpkins, Oden Hoerstman, and Charlie McCauley, the latter's opinion of much value, for he has filled the place I now hold for several years past, in the first administration of Mr. Roosevelt, and is, I believe, the best man in Washington to direct social affairs at the White House. He married, however, which, of course, cut short his career there. He did not go himself last night, as no married people were asked, but he called to tell me what others were saying.

Only a few days ago he told me that I would make a great mistake to have the supper in the ground floor or crypt. This change, however, made the ball, for it left the first floor free for the dancers, lounging, and promenading and general entertaining, whereas if the supper had been served there that floor would have been so congested that every one would have been uncomfortable and unhappy. As it was we served 440 guests at tables with a course supper in less than an hour. It was the first time that I have ever seen that number of persons entertained at the White House and yet have plenty of room. The old place never seemed so beautiful. Every door on the first floor was thrown open and the guests were free to rove any and everywhere. We did not use crash, and the polished floors shone like mirrors. There were over forty pieces in the orchestra, and twenty musicians played alternately, which made the music continuous throughout the entire evening.

Miss Ethel looked lovely in white. Mrs. Roosevelt wore a beautiful gown of blue brocade, which matched admirably the Blue Room, in which they received. I made the presentations, and some funny things happened. As some old friends would pass they would try to speak to me and shake my hand, but to each I gave a perfectly frozen stare and announced their names. The President was quite at a loss what to do. Being President and yet being limited to certain things which he could do made him very uncomfortable.

"My Southern nature never comes out so much," he said, "as when I am having a party. My desire is to mingle freely and introduce every one and see that the girls all know the men or vice versa, and to start the ball rolling, as they say in the West. But I can't do that, for the moment I attempt it I am about as foolish as the donkey who wanted to be the lap dog. Even you tell me that I must not go to supper, for everybody will promptly rise from the table, thereby checking the merriment of the supper. I am not complaining, but I only want you to know that being President and at the same time host to a real nice party is not a snap."

He talked this out while he, Mrs. Roosevelt, Mrs. Cowles, and I were resting in the Blue Room, while the others were all at supper. Mrs. Roosevelt said:

"Captain Butt can offer any excuses he wishes, but I don't want you to go to supper, for to eat at midnight gives you twinges of the gout."

I think we enjoyed ourselves as much as possible where we were. The President was in fine form and bubbling over with good humour. I did not eat any of the supper, but everyone said how good and hot it was.

The wine was some of that which was left over from Alice's wedding. We served something like ten cases, yet I did not see a single youth show any effect from it.

The tables filled the rooms, which correspond with the Red and Blue and the Green rooms and a part of the corridor. The prettiest effect was had in the long colonnade which is enclosed with glass and runs parallel with the corridor on the east. It is the first time that this glass corridor has ever been used, and it looked like Fairyland as one stood at one end of it and had the full view. Of course, I did not dance. As it was, I had plenty to do to keep me busy and several other aides as well, and at other times I had to remain with the President and his wife, for they are never supposed to be left alone for a moment at this function. If I had to go away for a minute I would call another aide to take my place.

I lunched to-day with Preston Gibson[1] and Lord Hartington, British Minister to Abyssinia. I found him most interesting. He has been in the East for twenty years and is so expatriated that conventional life at home bores him to death. His wife was Amy McMillan of Detroit, daughter of the late Senator McMillan, a millionaire from that place. Lady Hartington, as she is now, is extremely homely, but very clever and highly educated. I think it was a marriage based on admiration for each other's mental qualities.

To-morrow will be another busy day. I am interested in meeting the new German Ambassador, whom we are to present at 2:30. I am going to the White House to another "family dinner" in the evening. I am getting doubtful about these family dinners at the White House since the one Christmas Day. Mrs. Roosevelt starts out to have family dinner and by 1 o'clock the President has asked so many as to make it almost a state affair. He is certainly the soul of hospitality. He dearly loves a great number of people around his table. He is just as

---

[1]A Washington society man and successful playwright; a descendant of Patrick Henry; nephew of Chief Justice White; received the *Croix de Guerre* in the World War.

happy with a lot of schoolboys as he is with a lot of statesmen, a little bit happier, I often think.

Good-bye.
ARCHIBALD.

LXVI

Washington, D. C.,
December 31st, 1908.

MY DEAR SISTER:

I have seen some preferment in my profession and have been fortunate in the association of the President and his family. We have had something to be thankful for, and yet 1908 will always stand out clear as the most unhappy year of my life so far, inasmuch as it has robbed me of the companionship of the one person in the world whom I loved unselfishly and whose goodwill and admiration have spurred me on to do what little I have been able to accomplish in the world. Whatever I do now that is good or ennobling will be the result of her love and belief in my character.

Each day now has its incident, sometimes its series of incidents. Yesterday the newly accredited German Ambassador was presented to the President by the Secretary of State. While we have no great amount of form, yet there is enough to save us from the criticism of being absolutely barbaric in our diplomatic customs.

Colonel Bromwell was temporarily attached to the Ambassador and he called for him in the President's carriage at 2:30. Before his arrival his staff at the embassy came to the White House, where I met them with two other aides. We met them at the door and escorted them into the Blue Room. They were covered with gold lace and decorations, yet their uniforms did not look more imposing than those we wore, for ours were cut to the figure and we were at least erect and large; each one of us was taller than the Germans. We were eclipsed only by Stumm, one of the under-secretaries, who has a stunning uniform and wore it well. He was very small, like a little midget, but very handsome and dashing. Had he been tall he would have been wonderful. Even as it was he looked like one of Ouida's heroes.

Secretary Root came a little later leaning heavily on a stick, but always impressive in his appearance and manner. We conducted him into the presence of the foreigners with much dignity, something which has never been done before. A little later the German Ambassador, Count von Bernstorff, with Bromwell, arrived. He is a large man, nor is he especially impressive in his appearance. He looks more American than German and speaks English with only a slight accent. He was attired in as gorgeous plumage as the flamingo, yet the first thing the President said when I met him later was:

"Archie, did you notice the peculiar uniform of the Ambassador?"

I said that it was gorgeous.

"But did you not see that with all that lace and countless medals he had a white string tie over it all? If I ever permit myself to be decked out in such a costume, I will make it complete and have it surmounted by something else than a cheap-looking linen collar and a string necktie."

Really, nothing that is incongruous seems to escape him. He has the keenest sense of humour I have ever seen. Count Bernstorff, as he left, said that he had brought a book from the Emperor and an invitation from the great German university for him to deliver a lecture and in turn to receive some degree.

I knew the moment that the President told Professor Koch when he was here of England's invitation that

Germany would not rest until it had extended an invitation to him similar to those which had been given him by France and England.[1]

He made an engagement for the Ambassador to call this evening at half-past nine o'clock. I was on hand to meet him and when I went upstairs to find the President he and Mrs. Roosevelt were in her library reading something and laughing over whatever it was. The President asked me to bring the Ambassador to his study on the same floor and added:

"While I am in there you can remain in here and enjoy yourself."

He remained about an hour, and Mrs. Roosevelt and I had a good heart-to-heart chat.

I told her of the scheme of Edwards and others to have Major Mott as an aide at the White House; that Edwards had merely told me that he thought it would be nice to have Mott in charge of the horses and motor cars. I did not tell Edwards how impossible it would be, that Mott ranked me and that the position would be impossible for us both should he be there. I said this to the Secretary when I was in Augusta and suggested that Mott was an excellent man for my place, but for him to be given a subordinate place under me was impossible and that we could not exist side by side in authority. Mr. Taft said that he had no idea of permitting him to displace me, but I wanted him to know that I should not object to being displaced and that is what I think will come of it, if not at once, at least later in the year. It was the first chance

[1]Consult Bishop's "Theodore Roosevelt and His Time," chapters XIV–XVIII, for an account of Roosevelt's European journey written by himself in the form of a letter to the English historian Trevelyan. Lord Charnwood's Life of Roosevelt also contains valuable information about the journey. In my "Impressions of Theodore Roosevelt" and in the introduction to Roosevelt's "African and European Addresses" I have tried to re-create the *mise en scène* of that extraordinary pilgrimage.

I had to talk freely with Mrs. Roosevelt since I returned and she agreed with me that it was wise to be frank about the matter, for she felt as I did that it would be impossible for both Mott and me to remain on duty at the White House. I do not know why I feel so indifferent about the matter, but I am perfectly indifferent to the whole thing.

After the President returned, having dismissed the Ambassador, he came in the library bringing with him the book which the Kaiser had sent to him, elaborately inscribed on the fly page to the President and signed "William." It was accompanied by a lengthy letter written by a scribe and closed with some remark such as "I am, my dear sir, your sincere friend"—and we had added in his own handwriting "and admirer, William."

"This simplifies our personal correspondence in the future," said the President, "for heretofore we have always written to each other in our own handwriting, but I see he has not done so this time. I will let Adee conduct our correspondence in the future. I am glad he has called quits, for I imagine he writes as laboriously as I do." . . .

Good-night and God bless you,

ARCHIBALD.

January 1st.

P. S. I did not mail this letter yesterday, but kept it open to see if there was anything worth recording from New Year's Day. But nothing happened. The line was beautiful and the President received 6,665 persons, shaking every one by the hand, and we were all tired and hungry when it was over. Lunch was served in the state dining room to those of the receiving party, and every one had a chance to slip away for a cup of hot bouillon and an ice except the President, Mrs. Roosevelt, and Bromwell and myself. We had to stick it out and did not conclude until nearly three o'clock.

There were nearly two thousand people over last year, which would indicate that times are not as hard as they were a year ago, or else the hoi polloi have ceased to think it was due to the President alone that stocks went down. Good-bye again.

ARCHIE.

Roosevelt's allusion to his laborious work with the pen recalls the story of the illegibility of his handwriting, told by Hermann Hagedorn in his "Roosevelt in the Bad Lands"—one of the really valuable books for the student of Roosevelt's life and characteristics:

> He was to meet a hunter named John Willis, who was to take him and Merrifield out [in the mountains of Northern Idaho] after white goat. He had never met Willis, but his correspondence with him had suggested possibilities of interest besides the chase. Roosevelt had written Willis in July that he had heard of his success in pursuit of the game of the high peaks. "If I come out," he concluded, "do you think it will be possible for me to get a goat?"
>
> The answer he received was written on the back of his own letter and was quite to the point. "If you can't shoot any better than you can write, I don't think it will be."
>
> Roosevelt's reply came by wire: "Consider yourself engaged."

After at least one hair-breadth escape from death, Roosevelt got his goat—and got Willis, too, for the latter became one of his most devoted admirers.

LXVII

Washington, D. C.,
January 5, 1909.

MY DEAR CLARA:

I have had house guests for the past few days and therefore I have not had time to write to you or to chronicle in any form the number of interesting events which have taken place. If I pass over these matters while they are fresh in my mind or before my sober judgment tells me how trivial they really are I find that I do not refer to them later, so what has passed has gone into oblivion, for I will not attempt to rehash them to you. If they bore me to try to recall them they will bore you still more to be forced to read them.

This day, however, has been pleasant. I sat next to Miss [Anne] Morgan at lunch at the White House to-day, and she is really a most marvellous person. I did not know who she was, for her name meant nothing to me, but I was so impressed with her that after dinner I asked Mrs. Roosevelt and she laughed and said:

"You don't know that you took in to luncheon the daughter of Mr. J. Pierpont Morgan?"

She struck me as being a woman with a wonderful mind. She really ought to be poor and to be forced to make her own living. I think, however, she does a thousand and one things of importance in the world. For one thing, she asked me about a Miss Berry of Rome, Ga., and expressed horror when I could not tell her anything about her. She is interested in her and says she is the most remarkable woman in the South; that the work she is doing among the poor white people in the way of industrial education is simply wonderful.

She wanted to know if there was no way we could make the public men, our Senators especially, interest themselves in the work she is doing in Rome. I said it was not that which was needed in the South, but money for such work.

"Money is the least thing," she said. "We will raise the money if we can get help in other ways."

She, Miss [Elizabeth] Marbury, and Mrs. [J. Borden]

Harriman are in Washington to get the President interested in the matter of [their] undertaking [to do] just such work as the work which Miss Berry is doing in Rome, namely, to develop the poor white youths in the South, especially in the mountainous districts in Georgia, Tennessee, and Alabama.

"You know," she said, "there are such opportunities for careers in America now that it makes one restless where to begin. With the money that we have back of us and the energy we have stored up in us one hardly knows where to begin."

She said she scorned the idea of going to Italy to see the disasters at Messina out of curiosity, but she felt greatly tempted to go to see if there was something she could do. We talked of the horror of it all, and I said that it seemed impossible to take in the full scope of the calamity in Sicily; that the only way I could get into my mind at all the awfulness of it was to get the pictures of the inferno of Dante in my mind's eye and then study segments of them, and in that way I could reach some conception of how horrible it all must be.

"Not so," she said. "It is brought clearly to my mind by the serious discussion as to whether it were not the most humane thing after all to draw up a line of battleships and bombard Messina and thus destroy all alike, to bury the dead with the living."

She simply blue pencilled conversation, as I told someone later about her. She drew me out as to my detail at the White House, what interested me most in it, and if I said one word too much, or got on a subject she was not interested in she would promptly run her blue pencil through it and bring me to what did interest her. It was the first luncheon at the White House that I ever remember feeling indifferent as to what the President might be saying to the others in general conversation. And there were a lot of interesting people there, too.

Among them were Owen Wister and his wife and three of the dearest little children I ever saw; Mr. Garrett of Baltimore, First Secretary to our embassy at Rome, and with him was his bride of a few days. She was a Miss Warder and a great beauty to my way of thinking, a little uncanny possibly for the reason that she is so thin and dark, but very lithe and graceful. Mr. Barry, the artist, and Mr. and Mrs. White, whoever they are. I am afraid to-day to acknowledge my ignorance of any one since my ignorance concerning Miss Berry.

After dinner Miss Morgan told the President, when he said to her that he wanted her to meet his fellow Georgian, that I did not know of Miss M. Berry or her work.

"Then I repudiate you and you are no fellow statesman of mine," he said.[1]

I had a little chat with Owen Wister, and he told me that we were cousins in a way. It seems that he is a cousin of the Lewis Robertsons in Charleston and he spent most of his time with them while he was writing "Lady Baltimore." He had heard of us and introduced me to his wife as a cousin. He said, by the way, that he was somewhat unpopular in Charleston now; that while his friends there liked the picture he presented of Charleston, many of the people resented it. . . .

---

[1]Miss Morgan, Mrs. Harriman, Miss Marbury, and Martha Berry have been leaders in the constructive work which has so widely enlisted the interest of the present generation of American women. Miss Morgan founded the "American Committee for Devastated France" whose beneficent achievements are internationally known; Mrs. Harriman has been an important factor in promoting legislation for improving the conditions of women in industry; Miss Marbury is a recognized leader of women in Democratic national politics; and Miss Berry established an industrial school for self-supporting pupils in Georgia which has had a marked influence on industrial education throughout the South.

There were thirty at the luncheon, the others being largely the young society friends of Miss Ethel.

While at the White House this morning I asked the young lady to ride, but she could not do so as she had just refused to go with young Stumm, the Third Secretary of the German Embassy. Mrs. Roosevelt will not allow her to ride with any of the foreigners alone, but has no objection to her going alone with her American friends. She is very particular and at the same time shows her good judgment, for while many of them are fascinating, they do not have the same ideas as we have toward women. Stumm is an awfully nice fellow and I rather pleaded his cause, but Mrs. Roosevelt was quite firm.

"If I were to send a groom along he might feel insulted, but that is just what would happen in his own country were he to ride with a young girl. I don't mind them thinking us democratic, but I don't wish them to regard us as careless."

I have an awful blow to deliver to Stumm, poor fellow, but Mrs. Roosevelt has asked me to do it, and there is none other in the Embassy whom I know as well or like as much as Stumm. It is this:

Mrs. Roosevelt sent invitations to the German Ambassador and his wife, Baron and Baroness Bernstorff, for the diplomatic dinner and another invitation to the daughter to the dance. The acceptance was typewritten, and both acceptances were included in the one response. How the Kaiser would rave if he suspected such a thing! He would hardly do less than recall the new Ambassador, for it certainly shows frightful ignorance or very bad manners. Mrs. Roosevelt prefers to think it ignorance, but she has commissioned me to inform one of the Secretaries that responses in this manner are not received at the White House and that such acceptances are most distasteful. She laughed heartily over the matter and tried to think it due to some under-secretary or clerk, but she will never quite get over it and will be constantly on the lookout for bad manners in them in the future. She says it will make no difference in her feeling to them at all, but I know that her sense of the fitness of things is such that she will be unable to get this break out of her mind altogether. I shall invite Stumm to take a champagne cocktail, which beverage delights the souls of foreigners, the first time I see him at the Metropolitan, and over it I will diplomatically reprove his Embassy. A rather delicate mission, you will admit.

Senator Lodge came from Augusta yesterday, and he no sooner got back than he hurled discord into the Roosevelt and cabinet camps by announcing that he had been in Augusta two whole days before he was allowed to see Mr. Taft alone for a minute, that he was kept constantly under the watchful eye of either Mrs. Taft or of his brother, who is with him from New York. When I saw the President at 9:45 this morning at the office, he looked as if he had something on his mind and when he had the doors closed to the cabinet room and began to talk of Africa I knew that something more important was coming. Finally he asked me if I was assured that I would be kept at the White House, and when I told him I felt reasonably sure, he said:

"Because if you are not and know of anything I can do for you, I want you to let me know. I cannot leave my favourite aide hanging by his heels." . . .

I learned afterward from Mrs. Roosevelt that Senator Lodge had told the President that not one of the present Cabinet would remain unless it be Meyer, and he would remain only through outside pressure. He also told them that it was evidently the intention to get rid of every person who might keep President Taft in touch with the Roosevelt influence. He seems to think that they were determined that the Taft Administration should stand alone and that it would be impossible for any one to charge to it that it was but a continuation of the Roosevelt régime. I have always thought that this would be the case and I think Mr. Taft is big enough and strong enough to hew out his own policies and to make them successful. But I felt rather disgusted that Senator Lodge should come home and stir up discord between the two families.[1]

I frankly told Mrs. Roosevelt that Senator Lodge could hardly be considered a confidential adviser of Mr. Taft and that he might have exaggerated the feeling as he had conceived it to be. Lodge is so hopelessly selfish that if the Tafts did not kow-tow to him he would delight to make trouble between them and the Roosevelts, but it is my opinion that it is Lodge, and not the Roosevelts, the Tafts were guarding the President-elect from; but I could not say so, for they [the Roosevelts] are very fond of Senator Lodge and would never brook any criticism of him. He might make the President feel badly over it, but I venture to say that he would not be able to shake his faith in Mr. Taft, because he really loves him [Taft] and his faith in him is absolute. The fact that the President said nothing of what he was possibly feeling at the time I saw him would indicate that he preferred to await events than to judge too quickly on the say-so of Mr. Lodge.

I suppose everybody from now on will be trying to carry tales and make bad feeling between the families, and it will be my constant effort to rally their loyalty for each other.

---

[1]In a previous letter Captain Butt expresses his distrust of Senator Lodge. What he—or Roosevelt—would have said, could they have lived to see Senator Lodge supporting the payment of $25,000,000 to Colombia as "restitution" for Roosevelt's "taking" of Panama, can easily be imagined.

It may all come about as Mr. Lodge predicts, but if it does it will not reflect on Mr. Taft. I should want a clean slate if I were in their places and my only surprise is that they should show any disposition to retain me as an aide, for you certainly know by this time how I feel, and feeling as I do toward the Roosevelts, it will be difficult for me to serve with the Tafts without some mental criticism at least. Should he drop me I should not feel resentful at all. That you cannot serve two masters is as true now as in the time of the Christ. And the influence of Mr. Roosevelt over those around him is masterful and his friends become fanatical, e. g., to wit—I.

Good-bye. Yours at length to-day,

ARCHIBALD.

LXVIII

Washington, D. C.,
January 6, 1909.

DEAR CLARA:

I cannot help depicting the miserable state into which the poor old Ambassador from China has fallen during the past few days. No one could be more hopelessly wretched in appearance than he was to-night at the White House. He did not seem to be the same gorgeous creature he was the first day when he presented his credentials. On that occasion and the subsequent one, when he presented the Chinese students to the President, he was almost sublime in his Oriental dignity, never moving until someone approached him to act as escort and yet with a graciousness which denoted security, power, and prosperity. To-night he came to the White House alone, in deep mourning and pitiful in his appearance. His body seemed bent and he walked with a stealthiness which betokens fear.

It was scarcely a week ago that Marvin, the American manager of the Embassy, came to me to say that while the Ambassador could not accept any invitations to large affairs he would be honoured to be asked to dine informally at the White House, giving me the hint that such an attention was expected. I promptly communicated it to the President and he was asked to dine to-night. Since then his all-powerful friend Yuan Shi Kai has been dismissed from the office of Grand Chancellor and Commander-in-Chief of the Army, and his enemies, and it would seem also our enemies, have come into authority in the Chinese Empire. What it means our diplomats do not seem fully to know, though they believe that Japan is at the bottom of it and that it is a serious blow to our interests in the East. Straight said to-night that it was the end of something they [the Japanese] had been planning for years and yet it took them so by surprise that he could but laugh at the ridiculous figure he and all concerned were cutting now.

The Special Embassy is to be broken up at once and poor old Tang Fu starts for China Sunday, and they who understand say that he will be most lucky if he does not lose his head.

Marvin, our brilliant young American, who left the Consular service to become a member of the Chinese foreign office, loses his position, I am told, and certainly he looked pretty gloomy to-night at the club. Fletcher, who was here for a prolonged holiday, hastens to-morrow for the East again, and the chances are that the Chinese students, who were presented with such pomp the other day, will be recalled and whipped likewise.

There were only six at dinner to-night at the White House, as the Ambassador would regard a dinner with a greater number a "formal affair." There were only Mrs.

Beale, a daughter, you may know, of James G. Blaine, and a most charming woman; Senator and Mrs. Lodge, the President and Mrs. Roosevelt, and the Ambassador. The Ambassador was the last to arrive and, as I said, he looked hacked and unhappy. Can you wonder? Since he left his empire inspired with hopes of great things, the Emperor and Empress Dowager have died and a new ruler has been placed on the throne. Now comes the disgrace of the friend and his own recall. But the transformation is what shocked me, as it did Mrs. Roosevelt.

As she took his arm to go to dinner I heard her say to him: "You do not know what pleasure it gives us to have you with us, Mr. Ambassador," and by the way she said it I knew how her heart was touched for the sufferings of the old man. . . .

Good-night,
ARCHIBALD.

LXIX

Washington, D. C.,
January 8, 1909.

DEAR CLARA:

The diplomatic reception last night was a particularly brilliant affair, there being many more in attendance than usual. The old friends of the President and his family were anxious to show him that his invitations were still appreciated, and those who had not been there on former occasions were anxious to be at one of these receptions before he goes out of office. There are many society people here who never go to any of the receptions until the last season of an administration. Last night was a terrible one in point of weather, for the snow had been falling for nearly a day and a night and it was bitter cold.

The diplomats were, of course, all there. We herded

them in the state dining room before the crowd began to come. The American women among them were the most beautiful; in fact, there were no handsome women in the line of diplomats who were not American born. The Baroness Moncheur was by all odds the most beautiful among them and was the cynosure of all eyes. She is a daughter of Gen. Powell Clayton of Arkansas and a sister of Mrs. Grant Duff, whom you met in Cuba. She is a wonderful looking woman. Her figure is pronounced by the Baron Hengelmüller, who is said to be the authority on figures of women, to be the most perfect one he has ever seen. As she passed down the line last night I felt proud of her. I was in the state dining room before the reception began with a view of getting the diplomats in line.

I was talking with Mr. Jusserand, the French Ambassador, when the Baroness Moncheur passed. We both followed her with our eyes, and finally the veteran Ambassador said:

"Ah, Butt, truly the triumph of the American woman is her back!"

Several years ago when Wentworth Dilke of England, son of Savannah's distinguished relative, Sir Charles Dilke, was on a visit to this country and I was piloting him about Washington he caught a glimpse of the Baroness Moncheur at a ball of the British Embassy, I think it was. He asked me who she was, and when I told him he said:

"She must be Austrian. No other women have such backs."

"No," I said, "she is American. She is from Arkansas."

"Ah, ah, Arkansas," he grunted several times, readjusting his monocle. "Where is Arkansas? Is it one of your new South Sea possessions?" . . .

After the diplomats, came the society folk of Washington. It was noticeable how few Congressmen there were in line, but this was due to two reasons: One being that very few were invited and the other that many who were invited showed their resentment toward the President by remaining away. It made the reception all the more brilliant, for the fewer Congressional people there are at these receptions, the fewer incongruous costumes there are to be seen, and the fewer high-neck gowns there are to mar the general scene. We did not finish the presentations until midnight. The line was then formed, and the presidential party, headed by Colonel Bromwell, Commander Sims, Captain Cheney, and myself, filed through the great mass of people in the East Room and up the main stairway to the upper hall where supper was served.

There were some sixty persons in the supper party and they sat at small tables in the upper corridors. I sat between a Miss Ingersoll of Philadelphia and Mrs. Wallingford, a sister of Nick Longworth. The latter looks something like her brother and is a very interesting woman. I found her to be devoted to Mr. Taft, and one of his great friends among the younger set in Cincinnati. Mrs. Longworth came to the reception, but left early as she was suffering with a severe cold.

Old Nick was looking a little worried, I thought, but the situation at the House must be a most trying ordeal to him. He is very popular there and members tell me that he conducts himself with wonderful discretion. But to be a member of the body which feels itself insulted by the President, and yet retain his temper when that body attacks his father-in-law, is a difficult task, especially to one who is as devoted to Mr. Roosevelt as he is. As he said good-night to the President last night, the President hit him on the back, and said:

"Poor old Nick! What is he not suffering for love's sake these days!"

Nick laughed and said: "I think I am enjoying it about as much as you are, Mr. President."

"Nick," added the President, "it is a great pity they don't drop it. They may make me say some things which I don't want to say and which are true. I purposely took a back step and appeared even to retreat so as to give Congress a chance to simmer down, but if they push me too hard I may not be able to be so lenient as I was in my last message."

I met Nick to-day at the Metropolitan Club as I was coming to lunch and he said:

"I am playing hooky in real earnest to-day. They are discussing the resolution to be passed on the President's message. I don't want to take any part in the discussion, both for the sake of the President and myself. And I do not want to embarrass some of my personal friends there who may want to hit back for home consumption. But I wish they would get through with it so I could feel that every moment I would not have to skin out of the House to prevent voting to censure my own father-in-law."

Before going to the reception last night I dined with Mrs. Cowles, just the family party being present. She is famous for having the very best cook in the city. I sat on her left and we got talking about her mother and there was something very pathetic in the way she spoke of her mother.

"I seem to know everything about Georgia and Georgians that my mother knew. All the old jokes which are still told around the vicinity of Roswell I knew by heart as a child, and what makes my heart ache when I think of them now, is the fact that they represent the heart pain of my little mother. I could not know then what those constant recitals meant to her, but I do now. She must have been homesick for her own people until her heart bled in those early days. I never remember hearing her tell stories of any other part of the world; only of Georgia, and it was out of the very fullness of her heart that she used to tell us of home.

"She was only eighteen when she married, and just before that terrible civil war with all her feelings on one side. I shudder to think of what she must have suffered. I know the Roosevelts, and I should hate to have married into them at that time unless I had been one with them in thought. They think they are just, but they are hard in a way. I remember that Mother for a long time never came to the dinner table, but would have her dinner with us in the nursery, so that she would not be present during the discussions which, of course, would take place there.

"How delighted we were when she would tell us of Georgia! I see now it was a determination to keep her home constantly before her, as well as to implant in us a love of that home. She succeeded in doing this, too, for there is not one of us who does not feel loyal to her home and neighbours. My sister simply worships the Southern strain in us, and having married a man of Southern extraction she can better keep the sentiment alive. I feel that the only way I can help to make up to my mother for all the heart-aches she had is by keeping alive in the family and among my children the memory of her and of her home. I knew her when those years had been obliterated, and when she was surrounded by all that she held dear, so that my memory of her is not all sad; but when I think of her early married life and remember what each anecdote of her old home meant to her my heart throbs with something akin to pain. You and your devotion to your mother always make me think of my mother and what I lost in not knowing her in riper years when my sympathy and love might have obliterated the cruel scars of the past."

She said this in very much this way, only not in connected form as I have related it. But somehow it saddened me as it did her, for once or twice her eyes filled with tears which she soon concealed, and when I got up from the table I felt that I knew a little more of the President's mother than I did before, and that I understood some things in him which had been enigmatic up to this time. I felt that somehow he was trying, as was Mrs. Cowles, to make retribution to her for things which she had possibly been made to suffer, and that his constant and oft-repeated public statements about Georgia were not for political purposes, as is often charged, but with the intent of standing up for her beliefs and acknowledging her faith.

I had intended to tell you of a proposed ninety-mile horseback ride through the snow and how I circumvented it and how the President may yet take it with Admiral Rixey and myself, but it is too late to start on a long story which does not mean much, after all, but merely illustrates the fact that people had better not put up bluffs to the President unless they want their hands called.

Good-bye. With much love,

ARCHIBALD.

LXX

Washington, D. C.,
January 11th, 1909.

DEAR CLARA:

I am sorry the President has got into this awful rumpus with Congress, though I feel that he is not only justified but perfectly right in the matter, feeling, of course, as he does about the dangers of corruption in office. He thinks that is the most important issue which has ever presented itself to him. But these charges and counter charges worry Mrs. Roosevelt very much, and, in fact, they worry all of us connected in any way with the President. They seem to worry him least of all. I think he sees more clearly than any of the rest of us do, or else he has no nerves at all. . . .

In spite of the fact that he had only that afternoon given out the facts in the Tillman case, and the House of Representatives had tabled his messages, he was as spry as a boy and enjoyed himself hugely. In fact, we could hardly believe the report that he was dancing in the East Room with Madame Jusserand. Mrs. Roosevelt did not think it possible until he came in all flushed and told us so himself, and tried to get Mrs. Roosevelt to dance also. She refused to leave the Blue Room, however, until after the guests had all arrived, but agreed to dance later in the evening, which she did.

It was a very pretty sight to see them waltzing, and it created a great deal of interest, as you may imagine, though everybody was too well versed in the etiquette of the White House to pay any especial attention to it. It was about the prettiest affair I have ever seen at the White House.

There were only 370 persons present, and the dancing in the East Room appeared to be perfect. While there were some political people there, yet it was composed almost entirely of the smart element of Washington, irrespective of age; and the dressing quite eclipsed anything I have ever seen in the White House. All of the Ambassadors were asked and a few of the best of the under diplomats. The Austrian Ambassador, taking his cue from the President, danced with his wife and later with some of the younger set. The French Ambassador always dances if he has the chance, but this mixture of the social flippant with the "distinguidos" gave the evening a catholicity which was quite refreshing.

After the evening was over the President came up to where his wife was receiving those saying good-bye and remarked that it was the very smartest affair he had ever seen in the White House, and that his only piece of advice was to "keep the others on the same exalted plane!" . . .

He insisted that there were no frumps present, that everybody seemed of one class or set. She smiled at his enthusiasm, but was evidently pleased that he had commended her dance, for he usually gets horribly bored at the big affairs at the White House. . . .

The Duvalls and Senator Bacon dined with me last night and we had a pleasant homelike evening. The Senator cannot abide the President as President, but likes him as a man. He truly believes that the President has no respect for the Constitution, while others like Clay, his colleague from Georgia, think the President one of the greatest men in the world and with a profound respect for the Constitution. So after all it depends on one's viewpoint. Bacon's hobby is the Constitution, and he is always on the watch for someone who has not the same respect for it as he himself has. He told us the right of that story which was told on him after the last inauguration. He was one of the committee to attend the President when he took his oath of office. On reaching the White House reviewing stand, he said the President turned to Senator Lodge and said:

"Lodge, did you see Bacon turn pale when he heard me swear to support the Constitution?"

"On the contrary, Mr. President," Bacon replied, "I never felt so relieved in my life." . . .

I learned to-day that [Morgan] Shuster, in the Philippines, is to be beheaded officially. There is considerable feeling in cabinet circles that so few of his confrères are to be retained in the next administration. I think each member had hoped he would be the one picked out to remain, but it seems that Garfield, Straus, and the others are all to go, and there is gathering considerable criticism along the line.

I cannot see how any of the Cabinet except Mr. Meyer can hope to remain. Mr. Taft must be free if he is to carve his own administration into history with any individual imprint. I think the President feels that he is perfectly right in the matter, though he cannot be got to say one word. Only one thing I have heard him say. When some incense swinger was trying to make character by saying that he did not think the policy of the next administration would be as vigorous as this one, he said:

"The system may be different, but the results will be the same."

Good-bye,
ARCHIBALD.

LXXI

Washington, D. C.,
January 12, 1909.

DEAR CLARA:

I do not know when I will be able to write again, for I doubt after to-morrow I will be able to sit down for a considerable period, and I already imagine myself dining at the diplomatic dinner, standing. The fact is, the President has determined on that ninety-mile ride, and we leave to-morrow morning at 3 o'clock. We go by way of Fairfax Court House, down the old Bull Run road, on to Bull Run and thence to Warrenton, Virginia, and back again; presumably all in one day. I do not feel up to it by any means, for my life this winter has been more sedentary than for several years past, and that jolt I got on my spine last spring hurts occasionally now. But it is impossible to permit the President to go without an aide, and there is no one else who could get as far as Fairfax.

I have protested against his taking this ride, for he is not in fit condition, but he is keen to do it and so we are off to-morrow. Admiral Rixey, who proposed it, says frankly that he had no idea the President would take it up and he has asked Mrs. Roosevelt to intervene and get him to give it up. She will not interfere, because she says it would do no good whatever.

I am to spend the night at the White House and be called at 2:30. We will have breakfast and start promptly at 3:00. Admiral Rixey and Doctor Grayson are coming by for us. I told them to have a good beefsteak for us, as it will be many hours before we get another snack. I am going to sleep in the Rose Room, and expect to be haunted by visions of former Presidents and their dames. I would enjoy the night there if it was an entire night and not a mere chip off one.

We have had good weather for the last few days. It was that which decided the President to go to-morrow, but the bulletins this afternoon are predicting a blizzard, and the wind is howling on the outside now. A pretty prospect for 3 o'clock in the morning, forsooth! It is my own fault that I am in for it, however, for the President said that I need not go unless I wanted to, but his going makes it imperative for me to accompany him, and while it would be unfortunate for me not to be able to make the full ride with him, it would be nothing short of disgraceful not to make the effort. Before you get this I will have fallen by the wayside or else completed the ride. Now good night. I wish I could look forward to one. Love to Lewis.

Your affectionate brother,
ARCHIBALD.

The following letter vividly reveals one of Roosevelt's characteristics—his almost boyish zest in tests of his physical endurance and strength. His fox-hunt accident at Oyster Bay,[1] the exploits of his cowboy life in Montana,[2] his sufferings on the "River of Doubt" in South America,[3] his going down in a submarine on Long Island Sound in 1905, when submarines were not so well understood as they are to-day,[4] and his going up in an airplane in 1910 at Paris, when flying was still in the experimental stage,[5] were all manifestations of this trait. Nor were these exploits undertaken in a spirit of mere bravado. In every adventure—except possibly that of the hunting field, which was the result of exuberant joy in physical strength—the basic motive was a desire to help in promoting a spirit of courage and persistence in American life.

LXXII

Washington, D. C.,
January 14th, 1909.

DEAR CLARA:

I doubt if any of us know what we can endure until put to the test. As the President dismissed the carriage which had been sent to the Aqueduct Bridge to meet us last night

---

[1]See comment on Letter VIII.

[2]See Hermann Hagedorn's "Roosevelt in the Bad Lands."

[3]See "Impressions of Theodore Roosevelt."

[4]See "Roosevelt's Letters to His Children."

[5]See Introduction to "African and European Addresses."

and rode into Washington, he voiced the opinion of us all when he said:

"Had any one told me this morning when we crossed the bridge we would be crossing it again to-night feeling really in better spirits than we did then, I should have been inclined to put him in the Ananias Club. What has surprised me more than anything in this ride is the fact that no one has said a cross word, that we have had a good time, and that we returned laughing. And you know, Archie, that if we had not met this sleet storm, it would have been like taking candy from a child."

Really, Clara, that tells the tale of the ride. . . .

I had never ridden more than forty miles at a time and while the President had ridden as much as seventy, yet it was in good weather and over good roads and on good horses. Yesterday the roads were the very worst I have ever seen, the weather execrable and the horses, with the exception of those we owned ourselves, about as bad and rough as it was possible to turn out from a cavalry post. I knew this latter would be the case when the President refused to let me tell the commanding officers at Fort Myer why the horses were wanted and to what use they were going to be put. Had they known that he was going along, they would have sent the best in the stables, but as they thought they were for a party of navy officers they naturally sent their most inferior animals.

But it is just what he wanted. He was determined that this ride should be a test ride under just such conditions as the average officer would be required to take it. It was, in fact, much harder; for the test rides in the army are held only in the spring and fall, and never in extreme heat or cold. I am forced to bow to his judgment again and to acknowledge that what I feared might be a failure has been a great success, and that this ride has given me more respect for myself than all the honours which could have been heaped on me from the outside.

For this ride was each man's who made it. It took physical strength, but it took more moral courage and backbone than anything else. I realized as never before how easy it would have been to flunk had I stopped to think of it at all. I feel somewhat ashamed now, as I recall my feelings at 4 o'clock yesterday morning as we passed from underneath the portico of the White House. I had been somewhat under a nervous strain the twenty hours before and the wind cut round the corners of the old house like a knife. I felt distinctly resentful toward the President and indignant with the world at large. I had turned into bed at the White House by 10:00, but had been unable to sleep and was lying there reading when the President came in from dinner, given in his honour at Secretary Wright's. He knocked at my door to see if I was asleep and came in. He came ostensibly to say a word of welcome, but in reality what he came to say was this:

"I suppose I will be criticized again, Archie, for making a 'spectacular play for the benefit of the public,' but I don't think you know how I dread taking this ride at this time; but you would understand if you could see the protest from people against my last order prescribing the riding test for the navy. I believe that it has done so much for the army and will bear so much greater fruit later that I would undergo any hardship myself to guarantee the continuance of the order. I believe that Mr. Taft will continue the order, but I also know that a great coterie of both the army and the navy are only waiting for me to leave the White House to deluge the next President with applications to modify the order. I know the order is not too severe, but if it is, I also want to know it.

"If two naval officers,"—and with a comical smile added

in parenthesis, ("we won't mention the fact that they are Virginians and possibly born in the saddle")—"and you and I can take this ride of ninety miles in one day, we will never hear a word again in protest of the order. It will silence all critics, and the army and the navy itself will see to its perpetuation as a matter of *espril de corps*. And we are going to make it, so don't you feel worried a bit, but just go to sleep. I presume you have already said your prayers, but if you have not," he said, smiling, "add a word to have the predicted blizzard delayed for twenty-four hours."

I was asleep in five minutes and the next thing I knew he was hammering at my door to get up. He and I breakfasted together. We had little bread, but a considerable amount of rare steak and he drank two cups of coffee. Doctor Rixey and Doctor Grayson came before we finished and while we were merry apparently, I think our merriment was largely assumed, for it meant a good deal to each one of us, and there was no one in the party who did not realize it. For the President it meant prestige, a continuance of his orders; in fact, it would never have done for him to fail, and I don't think failure ever entered his mind, but it did in ours and we each looked most critically at him to see if he was in fit state. Doctor Rixey examined his heart and punched him here and there, which he resented in good humour, but submitted to it, as it was a part of his order for the riding test.

It was just twenty minutes to four when we mounted our horses. The President rode Roswell on the start and I had my old faithful Larry. The two Virginians had their own mounts also. We started on a dog trot down Pennsylvania Avenue and made the bridge in ten minutes. But, oh, the wind was cold! There were few clouds to be seen, and while everything was frozen hard there was no sign of a blizzard in the sky. We did not pass through Fort Myer, but took the road to the right. For the first six miles, in fact to Falls Church, the roads were fair and we made good time, but from Falls Church to Fairfax the roads were bad and we lost time.

If you can imagine the roads in Cuba during the rainy weather, frozen hard, you will have some idea of the greater part of the roads we travelled over. They had been deeply furrowed and cut up since the last thaw and snow, and had simply frozen in this way, but we managed to reach Fairfax by ten minutes past 6. Here we found the first detachment of horses waiting for us, in charge of a trooper from Fort Myer. As we had not decided to go until 10 o'clock Tuesday morning, it was after 12 before I could perfect arrangements to have the relay horses sent out. Then I simply ordered four horses and two orderlies to report to Doctor Rixey's farm, near Falls Church, for the use of some officers, presumably of the navy, and so no one knew what they were really to be used for. Orders were given to the orderlies to leave two horses at Fairfax, two more at Bull Run, and two more at Buckland. I had also sent from Washington the President's bay mare Georgia for him to ride from Fairfax to the second change, but to my chagrin when we got to Fairfax I saw that Georgia was not there and inquiry developed the fact that Doctor Rixey, thinking I had sent too many horses, had ordered one to be left back, and as luck would have it, Georgia was the one chosen. I thought the President would be furious, as he had every right to be, for he had told Doctor Rixey that he would have Georgia sent over for the trip, and I had given most specific orders, yet all he said was:

"I am keenly disappointed, for I wanted Georgia to be in on this ride as a matter of sentiment if for nothing else."

It was 6:20 when we arrived at Fairfax Court House, and it took only fifteen minutes to change horses, and without waiting a minute we started at a brisk trot toward Centerville, which we reached at 7:20. Two miles farther on we came to Cub Run, where we found our second change of horses, and the change for the President and myself was for the worse; for the horses we got in exchange for the ones we were on were rough, slow, and mine was vicious. We passed the battlefield and saw some of the monuments erected to some of the New York regiments, which led me to repeat the story which always struck me as rather good:

"When one old General was talking of the Battle of Bull Run, one of his listeners asked, 'Did you run, General?' to which he promptly replied, 'All who didn't are there yet.'"

The whole way the President was in the best of spirits. We only saw the sun that day for a minute, and as it came out somewhere near Bull Run the President turned in his saddle and said:

"Let Tillman rage and let Foraker imagine a vain thing, we will enjoy this day in spite of them, the secret service and the resentment of Congress."

The conversation was in patches, for no one attempted to carry on a discussion of any kind. The President's keen wit was like wine when our spirits began to flag. He joked Admiral Rixey about the Virginia roads and wondered what the old vets would say if their spirits could come back to earth and see him riding over Bull Run road with three rebels, as he called us. We had thought of the fact that his companions were all Southern men, two Virginians and one Georgian, but did not know that he had.

"It is strange how I get along with Southern people," he

said to me. "When I look back, the aides who have been closest to me were from the South. Either I have more Southern ways in me than I realize or else it is natural for the Southern man to take the pursuits which seem to appeal to me."

I told him that not only himself but all his family had more of the South in them than they knew and that I was constantly seeing mannerisms and hearing sentiments which were common in Southern families, and which always surprised me when I met them elsewhere.

"I have no doubt," he said. "My dear mother evidently implanted in us more of her section than any of us knew, even more than my father suspected. Then, too, we always admired her relatives whom we met and I think the character of her brother, my Uncle Bulloch, who was in the Confederate Navy, appealed to me more strongly than any man I ever met in life. I used to think him very much like Colonel Newcomb, and now I still see a strong resemblance."

He loves to talk about his mother, and her personality is a very real one to him.

"I can see her now, when, in order to show my resentment to her for some disciplinary measure she would enforce, I would pray for the success of the Union forces or, as I was wont to speak of them, the 'Yankees.' She always heard our prayers at night, and when I could not vent my anger any other way I would close my prayers with asking God to bless the Yankees. And when we wanted anything which she would not give us we often resorted to the stratagem of calling God's blessing on the rebels, too. This frequently secured a respite for us from bed for another half hour."

By the time we reached Gainsville we all felt that the trip would be a success. Each had measured his strength, as it were, and knew about what we could do, and, as the President said, "As our physical condition would weaken our morale would rise," so that when we reached Buckland at 9:35 we were in a fine humour.

We changed our horses there and started on our last lap to Warrenton. We had planned to reach the town by 11:00, but it looked hopeless for a time, as part of the road was so furrowed and cut up that we could only make any time by keeping off the roads and riding on the embankments. We took advantage of every good stretch, however, to gallop and just as the town clock struck 11:00 we entered the main thoroughfare of the town. No one knew of our coming, but several persons recognized the President and soon the news spread to all quarters of the city. In less time than it takes to tell it there had gathered upward of a thousand persons in front of the old Warren Green Hotel and I was detailed to go out to see them.

They would not believe that we had ridden from Washington and they begged me to say to the President that they would like so to meet him. I knew he would have to see them so I told them, or the leading men, who acted as spokesmen, that the President was as anxious to meet the people of Warrenton as they were to meet him, and when I got him to appear five minutes later, they gave him a rousing cheer. He is the first President to visit Warrenton since Franklin Pierce, and they made him welcome. He made a short address to them and shook each one by the hand, I presenting each by name just as I would do at the White House, and to each he had some special word to say. The result was, however, that he had to eat his lunch in ten minutes. He drank two cups of tea and ate some soup. The rest of us swallowed hunks of beef, but none of us took anything in the way of alcohol, although Dick Wallack and Evans, the master of the

Manigault Park, Library, and Breslin Tower of the University of the South at Sewanee, Tenn., where Archie Butt was graduated

hounds, for you know it is a great hunting country, tried to press on us the hospitality of the Farquier County Club.

We left Warrenton at 12:15 and did not reach Buckland on our way back until 1:35. I had a horse which fought the bit the entire way, and once when I got off to look after the girth on the President's saddle I was fifteen minutes getting back on again. He would plunge and rear, and once he struck at Doctor Grayson and came near putting him out of business. Finally I made a flying leap for the saddle and made it. I was mighty well glad to turn him over to the orderly at Buckland, I can tell you.

Between Buckland and Cub Run our vitality was at its lowest. Admiral Rixey was on a fine animal of his own, and he had set the pace at a jog trot, which was all right for him, but it was hell on the President and myself, who were riding about the roughest troop horses which Fort Myer could turn out. Finally as we reached Cub Run and started afresh the President ordered Rixey to the rear and told me to set the pace. I set it by walking slowly when the roads were bad and galloping like mad when they were good. We made better time in this way, although one is not supposed to; but this pace had the effect of resting us up when very tired and when galloping to warm our blood and exhilarate our spirits.

Just before we reached Centerville we met the blizzard, which came from the north in the shape of a blinding sleet storm, and this storm was continuous from this point to Washington. The wind was blowing a gale and the ice cut our faces so that I thought that mine must certainly be bleeding. We kept up a fast gait to Fairfax, however, for every mile covered now was that much made certain, for it was beginning to look doubtful whether we would be able to make Washington on account of the heavy fall of sleet. When we reached Fairfax we got the horses on which we had begun the ride, and I never felt more relieved in my life than when the orderly told us that both Roswell and Larry were in good condition and not lame from the ride in the early morning. On any other horses I don't think we would have made Washington without an accident, if indeed we had made it at all.

We left Fairfax in inky blackness and walked practically the entire way to Falls Church. From Centerville the President had been going it blindly, for the ice would cake on his glasses so that he could see nothing ahead of him. He simply trusted to Roswell now. I took the lead and he came immediately behind me, followed by Grayson and Doctor Rixey.

I dared not trot or gallop, for we were too near our goal to run the risks of an accident. Once, when I began to trot, the President's horse went into a ditch, but luckily recovered himself without injury to himself or his rider. At Falls Church we began to trot, for the roads were better, and, strange to say, by the reflected lights of Washington, nine miles away, we could keep fairly in the roads. Enough snow had fallen with the sleet to make them fairly safe, so we trotted the entire way into the Aqueduct Bridge. As we turned into the lighted approach, we saw the carriage from the White House which I had ordered to meet us before we left Fairfax. I did not believe it would be safe to cross through town on the asphalt and had taken the precaution to tell the orderly to 'phone to the White House to have something to meet us. When the question came up as to whether the streets were safe, the President settled it by saying:

"By George, we will make the White House with our horses if we have to lead them," and we started across the bridge.

Mrs. Roosevelt was watching for us from the window

of Miss Ethel's room, and by the time we alighted she was standing in the doorway to welcome us. It was a perfect picture. She had on some light, fluffy evening gown and I don't believe that Dolly Madison, even in her loveliest moments, ever looked more attractive than did Mrs. Roosevelt at that moment, standing there, framed in the big doorway with the strong light on her and the wind blowing her clothes in every direction.

We were all covered with ice, but the President in his black riding jacket, with fur collar and pockets, and broad-brim black hat, looked for all the world like the pictures of Santa Claus. Mrs. Roosevelt made us come in and gave us each a julep, which was the first drop of liquor any of us had during the entire ride.

I am stiff to-day and did not feel like getting up this morning, but I was out of the house at the usual time and reported to the President by 10:00. I could not refrain from stopping in the club and showing myself in passing, for I knew that everyone there would be expecting us to be laid up for several days.

With love,
ARCHIBALD.

LXXIII

The White House,
Washington,
January 15, 1909.

MY DEAR CAPTAIN BUTT:

I desire that this letter be filed with your record. On January 13th, you rode with me from the White House, Washington, to the inn at Warrenton, Virginia, and back, a distance which we have put at 98 miles, but which I am informed was 104. We covered the distance between 3:40 in the morning and 8:40 in the evening, including an hour and a quarter at Warrenton and five or ten minutes at each of the places where we changed horses. We rode first to Fairfax Court House, where we changed, getting on fresh horses; then to a farmhouse near Bull Run, where we again changed; then to Buckland, where we again changed; and then to Warrenton, using the same horses back to Buckland. On the return trip we thus covered each stage with the horses we had used upon going out. After the first stages the horses were ordinary cavalry horses, and two of yours were hard animals to ride, which materially added to the fatigue of the trip so far as you were concerned. The conditions of the weather and of the roads materially increased the difficulty of the ride, for from Centerville in a blinding sleet storm drove in our faces, and from Fairfax Court House in we were in pitch darkness going over the frozen roads through the sleet storm. You and Doctor Rixey alternately led the way and set the pace. You as well as the rest of the party returned in fine condition, convincing me of the fact that the test provided for the army and navy was not excessive.

Sincerely yours,
(Signed) THEODORE ROOSEVELT.

Capt. Archibald W. Butt,
A. D. C. to the President,
Washington, D. C.

LXXIV

Washington, D. C.,
January 20, 1909.

MY DEAR CLARA:

The personal side of the President these last few days seems to be at the minimum and the presidential side at the maximum. Things official have been happening so rapidly that there has been little time to indulge in the personal pursuits in which I am usually his companion and at which times I find much to study in him and to enjoy. His trouble with Tillman and Foraker has brought out some of his old-time fighting qualities, and the attack of Willet on him in the House was positively enjoyed by him. He had not heard of it until he came from the office for dinner, when Mrs. Roosevelt told him of it.

I had come to the White House to accompany him to the big Methodist meeting at the Metropolitan Church. As he came out from the dining room he called for the afternoon paper and went to the library, where he read the attack out loud. Mrs. Roosevelt was furious, but the President did not mind it in the least, and laughed heartily over some of the expletives of the irate Congressman.

As he finished he said:

"Well, my dear, this does not bother me nearly as much as this Methodist meeting, for this is behind me and the meeting is ahead of me. I am very tired and do not feel like leaving the house, but, thank heaven, I have not got to listen to any one else talk, but will do the talking myself. I do not regard myself as a great orator. In fact, my style of oratory in any one else would bore me to death, for all speaking bores me, but if I have got to hear someone reel off English by the hour I much prefer to administer the torture than to have it administered by someone else."

I could not help but think of this remark as I listened to him a half hour later. He sat among the great divines of the Methodist Church, and finally delivered a sermon which held even me spellbound for an hour. It was an odd mixture of religion and politics. He sandwiched in his appeals for the missionary work of the church a lot of world politics about England and India, the Dutch and Java, and California and Japan.

As he left the church and we were driving home he said:

"I would rather address a Methodist audience than any other audience in America. You know, for one thing, that everyone there is an American. You do not have to think about placating this element or that element, for the Methodists are Americans, and all you have got to do is to hammer facts into them.

"Next to the Methodists I prefer to address Episcopalians. They are all Americans likewise, usually representing the higher or else the lower social class. The Methodists represent the great middle class and in consequence are the most representative church in America. I think the Methodists and the Episcopalians increase more rapidly than any other churches in this country. They appeal to the genius of our institutions more than any other denominations. The growth of the Episcopal Church in the cities is marvellous. The Methodists do not seem to make much advance in the cities, but its growth is largely in the country and in new territory.

"I think the organization of the two churches is very similar, and, after all, organization tells in the long run. I should not like to be quoted, especially after my appeal for religious tolerance, but the Catholic Church is in no way suited to this country and can never have any great permanent growth except through immigration, for its thought is Latin and entirely at variance with the dominant thought of our country and institutions.

"The Episcopal Church has a wonderful future ahead of it here. It is so closely akin to our civilization, and it appeals not so much to wealth (as is sometimes charged) as it does to conservatism. It just so happens that the conservative class is usually the wealthy class. While I would have liked one or two of my children to have become members of my church, I feel greatly comforted that they are in their mother's church. Somehow I feel they are safer there, that they are well anchored."

I have had the opportunity this past week of seeing Mrs. Roosevelt in quite a new light. She has always been particular as to whom she invites to her private entertainments, but I did not expect to see her take cognizance of any "affair" to the extent of barring the offenders from the public reception at the White House. . . .

But last week, much to my surprise, she sent for me to discuss a very delicate situation, as she expressed it. She had heard rumours of an entangling alliance between the wife of a certain high official and a member of the diplomatic corps. In consequence she had gradually eliminated the parties from her dinners, but she had invited them to her dances, for she was not ready to believe the gossip she heard. But she saw something herself at her last dance that angered her, and after the diplomatic dinner she joined a party of ladies in the East Room and heard them discussing this American woman and the diplomat.

They tried to stop the conversation as soon as she came up, but enough had been said for her to know what they were talking about. The husband of the woman in question is a high government official and one whom it would be most momentous to offend. Then, too, she was anxious not to humiliate him, so she had decided that the matter had to be settled through me. Imagine my feelings when I learned that I was to convey the message to the lady that if this affair did not instantly stop neither she nor her husband would be invited to the White House again and the invitations which had already been sent would be recalled.

Both the woman and her husband were friends of mine and had entertained me frequently in the past, and last

Christmas had sent me quite a handsome present. Then, too, I am no saint.

However, I made the engagement over the 'phone and called to see the woman. I found her in a highly nervous state and when I gave her the message she simply raged. Finally she broke down, and putting her head on my shoulder, sobbed as if her heart would break. She acknowledged her love for the man and told me of his love for her; she assured me that they had done nothing to be ashamed of and read me certain letters from him which convinced me that she was speaking the truth.

I made her write Mrs. Roosevelt a letter, which I dictated and which fixed her status for the time being. Mrs. Roosevelt, when she learned of the true state of affairs, was grief-stricken herself and is now bent only on saving the woman's reputation and protecting her family. She, as others believed, thought the affair only one of those scandals which so often jar Washington society; that the affair was deep rooted and tragical in its nature called forth all the motherly instinct in Mrs. Roosevelt.

The diplomatic member called on me the next afternoon and told me in the most childlike way his worship for the woman and of his deep sorrow for the husband. It seems that the husband knows of this love, but believes implicitly in his wife, just as I do now. The diplomat showed me the secret cablegrams in which he had appealed to his home Government to transfer him, but he does not want the woman to know anything about it until it is *un fait accompli.* With tears in his eyes he begged me only to save his reputation with her after he had gone.

"She will think me disloyal to her; she will think I am running away and deserting her, and so when I am gone tell her that you know the sacrifice I make now for her, and that if I did not love her as I do I would remain."

He made me promise to see Mrs. Roosevelt and to tell her all that night. It was Saturday evening and Mrs. Roosevelt was alone, the President was working in his study. I told her everything, for the scene with him had been depressing, and several times he had to stop to control his feelings.

Just as I was about to go the President came in and Mrs. Roosevelt told him the result of the interview. His only comment was:

"Poor Archie! I feel only sorry for him. His duties as aide are certainly complex. One day he has to ride a hundred miles with me, and the next he is called in to straighten out some *affaire de cœur.* However, I have no sympathy for the husband, for if he had the heart of a rabbit and the courage of a guinea pig he would throw the man out of the window and chastise his wife into obedience if not affection."

Now that I have got mixed up with this love affair, I presume I will have many more harrowing scenes until the diplomat has gone and the woman has recovered.

As the President said good-night he added: "However, as I am writing a sermon in the next room I cannot let my mind dwell too long on these earthly doings," and with that he passed through the panel door which leads from his study into the library, to finish the sermon he delivered to the Methodists as above stated.

You remember my writing about the little sofa that Mrs. Roosevelt wanted to take with her to Oyster Bay. She has decided not to take it, and even her desire to take it has led to much embarrassment for her. The President, when he heard she wanted it, wrote a letter to Speaker Cannon and asked to be permitted to take it and to replace it with a new sofa. As soon as she found out that the President had written to Congress about the matter she got me to ask Mr. Loeb to have the letter withdrawn as she thought the incident too trivial to be made a subject of official correspondence. She had given up all ideas of taking the wretched little sofa and thought no more about it until a few days ago, to her surprise, she saw the whole incident in the newspapers, and it was made to read that the President wanted to take the furniture out of the White House without paying for it.

The letter had not been entered at the Capitol even and had only been seen by the Speaker and his secretary, so that its publication was with malice and was done merely to get back at the President in part for his secret service incident.

The President never minds what Congress does, as is shown by the fact that when they are storming about the loudest, he can with perfect poise of mind write a sermon or take a ride.

But Mrs. Roosevelt said to me regarding the matter: "Before I leave Washington I am going to tell Speaker Cannon what I think of his action, how petty and little I think it to be. It is the first time since I have been in the White House that I have been dragged into publicity in a matter of this kind. I have always liked Miss Cannon and I have always tried to be nice to the Speaker."

This is the first time I have ever seen Mrs. Roosevelt show anything akin to anger. Unfortunately the President mentioned in his letter to the Speaker that the sofa was one bought by Mrs. Roosevelt and for which she had many pleasant associations. She says she would not have it now that all the associations with it are of a most disagreeable character.

Good-night, dear Clara. This letter comes nearer the court gossip of de Gramont than any I have yet written.

ARCHIBALD.

LXXV

Washington, D. C.,
January 23d, 1909.

My dear Clara:

Friday, that is, last night, we had another large dinner at the White House, of over thirty covers, and the President was apparently in good humour again. After dinner the women went into the Green Room to drink coffee and to gossip, and the men into the private dining room to drink *liqueurs* and to gossip also. The President was at the large table with the German Ambassador on his right and Senator Carter on his left. I gathered a small table in the corner with Stumm, Prittwitz of the German Embassy, Billy Phillips, and Straight, and one or two foreigners without any special attributes to remember them by.

Stumm is most charming, very handsome, and has something about him which an American or an Englishman can comprehend and get hold of. I was so struck by this that I asked him what it was about him that was not Teuton. He laughed and said his grandmother was a Miss Grimes, either of Virginia or South Carolina, that he always felt at home with a Southern man in spite of the fact that he usually hid the fact of his American blood, preferring to be considered all German for political and other reasons. The Stumms, from what I gather, have in Germany a position similar to that held in this country by Carnegie and other big steel folk. I know he is very wealthy, but yet very simple, direct, and possesses great charm. . . .

Well, I am rather getting off the track; for I wanted to follow the President's humour. During the dance he occasionally came to the Blue Room to receive with Mrs. Roosevelt and was certainly not at ease. Finally he said:

"I am going to my study, but if Senator Clark [of Wyoming, I think the state was] comes in I wish to know at once."

Here is where I am a poor chronicler, for I could easily find out what state this particular Senator Clark is from by looking it up in the Congressional Directory, but I prefer to be vague and uncertain rather than take the trouble to go downstairs for a book, which would involve hunting for matches and lighting lights and possibly getting in a bad humour before I returned.

It was a half hour later when Senator Clark came in and as soon as I presented him to Mrs. Roosevelt I sent a junior aide to notify the President that Senator Clark had come.

The President came down, passed in and out of the rooms, waltzed once with Mrs. Richardson, once with Miss Ethel and then "chanced" to run across Senator Clark. They talked in the Green Room for a few minutes, and then I saw the President take him by the arm and lead him away, I presume to his study. Later in the evening, when he appeared, he was his old self again. He joked, petted his wife's hand, and he and Alice sat in the Blue Room, and laughed and talked for a half hour.

The dance was not quite as brilliant as the first one, I may mention in passing, but far nicer than the second.

Well, to continue to camp on the President's trail: When I reached the White House office this morning at 9:45 he had not come in, and only Assistant Secretary of State Bacon[1] and I were waiting for him. When he did arrive it was with a rush, and we stood ready to see if there was anything he wanted and to leave as soon as possible.

---

[1]Rotber Bacon, member of the firm of J. P. Morgan & Co., 1894–1903, Assistant Secretary of State, 1905–1909, Secretary of State, 1909, in active service in the World War, died May 29, 1919.

He made us both sit down until he had looked over his engagements and then said:

"Do you know I am glad I learned to play poker when I was young. If you two do not know poker, learn it even if costs some money, for it may stand you in good stead some time. The Senate through Clark laid down its hand last night, and I am inclined to think my bluff went. However, I am inclined to keep my pistol ready, for sometimes after the cards are on the table the stakes are still in danger.

"I have really had a very disagreeable two days. The Senate called for certain papers in the Bureau of Corporations this week and on Thursday ordered Herbert Knox Smith to transmit all papers on a certain subject in his office. He came to see me and to tell me that most of the papers were given in a confidential way; that if they were made public no end of trouble would ensue. I ordered Smith to get a decision from the Attorney-General that these papers should not be made public, and yesterday the Committee on Judiciary of the Senate summoned Herbert Knox Smith before it and informed him that if he did not at once transmit these papers the Senate would order his imprisonment at once or the committee would. As soon as he reported this to me I ordered him in writing to turn over to me all the papers in the case, so that I could assist the Senate in the prosecution of its investigation.

"I have those papers in my possession, and last night I informed Senator Clark of the Judiciary Committee what I had done. I told him also that the Senate should not have those papers and that Herbert Knox Smith had turned them over to me. The only way the Senate or the committee can get those papers now is through my impeachment, and I so informed Senator Clark last night.

"The Senator informed me that the Senate was only

anxious to exercise its prerogatives and that if the papers were of such a nature that they should not be made public the committee was ready to indorse my views. But, as I say, it is just as well to take no chances with a man like Culberson, who is behind this thing, so I will retain those papers until the 3d of March at least. Some of these facts which they want, for what purposes I hardly know, were given to the Government under the seal of secrecy and cannot be divulged, and I will see to it that the word of this Government to the individual is kept sacred."

We did have such a nice dinner this evening at the White House. The President and I were the only men and the women were all intimate friends of Mrs. Roosevelt. . . .

The President had to go to another dinner at the Shoreham at 10:00, given by the New York delegation to Vice-President-elect Sherman, but we had about an hour all together in the library. We all sat round in a circle and Miss Tuckerman began by saying:

"Mr. President, tell us some state secrets."

"Emily," he said, "I have never been asked in quite so open a way before to betray my country, but go ahead. I will answer any question which you have a mind to put. . . ."

"Mr. President, do you really think the German Emperor gave out those interviews to Hale[1] and others about the English which it was reported he gave out?" asked Miss Tuckerman.

"I am sure of it," said the President.

---

[1]William Bayard Hale sent to the *Century Magazine* an interview with the Kaiser which was mysteriously suppressed. Hale, who was originally a clergyman, became later a confidant of President Wilson, achieved some notoriety for his pro-Germanism in the World War, and recently died, an expatriate, in Europe.

"How do you account for it?"

"He had a brain storm—that is all. He has said practically the same thing to me. He once wrote to me of those 'filthy English lies.' There was never a better expression than that of brain storm to describe certain conditions which sometimes arise in perfectly sane men."

Mrs. Lowndes said she felt very apprehensive about the coming cabinet on account of the appointment of Knox as Secretary of State. Each took a turn at him. Miss Tuckerman said he could not be a big man, because several years ago he took her out to dinner one evening and showed considerable agitation because he had not gone out according to his place in line, and that when they got up from the table he said to her: "Come with me, my place is ahead of the Postmaster-General, and I do not like to waive my prerogatives."

Finally they all agreed that Mr. Roosevelt should be consulted in the formation of a cabinet and so said. He laughed heartily and said:

"Some say I have not been altogether successful in regard to cabinet-making. I am sure, Mrs. Hopkins, that from your elevated post you must have condemned some of my selections at times."

"Yes, at times," she murmured bravely, "but you always had a great Secretary of State, and that after all is what we want to be well made."

"If Mr. Taft were to ask my advice as to his cabinet I would not know what to say. I would possibly suggest to him to retain the present Cabinet and to make changes as he saw fit, but he cannot ask me and I cannot volunteer advice in the matter. If he should ask my advice he would feel compelled to take it, whereas if he asks Root's advice he can take it or not as he chooses.

"No, Taft is going about this thing just as I would do,

and while I retained McKinley's cabinet the conditions were quite different. I cannot find any fault in Taft's attitude to me," he said most seriously.

"It is a difficult thing to find a Secretary of State. There are not many Roots lying above ground to be picked up at random. Knox is a great lawyer, and I think he will be a splendid cabinet officer. I say this, too, recognizing also that he is not a man of the world and limited in his knowledge of other countries and the affairs of other governments.

"Taft will also have trouble finding someone for the Court of St. James's. Everyone is trying to get my indorsement for President Eliot, who has just retired from the presidency of Harvard, but I cannot take any part in it. In spite of my own feelings toward Whitelaw Reid, I should like to see a very poor but cultured man succeed him. We have all the prestige abroad which money gives, and what I should be proud to see now is a very strong contrast. I am getting tired of seeing our Ambassadors entertain. I want to see them entertained instead, but this discussion would lead me into criticism of the Reids, which I am not willing to be led into, however much I desire to see education and culture made the standards for preferment. I cannot forget, either, while possessing great admiration for Eliot, that he did not support Cleveland in his Venezuelan message, which to my mind showed a great want of judgment, certainly a lack of breadth of character, which a successful Ambassador should always possess."

Just then the usher announced that the President's secretary had come to accompany him to the Sherman dinner, and he said:

"Oh, how I hate to go! I am having such a good time gossiping with you dear people. I have been as indiscreet as the German Emperor, but if you feel repaid I have no regrets."

I don't think I told you that the diplomat whose attentions to one of the "Court Circle" shocked Mrs. Roosevelt stopped in front of the President, at the judiciary reception, and informed him that he had asked to be relieved. The President did not take it in at first, but grasped his hand again and told him how very sorry he would be to see him go and that he hoped the request would not be complied with. Mrs. Roosevelt, who had heard the President's remarks, straightened it out by saying, as he shook hands with her, that she would hate to see him go, but that she felt he was acting most wisely. The lady in the case wrote declining the reception and the dance, but Mrs. Roosevelt got me to tell her that it was her wish for her to appear at the reception, as she would have to appear some time, and that if she did not come she might cause comment.

After I delivered the message I also reminded her what Madame de Staël had said—that a good fitting gown was more support than a good conscience—so to be sure and wear her most becoming frock, which she did. As she came down the line Mrs. Roosevelt held her hand quite a time and asked her to remain for the supper, which promptly gave her cachet in the eyes of fashionable Washington which was gathered behind the lines. . . .

ARCHIBALD.

LXXVI

Washington, D. C.,
January 25 [1909].

DEAR CLARA:

The other day John L. Sullivan, who was in town, called on the President and presented him with a gold-mounted rabbit's foot, and the President brought him to luncheon.

The President and Sullivan are really pals when they get together. The President says he is the cleanest prize fighter we have ever had, that he always fought squarely and never sold a fight.

The talk was all prize fighting, much to the disgust of Mrs. Roosevelt, and when one of the guests started to describe a prize fight at the table to-day Mrs. Roosevelt stopped him and said that she would not permit more than one prize fight discussion a season in the White House. It was ex-Mayor Phelan of San Francisco who started the discussion to-day, and she gently reminded him that the Japanese trouble now going on in California was as near a fight as she would listen to. . . .

Good-bye for to-night.

ARCHIBALD.

LXXVII

January 27 [1909].

DEAR CLARA:

I have just returned from the New Willard, where the President went at 10:30 to-night to make a final address to the conference on the care of dependent children. . . . As we drove home he was speaking of Postmaster-General Meyer and from him got on to the Cabinet.

"Meyer and Garfield are the ideal cabinet officers," he said to me after a while. "They are not Tafts or Roots, but the Government would soon go to the bow-wows if the entire Cabinet was made up of men of the type of Taft. Root, of course, is quite unique. He is a great national figure, but at the same time he is a great executive of a department and he has done wonders with the State Department, and his reorganization of the Consular service is as enduring as the work he did in the War Department.

"I realized the War Department suffered through Taft's

activity in politics, but one such big-brained man is necessary for each administration, for he can say and make explanations which the President cannot do. But one such officer in a cabinet is sufficient, and more than one is a distinct disadvantage in my opinion. What is needed in cabinets is men who can forego the pomp and prestige of their office, or who will accept them merely as an incident, and who will keep strict office hours and keep the executive mill grinding rapidly. If one of the departments gets clogged, it slows up the whole Administration.

"I have been criticized for shifting and changing my cabinet so often, but I do it with a purpose. Just as soon as a Secretary of the Navy or Interior or any other department gets rusty or else settles down to ease and comfort I transfer him so that he will use the energy, which made him valuable in the first place, in some other department which needs bolstering up. I have not hesitated to drop cabinet officers when I found them inefficient, even though my affections for them urged me to retain them. It is so easy to put one's personal affections for men above the public service.

"Meyer, Garfield, and Straus are ideal cabinet officers for me. They keep up the routine, and when it is a matter of national or international policy they promptly bring it up to me for a decision with a clear-cut recommendation."

I learned at the White House this morning that the three dining-room waiters had applied to be transferred to other departments and all expected to leave on the 4th of March. . . .

Mrs. Roosevelt is a trump. When I told her about dining-room servants leaving she sent for them and told them that they would remain on until Mrs. Taft discontinued their services or she would let them go at once. So when Mrs. Taft comes in on March the 4th she will find a good lunch and well-trained servants, and if she would take my advice she would continue them as long as they were faithful to her and did their work properly. . . .

ARCHIBALD.

LXXVIII

Washington, D. C.,
January 28, 1909.

DEAR CLARA:

We had such a nice lunch party at the White House to-day. It was made up of as smart a set as the one yesterday was deadly and ordinary. There were the Postmaster-General and Mrs. Meyer. . . . To me she is simply a very charming woman of the world, witty, humorous, but who does not permit the rabble to get a foothold in her home. Mrs. Fred Vanderbilt was there with strings of pearls, but otherwise simply gowned. Her manner is unaffected, and I understand she goes in for charity to a great extent. Mrs. Longworth is always good fun, and Mrs. Townsend was at her best.

As the President came in he said as he passed me: "You old trump; I love to see you about here."

When he says anything in that vein I know his mind is clear and not befogged with politics or disturbed with international problems. He was in good humour, and someone started him on the subject of Pittsburgh and New York.

Forgetting that Mrs. Vanderbilt was the centre of the set he despises he said:

"While Pittsburgh is vulgar and common, it is not so sordid as New York. Our worst influences come from New York, not from Pittsburgh. Edith, my dear, why are you frowning at me? Oh, I see, dear Mrs. Vanderbilt, Edith seems to include you in that category I am about to denounce. You see, I know you better and think more highly of you than my excellent wife does, but for fear I may be led into an indiscretion about some in-law, or rather out-law, of yours, I will change the subject."

Which caused a good laugh, and no one enjoyed it more than Mrs. Vanderbilt.

ARCHIBALD.

LXXIX

Washington, D. C.,
January 30, 1909.

DEAR CLARA:

He [the President] was feeling a little cast down, I thought, when I saw him this morning. He had just heard that the Ohio Society in New York at its banquet had not drunk his health and that this formality had been lacking at the New England banquet[1] a few nights ago. I had just read him a letter from General Barry in Cuba, in which the General told me of what the President's order had done for the army and his belief that it would add 50 per cent. to the efficiency of the army, navy, and Marine Corps.

"It is fine to get such letters as that, for just now I do not hear from my friends, but all the little hounds who have been afraid to bark in the open heretofore are coming to the front. I cannot believe there is any change toward me on the part of the people, but my enemies are certainly getting in their work now. I have not time to hit back and would not bother with them if I could, but it makes me a little cynical, to say the least, when the Ohio banquet refuses to drink my health.

[1]What "New England banquet" is referred to is not clear. It was not the annual dinner of the New England Society in the City of New York held, as usual, on December 22nd. Mr. H. A. Cushing, secretary of the Society, writes me that the first toast of the 1908 dinner was to "the President of the United States" and that the Year Book of the Society for 1909 contains the remarks of the presiding officer, Mr. Seth Low, in proposing the toast.

"It was the more surprising because Charley Taft was there. I do not believe that it was done with a view to aid in the divorcement of Taft and myself, as some friends seem to think, and I believe it will distress Taft when he hears of it more than it has me, for after all I don't give a rap. I see a tendency, and I think it but natural,on the part of the friends of Taft to discredit what I did for him in the campaign.

"They little realize that Taft is big enough to carve out his own administration on individual lines, and if he were not, this sort of thing would only add ungratefulness to other charges which are bound to come up. I predict a brilliant administration for him. I felt he was the one man for the Presidency, and any failure in it would be as keenly felt by me as by himself or his family. You have heard some things said against my administration, Archie, but they are nothing to what you will hear when I am completely robbed of power and in Africa; but when the history of this period is written down I believe my administration will be known at least as an administration of ideals. Certainly it will not be looked upon as a Capua in American history." . . .

We had such a nice luncheon to-day at the White House. No one but the family and the Douglas Robinsons and Mr. Sheldon, the treasurer of the last Republican Campaign Committee. Mrs. Douglas Robinson is his youngest sister, and she is extremely pretty and looks hardly more than forty, yet she has several grown children. She has a great deal of the personal charm of Mrs. Cowles and the intellectual vivacity of her brother, the President. They discussed the Panama libel suit, and both the President and Mr. Robinson think that they will put —— in prison for criminal libel.

Mr. Robinson told a funny incident of receiving a call

from a reporter from the New York *Sun* at his house in New York the other day relative to the libel suit. It seems that the reporter mistook him for an English butler (he is Scotch), and tried to pump him about the private life of Mr. Robinson. Mr. Robinson said it would be worth as much as his job if he revealed anything about his master and the reporter told him he would well make it worth his job, that he would not only get him a better job, but give him considerable cash to boot. The President enjoyed this very much, but said:

"Douglas, if you are such a successful perjurer, I don't know whether I was wise in bringing this criminal libel suit in your name."

Mrs. Robinson then told of an incident when her husband was receiver of some street-car line in New York and being once on a car on which there was a drunken man who was asking all the women to sit in his lap. Mr. Robinson stood this as long as he could and when he got to Twenty-third Street he called a big burly policeman who stands there, and whom he knew well, to remove the drunk. The policeman yanked him off the car by the collar and Mr. Robinson got off at the same time. The policeman then told him that it was illegal for him to have taken the drunk off the car until the conductor had asked him to leave and until the drunk resisted. He said:

"Now, Mr. Robinson, you will have to stand by me and we may both get into trouble, but if you will swear that he refused to get off the car and that he resisted the conductor, then we may get through all right, unless he gets some witnesses and sues you for damages."

Mr. Robinson said that none of these things suited him, and they stood there in a quandary while the crowd continued to gather. The drunk could not stand, and in despair Mr. Robinson asked the policeman what he could do.

"I hate to suggest it, sir, seeing what trouble you have had to get him off, but if it was me alone I would put him on another car."

Mr. Robinson said that the suggestion was an inspiration and forthwith they stopped the next car and piled the drunk into a corner seat and left him. Mr. Robinson is a huge, good-natured looking Scotchman—rather, his father was a Scotchman—and he is witty and brimming over with fun. He had the table convulsed with laughter before he finished the narrative.

To-night Mrs. Longworth and Miss Elkins with several friends are coming to play poker at my house. Nick Longworth has a bridge evening every Saturday, and Mrs. Longworth is having this poker party at my house to even things up with her husband for leaving her alone.

I have seen a little of Miss Elkins since she returned. She speaks quite frankly about Abruzzi and refers to him as the Duke. Their friends are still in the dark as to the reason they don't marry, and every now and then it is given out that he will defy everyone and renounce his royalty to wed the American girl. I believe myself that she cannot make up her mind to marry him. I do not think she loves him in the least, and I rather suspect her of being enamoured of a young American in Washington society.

She may, however, want to wait to see what time and nature will do for her before discarding the Duke entirely. She is certainly handsome, dresses beautifully, but is not to my thinking a wondrous beauty by any means. Nor was she considered beautiful at all until the approval of royalty was put upon her. She is, however, straightforward, honest, sincere, and clever, and while she lives what appears to be a fast—that is not the word, either, but an advanced, worldly existence, she has never been regarded as either rapid or even indiscreet, but, on the contrary, she puts her disapproval on men whose morals are not supposed to be up to standards she has set for her friends. A roundabout description, but it gives you some idea of this very stunning girl.

ARCHIBALD.

LXXX

Two allusions in the following letter deserve some amplification. Miss Margerie Ide, who was one of the guests at Archie's hospitable party, is a sister of Annie H. Ide who married the distinguished Democratic orator and Congressman, the late Bourke Cockran. Miss Annie Ide's name has been given a kind of literary immortality by Robert Louis Stevenson. The father of the two Ide sisters was Henry Clay Ide, Chief Justice in Samoa under the American Administration of the islands of that group. In 1891 Robert Louis Stevenson was living in Samoa and wrote to Mr. Ide the following delightful letter, which will be found in the edition of Stevenson's works edited by Sidney Colvin and published in this country by Messrs. Charles Scribner's Sons.

Herewith please find the DOCUMENT, which I trust will prove sufficient in law. It seems to me very attractive in its eclecticism; Scots, English, and Roman law phrases are all indifferently introduced, and a quotation from the works of Haynes Bayly can hardly fail to attract the indulgence of the Bench.

Yours very truly,
ROBERT LOUIS STEVENSON.

I, Robert Louis Stevenson, Advocate of the Scots Bar, author of The Master of Ballantrae and Moral Emblems, stuck civil engineer, sole owner and patentee of the Palace and Plantation known as Vailima in the island of Upolu, Samoa, a British Subject, being in sound mind, and pretty well, I thank you, in body:

In consideration that Miss Annie H. Ide, daughter of H. C. Ide, in the town of Saint Johnsbury, in the county of Caledonia, in the

State of Vermont, United States of America, was born, out of all reason, upon Christmas Day, and is therefore out of all justice denied the consolation and profit of a proper birthday;

And considering that I, the said Robert Louis Stevenson, have attained an age when O, we never mention it, and that I have now no further use for a birthday of any description;

And in consideration that I have met H. C. Ide, the father of the said Annie H. Ide, and found him about as white a land commissioner as I require;

Have transferred, and do hereby transfer, to the said Annie H. Ide, all and whole my rights and privileges in the thirteenth day of November, formerly my birthday, now, hereby, and henceforth, the birthday of the said Annie H. Ide, to have, hold, exercise, and enjoy the same in the customary manner, by the sporting of fine raiment, eating of rich meats, and receipt of gifts, compliments, and copies of verse, according to the manner of our ancestors;

And I direct the said Annie H. Ide to add to the said name of Annie H. Ide the name Louisa—at least in private; and I charge her to use my said birthday with moderation and humanity, *et tamquam bona filia familiae*, the said birthday not being so young as it once was, and having carried me in a very satisfactory manner since I can remember;

And in case the said Annie H. Ide shall neglect or contravene either of the above conditions, I hereby revoke the donation and transfer my rights in the said birthday to the President of the United States of America for the time being;

In witness whereof I have hereto set my hand and seal this nineteenth day of June in the year of grace eighteen hundred and ninety-one.

Seal
ROBERT LOUIS STEVENSON.

Witness, LLOYD OSBOURNE
Witness, HAROLD WATTS

It is surprising, but unfortunately true, that the allusion to Mrs. Cleveland apparently needs explanation. When the passage containing her mock protest against her life in the White House appeared in the newspaper publication of Archie Butt's Letters it was taken by some otherwise intelligent people as a confirmation of the baseless gossip about President Cleveland and his wife. It seems as if it ought to be perfectly apparent to the most simple-minded that Mrs. Cleveland was speaking ironically. Her resentment against these cruel slanders of her illustrious husband is fully recorded in the recently published authorized Life of Grover Cleveland by Professor McElroy of Princeton University. When Cleveland's first child, Ruth, was born he wrote to his old friend and law partner W. S. Bissell (who became Postmaster-General in the second Cleveland administration) as follows:

I feel an impulse to write to you. And I feel, too, that unless I make an effort, I shall write in a strange fashion to you. I who have just entered the real world, and see in a small child more of value than I have ever called my own before; who puts aside as hardly worth a thought all that has gone before—fame, honour, place, everything—reach out my hand to you and fervently express the wish—the best my great friendship for you yields—that in safety and in joy you may soon reach my estate.

Mr. Cleveland wrote this in 1891 between his first and second terms in the White House. In 1907, after he had become an honoured private citizen of Princeton, and while he was on a hunting trip in the South, Mrs. Cleveland sent him a birthday greeting which she has permitted Doctor McElroy to publish. It probably now only sees the light as her protest against the innuendoes circulated about a notably happy family life. This birthday greeting reads as follows:

Princeton, N. J.,
March 15, 1907.

MY DEAREST:

I am so afraid that I will not get your birthday letter to you in time that I suppose it will be a day ahead! And maybe you will reach home anyway and so not get it, but in that case I think I might be able to express my birthday thoughts to you. I hope you will be well on Monday, just as well as you can be, then things will look bright to you and your new year will begin happily. Then I hope you will keep well, and it will go a long, long way toward making your year happy. I hate to have you away on your birthday, but I realize that it will save you some strain—for many people seem to be thinking of you at this time. We all send much much love, and all the deepest best wishes of our hearts—and my heart is full of gratitude for what the years of your life have meant to me. You know how dearly I love you. You do not mind my saying it over, any day, and you won't mind it on this especial day—so I repeat it and repeat it, and I ask God's blessing on you for all the days.

Your loving wife,
FRANK.

The White House for a hundred years has been distinguished for the happy family life within its walls and it is not inappropriate, I think, to place here, in the record of a great Republican President who believed that the family is the cornerstone of American life, this testimony of a similar belief held by a great Democratic President.

Washington, D. C.,
February 1 [1909].

DEAR CLARA:

My poker party Saturday night was a great success. I invited five intimate friends to play with Mrs. Longworth, and before the end of the evening there were eighteen people in the rooms. I told her she could ask whom she wanted, and every now and then during the day my telephone would ring and someone would ask if he or she might not come in for the fun of it.

Larz Anderson from his palace on Massachusetts Avenue was hurling denunciations at both of us every time one of his guests went to say good-bye to him. He accused Mrs. Longworth of getting up a rival party just to make his a failure. It is true that we had the cream of his party and he had a right to be angry with his guests, possibly, for coming, but not with us, for when we decided to have our poker game we knew nothing of Larz's party. . . .

Mrs. Longworth . . . is still the drawing card in Washington society, and people will forsake palaces and feasts to have a crust of bread with her. She has that indescribable thing called charm, and she will be just as popular after the 4th of March as she has been, if not a little more so. She refused to go to the Andersons' because she heard of his criticizing her father, and that is the one unpardonable sin in her eyes.

We had a large turkey on the table, two dishes of fruit salad, a Virginia ham, and sandwiches made of cream cheese and guava jelly. Miss Emory presided over a chafing dish and cooked crab flakes à la Newburgh. We had Scotch and soda and beer. The guests would saunter in the dining room, eat what and how they wished, and continue their game, which, by the way, was for only a penny ante and 50-cent limit. The largest amount lost was only $8, so don't think your erstwhile religious brother-in-law has turned gambler.

The crowd did not leave until 3 o'clock, and the evening was voted one of the best of the season. Willard Straight brought his guitar, and early in the evening Nick Longworth forsook his bridge party to join us. A number of friends came uninvited, such as George Howard and his wife, Clarence Edwards, Billy Hitt with two friends, Terry and Hare. I never heard of them before, but they are both good chaps and they all knew they would find a welcome. Ovey of the British Embassy and Von Stumm of the German made up the foreign contingent.

When I called up Margerie Ide and asked her to come she asked: "How can I, when you have never called on me since I came to Washington?"

I told her I had called enough on her in the Philippines to last a lifetime. She agreed to set aside formalities, not on account of my sophistry, but because she wanted to come, as she could guess at the crowd who would be here. I never saw Katherine Elkins looking lovelier, and I must take back what I wrote about her [in my last letter], for she really looked regal and lovely, too. . . .

I asked her [Mrs. Roosevelt] if she had any regrets at going, and she answered me by relating a conversation which Mrs. Cleveland had with Mrs. Douglas Robinson at the time Mr. Cleveland was being urged for another nomination. Mrs. Robinson asked her if she would like to be again in the White House and Mrs. Cleveland's answer was:

"What! There where my husband was accustomed to drag me about the house by the hair and where my children were blind, deaf, and deformed? Never! I prefer Princeton, where my husband is not a brute and my children remain normal and free from disease."

This morning Mrs. Roosevelt showed me the President's new cards bearing only the inscription of Theodore Roosevelt. His cards now read only The President, and of course he cannot use them after March 4th, but Mrs. Roosevelt wanted his new cards to have the mister on them, but he would not yield to her opinion as he did about the uniforms. I said I agreed with him that simply Theodore Roosevelt was most distinctive and he was certainly sufficiently known to need no descriptive adjectives.

"I might have known the true Georgians would stand together," she laughed. "Why should he not have *Mr.* Theodore Roosevelt, as any other gentleman would have on his card?"

"Because he is not like any other gentleman," I said.

"Then why not simply have Roosevelt or Theodore, or even The ex-President?" she said. "I want him to be the simplest American alive after he leaves the White House, and the funniest thing to me is that he wants to be also and says he is going to be, but the trouble is he has really forgotten how to be. I try to think of his year in Africa and my year in my sister's little cottage on the Mediterranean as having the effect the forty years of wandering had for the Jews. At the end of that time we will enter the home at Oyster Bay as gladly and as meekly as ever the Children of Israel entered the Promised Land."

We do have such nice times in the morning in the upper corridor. As soon as I see the President [in the adjacent Executive Offices] I go to the White House to see if there is anything to be done. There is usually a question of precedence to be decided, or whether this or that person ought to be invited to dinner, or whether a mere invitation to a reception or a dance will be sufficient. I found myself sitting each morning later and later until I began to see myself in the tame-cat attitude. I announced my intention to go at once and not to come again unless there was some actual work to do. She laughed softly and said to Miss Hagner, "Belle, he is only leaving the sinking ship," which brought much laughter from Miss Hagner and violent protestations from me. I really feel that I cannot see too much of this family before they go. Everyone whom they have received into their home life feels the same way. Two more of the servants announced to me to-day that they were going to quit because they were not willing to remain after Mrs. Roosevelt leaves. Yet she keeps them all up to their work, but she is thoughtful of them when they are sick and helps them when they are in trouble.

I don't think any one realizes what a lot of charity she does. She gives through clergymen and doctors mostly. I heard her tell Miss Hagner the other day to send a hundred dollars to some minister of some small Episcopal church in the southwest part of the city—for some poor family where there is sickness, she stipulated, solely. Six years ago she said she had gone to Christmas Eve service there and was so greatly benefited by the service at that particular time she felt that she could never pay the debt. Miss Hagner told me confidentially afterwards that she did a great deal of good just in this way, and one of her favourite ways of giving was to have the doctors hand a certain amount to charity patients when they were discharged from the free wards in the hospitals. . . .

I got Carpenter to cable to the Tafts in Panama to-day suggesting that they let us know how many they will have at lunch on Inauguration Day, whether they want a set lunch served at the table or a buffet lunch such as the Roosevelts had the last time. After the ceremonies at the Capitol it is customary for the new President to drive to the White House and have lunch with such guests as he may ask, after which he goes on the stand in front of the White House and reviews the troops. Heretofore the retiring President and his wife, if he is fortunate enough to have one, have always been at the White House to receive the new Chief Executive and his party, and forthwith scuttle out of the back door, which is in reality the palatial south entrance, and drive to the station. Mr. Roosevelt, however, is going direct from the Capitol to the station, where Mrs. Roosevelt will be waiting for him. . . .

ARCHIBALD.

LXXXI

Washington, D. C.,
February 3 [1909].

DEAR CLARA:

When I left the White House this morning I said:

"Mr. President, Major Winship and Colonel Grebble arrived from Cuba this morning, and Colonel Grebble sends his sincere compliments and says he will not call to bore you with Cuba, but he thinks the Government there will last much longer than the dispatches from there would indicate. He does not anticipate a revolution there, at least not for a very long time."

He looked up from his desk and said:

"No, Grebble is right. I do not think about Cuba now. It is not our fault if things go badly there, but it is our fault if the people of this country force trouble on themselves from Japan. Nevada, not Cuba, is what is worrying me this morning."

He got up and struck the desk with his fist and added:

"Nevada trying to dictate our foreign policy is as absurd as Jo Blackburn trying to guide the destinies of the Established Church of England. It has only been three years since Nevada was calling upon me to police the state with the United States Army because it could not control a few striking miners, and now she sits a sovereign state in the Union, with sixty thousand inhabitants, and thinks herself capable of settling international affairs."

He is very much wrought up over the Japanese situation. He fears that the West is going to force Japan to war with the United States and that if trouble comes it will be through just such thoughtless action as that taken by the Nevada Legislature.

The officers who were with me in Cuba have nearly all returned, and most of them have come to Washington to make their reports to headquarters. Colonel Slocum, Colonel Grebble, Major Winship, Colonel Black, and Major Kean dined with me to-night. Nothing seemed to delight them as much as the oak fire in the library. Although it was a warm night, they hovered about it and never tired of looking at the flames.

How the open fireplace stands for home to the average man of Anglo-Saxon descent! . . .

ARCHIBALD.

LXXXII

Washington, D. C.,
February 7, 1909.

DEAR CLARA:

The ball rolls faster as it nears the bottom. This week has been to those at the White House the busiest of the season. Receptions, dances, balls, and luncheons have filled every minute for the President and his wife and Ethel.

Now that the Administration is nearing its close the President and Mrs. Roosevelt, too, remember someone whom they have not had at the White House at all or recall some friend whom they want to have once more before they leave the White House altogether. Every morning, nearly, Mrs. Roosevelt receives memoranda from the office containing names hastily written in pencil, with simply a request that he or she or whosoever they may be have invitations for some meal at the White House. . . .

We have had the carpenters pretty busy this week packing and boxing. We at last got the books divided and sent the undesirable ones to the second-hand store, and the ones we thought worthy to be kept we have had shipped to Oyster Bay. After I had finished the work I had a list made out of those I thought should be sold and submitted it to the President. He looked over it and said:

"I would not have believed that so many worthless books had been printed during my administration. I would gladly give them to a library if I did not feel that I would be doing an unkindness, and I do not like to destroy them."

He allowed me to sell them, and when I told him that I had received more than a hundred dollars for them it looked incredible to him and forthwith he directed Mrs. Roosevelt to turn the amount over to some charity.

Both the President and Mrs. Roosevelt have a good deal of sentiment in their makeup, and they want each person who has been associated with them in a close personal way to have some memento of their stay in the White House. But she has had to take this matter in her own hands, as the following incident will show. She had come home late from a supper the other night and went at once to her room. This she told me, laughing, the next morning. She went to bed, but did not hear the President go to his dressing room. She thought it strange. She rang the bell and asked where the President was. She was told that he was in the study with some of the house guests. It was only that evening that they had been talking about their belongings, what they wished to give to this person or that person, and she jumped to the conclusion that he was distributing gifts at that moment. She sent for Ethel and told her to go to her father and see what he was doing.

She returned in a few minutes and said: "Why, Mother, he has given away nearly everything in the study, and

Aunty Corinne and every other guest in the White House have their arms full of pictures, books, and souvenirs."

Mrs. Roosevelt said she could not help laughing, and, knowing that it was too late to say anything, she waited patiently until he came in, and then watched him tiptoeing about, knowing that he had been doing something naughty and afraid to be caught at it.

The Douglas Robinsons returned most of the gifts of the night before, as they have had to do this at other times; but the other guests got away with their loot.

Whenever he asks for anything new Mrs. Roosevelt says: "Oh, that! Yes, my dear, you gave it away the other night," and so she has got his promise to give nothing else away until they two have agreed on what it shall be and to whom it shall go.

She loves Miss Hagner as if she were one of her own children, and so yesterday she asked Belle to accept the silver vase which has stood on her writing desk ever since she has been in the White House and which has been filled with fresh flowers every morning. She is very fond of Mrs. Garfield, and has given her an engraving which she once heard Mrs. Garfield admire. And so on, each friend whom they have will get some little souvenir, but she says if the President is going to play Santa Claus every time he feels in a generous mood there will not be enough gifts to go round. . . .

I wonder what Chartran would think if he could see the portrait of the President being destroyed. It was painted by the famous Frenchman when he was commissioned to paint the portrait of Mrs. Roosevelt for the Government. Senator Knox, then Attorney-General, I think, thought it a fine chance to have the President painted by a famous artist, and so gave Chartran the commission. The frame alone cost several hundred dollars, but neither the President nor his wife has ever liked the portrait. It was hung in the upper corridor, in the darkest spot on the wall, and by the family it has always been called the Mewing Cat.

Chartran was no more fitted to paint Mr. Roosevelt than I would be. I, at least, would know something of the inside of the man, whereas Chartran had no conception of the President. He painted him in a coy attitude, with his head on one side, looking sentimentally out from the canvas, hence the apt appellation of the mewing cat. What to do with it has been hanging over the family for some time, but the other night it was taken up, and there not being a dissenting voice, it was condemned to be burnt.

As valuable as it might be purely as a work of art, I told the President that, should it be given to me, I would receive it only to destroy it, and when Alice said she would not have it in her kitchen Mrs. Roosevelt said:

"Well, if Alice would refuse it, then it must be bad indeed, and so I will consent to having it burned."

This reference to Alice came from a remark which Charley McCauley made some years ago when everybody was trying to give presents to the White House. Mr. Roosevelt had adopted the plan to refuse everything in the way of gifts and not to permit Mrs. Roosevelt to accept anything except from intimate friends. But Alice, being a law unto herself, would accept anything she had a mind to, and at the time of her marriage, when presents would come which the President thought ought to be returned, Alice would accept them. Charley McCauley one day after one of these discussions said:

"Alice will accept anything but a red-hot stove, and will take that if it does not take too long to cool."

Ever since then presents have been referred to as red-hot stoves. The other day, for instance, Mrs. Roosevelt brought out from the President's room a suit of leather made after cowboy fashion and, seeing me, said:

"Archie, here is a red-hot stove, but you can have it if you want it."

Red-hot stove or not, I took it and will always value it. Apart from its intrinsic value and beauty, it was made for the President, and while Mrs. Roosevelt does not care for it, he likes it, and nothing would please him more than to put it on and mount a pinto and swing a lariat. . . .

The dance Friday evening was brilliant. The President danced a number of times, and more often with his daughter and Madame Jusserand than any one else. He talked more with Madame Hengelmüller than with any one else, because he had to make up with her for not asking her to dance. She dances abominably, and he knows it. But she is a great admirer of him and, moreover, he would not offend her or her good husband for the world; so whenever he would dance with Madame Jusserand or that exquisite little woman Madame Loudon, he would steal back guiltily to Madame Hengelmüller or the Baroness Takahara, and once sat a long time with Madame Nabuco, the wife of the Brazilian Ambassador. This is called doing penance for his pleasures. He felt so guilty about the Austrian that he has accepted an invitation to luncheon there on the 25th of this month.

He was sitting with her in the north side of the Blue Room when I heard him call to me. I left Mrs. Roosevelt and went over to him. He took my hand and said, with a queer, humorous twinkle in his eye:

"Archie, the Baroness wants me to lunch with her on the 25th, and in order that I shall not take an unfair advantage of my fellow Georgian she has agreed to ask you also, and I now order you to accept."

She did not understand his reference to "unfair advantage," but she looked knowing and was most gracious in her invitation. She is really very nice and certainly a great power socially.

A little after 12 o'clock Mrs. Longworth and Ovey of the British Embassy came to me and asked for the key of my house, and the next thing I saw was those two inviting people to a supper there. They had sent Oden Hoerstman over to the club in advance for raw oysters and eggs, and they knew I always keep well stocked with Scotch whisky, soda, and beer.

Well, when I got home at a little after 1 o'clock I found the chafing dish working and Margerie Ide presiding over it. The table was covered with dishes of indiscriminate sizes and shapes, and a half-eaten turkey was sitting in the midst of the Japanese china in a kitchen bakepan.

Around the table and scattered throughout the house was the jolliest-looking party I have seen for many a day. Mrs. Longworth had brought Miss Sears of Boston, Miss Ide, Miss Terry, and Blanche Emory, and Miss Emory had brought her sister and brother-in-law, whom I had never seen, and then there were Clelland Davis, Nick Longworth, Baron Stahl, who had no idea what it all meant, Richie Simpkins, Preston Gibson, and others.

They cooked the oysters after the eggs and in the same chafing dish, and, I think, without washing it. I had a fruit salad, which we had not touched for dinner, which came in well, and altogether it was a very enjoyable evening.

Your affectionate brother,

ARCHIBALD.

LXXXIII

Washington, D. C.,
February [1909].

DEAR CLARA:

I am often amused at people saying that Mr. Taft has such a wonderful memory for names. In manner he is the politician carried to the *n*th power. I have presented the army and public to him both in Washington and the Philippines, and he never receives a delegation without someone to announce their names. His instructions to Cloman and myself have always been never to let a person get by without getting his or her name, but when they do get by, as they often will, especially when they think they are old friends and, therefore, want to demonstrate the fact that they are remembered as such, it would be impossible for any one not knowing him well to realize that he has no idea whatever who they might be.

I shall never forget once, several years ago now, trying to get a visitor to give me his name, and he simply refused to do so, saying:

"Oh, the Secretary and I are old friends and were schoolmates."

"That may be so," I said, "but it is my duty to announce you by name."

"Oh, that does not make any difference; he will remember me."

As he got up to the Secretary I saw him stretch out his hands in a peculiar way old friends have of doing, which gave the Secretary some idea as to what his expectations might be. The Secretary turned hopelessly to me, but I was unable to help him out, so he drew back his arm as if he were going to strike the man and made a sweep through the air and grasped his hand and gave a greeting that no one else had had during the day.

The guest began to pin him rather closely, so to extricate himself he said:

"Helen" (or "Nellie," as he calls her, I think), "you remember our dear old friend here."

Before "Nellie" could say she did not, which she would have said had she been given the chance, the Secretary was busy recognizing some other old friend.

At the first lull in the line, Mrs. Taft turned to the Secretary and said:

"Will, I never knew that man's name even. I wish you would give the names of your intimate friends when I am expected to be especially cordial."

"My darling, I have not the faintest idea who he is, but I saw he was an intimate friend by the way he stood poised on one foot waiting to be recognized."

I could but laugh later when this same man passed me in the hall with his coat and said: "I told you there was no need to present me."

When the President does not remember a name or face he gives a cordial greeting, but he never makes any effort to deceive the man or woman into the belief that he does remember them when he doesn't. . . .

Good-night,
ARCHIBALD.

LXXXIV

Washington, D. C.,
Sunday, February 14, 1909.

MY DEAR CLARA:

Just a short letter to tell you that I got back safely from Lincoln's farm and that it was an extremely interesting event.

I cannot get out of my mind the meanness and sordidness of that cabin and wonder how anything like unto Mr. Lincoln could have breathed his first breath of air in it. A door and one poor little window were all that could be opened to admit the sunshine and light. It was smaller and meaner and more badly built than most of the Negro cabins you see in the outskirts of the villages in Georgia. The country was poor and the roads were terrible, and I never felt as sorry for Lincoln the man as I did for the poor little boy who had to tramp such byways, or for the mother who had to go through her travail in such surroundings. In the present day a Negress to be confined would be moved out of such a hut by the health inspector. My mind was not occupied nor my heart moved by the wonderful things which each orator pictured the President to have done, but it bled for the mother and child and the sordidness and misery of their early days together.

None of the Lincolns was present, and if it be true, as I hear, that Bob Lincoln, ex-Minister to the Court of St. James's and railroad millionaire, does not relish the perpetuation of this cabin, I cannot blame him. The very thought of it, having seen it once, would make him or any member of his family shudder with horror. It does not bear the stamp of poverty alone, but degradation and uncleanliness. If there was anything to put the final touch of pathos on the life of Lincoln it would be rehabilitation of the cabin in which he was born. It needed not a civil war to put that stamp of sorrow on his face, for the mere thought of one's mother suffering in such a hovel would be sufficient to cast a gloom over one's life for ever, it would seem to me.

The President delivered a great speech, I thought. It was one of the very best bits of oratory I have ever heard him deliver. He stuck closer to his text than he usually does, and I was glad that he did not take advantage of the opportunity offered to wield the big stick or lecture Congress. The papers all seemed to think he would use the chance to give one final whack at corruption, but he fooled them completely and devoted all his time to Lincoln, the result being a really marvellous piece of oratory. He delivered it, too, under the most trying circumstances. The rain was coming down and the wind was flapping the canvas, and it was difficult for the audience to see him, much less hear him, but with characteristic independence he called for a chair, and there were none to be had but those frail camp chairs, in which it is hardly safe to sit, much less to stand. But he climbed into one of these and stood immovable from his knees down, for any motion would have upset him. Governor Wilson sat back of him to try to steady the chair, but we expected to see him fall in a heap to the floor, but fortunately his crag-climbing proclivities had taught him to steady himself, and so he came through without accident.

We left [Washington] at 11 o'clock Thursday and did not reach Hodgenville until about the same time Friday. We made a few minutes' stop in Louisville, where we held the train until we could get some rubber shoes for the party, and during that time I had the chance to see Charley Haggerty, General Castleman, and a few friends who had come down to the station to greet me.

The President had a great reception at every town through which we passed. He rather expected a diminution of popular demonstration, I think, and for that reason gave the strictest orders that the time of our departure and the route would not be made public. For the first hour there were no yells, and it seemed to me the President saddened at the thought that it was the last trip he would take by rail as President and that he missed the demonstrations to which he had grown so accustomed. We did not have to wait long, however, before the whole country through which he was to pass knew the schedule time, and at each station there was always a great crowd to watch his train shoot by. At Altoona there must have been 5,000 people, and the same reception was given him at all the larger towns.

There were no stops to speak of, for we were travelling on a special train making record time. He jumped from his seat as readily for a half-dozen people at a road crossing as he would for a crowd at a station. As we would get a glimpse of some two or three people looking wistfully at his car we would call his attention to it, and he would pop up and be at the door in a minute waving his handkerchief, and the sight of that handkerchief was always a signal for a shout of welcome. Once Mrs. Roosevelt called his attention too late, and by the time he reached the platform there was nothing to be seen but an old Negro woman. As he entered the car he said:

"Edith, my dear, there was no one there but a large fat coloured lady who thought I wanted to flirt with her. She turned from me with scorn as I waved to her."

This led him to tell me that once when he was out on a similar trip he found himself waving frantically at a herd of cows.

"It is needless to say that I met with an indifferent, if not a cold, reception. But I think a public man who does not understand this sort of thing, who is unwilling to make a show of himself as I am doing now, fails to see the point of view of just such people as we are passing now. It is some trouble for him to jump up from his meals as I have been doing all through lunch, but if it gives any of these poor people any pleasure to see their President I have no right to deny them that spark of brightness."

I watched the upturned faces in every crowd he addressed or yelled "Good luck!" to, and there was always that unmistakable look of personal affection in the individual face as he appeared, and as he swept his eyes over the throng there was set up instantly, it seemed to me, a personal hand between him and every man or woman present. It was not the look which comes from admiration, and curiosity seemed to be absent entirely. It was purely one of affection. It made me think of a remark I heard Ambassador Bryce make only a few days ago:

"Nobody likes him now but the people."

He is certainly as strong as ever there, and if I mistake not they will be heard from before the next four years are over.

Secretary Wright was with us and added a great deal to the trip. The President was not so genial or enlivening as I thought he would be. The end of the car was a general sitting room and dining room, too, and our little party at meals was made up of the President, Mrs. Roosevelt, Miss Ethel and Secretary Wright, Mr. Loeb, Doctor Rixey and myself. The President read almost constantly. Secretary Wright memorized his speech on the way out, and Mrs. Roosevelt, Miss Ethel, and I played solitaire or chatted.

The President has the greatest power of concentration I have ever seen. When he is reading or thinking he does not seem to hear anything which goes on about him. Once when we got into a discussion and became rather loud and then got to laughing I suggested that we would disturb the President. Mrs. Roosevelt said it made no difference to him, that he would not hear us; and so we paid little attention to him after that if he was reading. Doctor Rixey and I carried on a conversation about him once in chairs next to his and he did not even hear us, not even when we mentioned his name. I got a good deal of pleasure from merely watching him on this trip.

He spoke of Mr. Taft only once, and then only by reference. He said that he was very proud of his Secretary of War, while congratulating him [General Wright] on his speech on the return trip, and added:

"I am distressed, General, that you will not continue to be Secretary of War, but unfortunately you have been too close to me, I fear."

I learned from Mr. Loeb that you cannot get him to say anything, but he feels very deeply, nevertheless, the fact that Mr. Taft seems determined to sever all the ties which have bound them together in the past. He was the only one who did not foresee this, and I think he will be bitterly disappointed when he sees many of his policies reversed. He was so cocksure that Mr. Taft would continue all his policies, and I fear that a general reversal will be nearer the line he will follow. It will be a dangerous thing for him to do, for it will relieve Mr. Roosevelt of all responsibility of breaking the bonds and afford him every excuse to make the race in another four years if there is any demand for him from the people.

As tiresome as the trip was, it was a great rest for Mrs. Roosevelt, who looks utterly fagged out with her social duties of the past two months. It was no rest for him, for he never rests. Mrs. Robinson, whom I called on to-day, told me of the time when he rushed into the house in New York and announced that he had a month's holiday and was going to spend it with her.

"I am so glad, Theodore," she said, "for now you can take a good rest and you have deserved one, too."

"Yes," he responded, "I am going to take a complete rest. I shall do nothing in that time but write a history of Oliver Cromwell."

I was so ignorant of his works as to ask:

"Did he do it?"

She then told me that he not only did do it, but in the time he had allotted for his rest.

Two remarks seemed to amuse him on the trip very much. One came from Sloan, the secret service man. It was just after we left Altoona, where there was the first big crowd and where he climbed on a truck to make a speech to it. As we entered the car Sloan said, with what seemed to me to be tears in his eyes:

"Mr. President, we are not dead yet."

The President gave him a pat on the back and said:

"Dear old faithful Jimmie, no, we are not dead yet, but we soon will be."

The other was when the President, Secretary Wright, and I were in the car by ourselves, and he turned to Wright and said:

"General, I think that was one of the best speeches I have ever heard on Lincoln and so just from your point of view. Don't you think so, Archie?"

"I think he presented our side most admirably, Mr. President."

He laughed heartily and added:

"It has struck me just now for the first time that I made this trip to Lincoln's birthplace with three Southern men, you, Wright, and Rixey, for I am sure you still believe in the right of the Confederacy to secede."

General Wright said:

"Mr. President, you will notice that I have never attempted to apologize for the position of the South, and I am glad to say that the North, too, is admitting more and more every day the right of the South to do as she did."

"And you, my dear General, have never heard me criticize the South for so doing."

The end is in sight. The carpenters are busy day and night erecting the reviewing stands for the inauguration of Mr. Taft, and there is the same rush for rooms and houses as at all inaugurations, no greater, certainly no less. Mrs. Roosevelt will have her last dinner party on the night of March third and has included me in it. The Tafts will be there, and it ought to be replete with interesting incidents.

Good-night again. With love,

ARCHIBALD.

LXXXV

Washington, D. C.,
February 15 [1909].

DEAR CLARA:

. . . I have always contended that there is no way that one can possibly keep a footing of informality with occupants at the White House. Even the President's sisters, when they are not visiting there, cannot run in and out when they choose, and if they wish to see Mrs. Roosevelt they are forced to make engagements ahead, just as a stranger would have to do. The moment one ceased to be a part of the household, that moment places a barrier between him and the house itself. I was walking by there with Winship a few nights ago, and I made just this comment:

"No one aide has ever had the run of the White House I have had since my term of service there," I told him, "yet were I to be relieved to-morrow there would be no way I could make my way into that house without the greatest formality. The very nature of the life there prevents it. It would be as if I had never been there at all."

Yet think of it. This morning when I went there Mrs. Roosevelt was going out, and she stopped long enough to ask me to destroy the Chartran portrait and two others which she had taken from the walls and which were leaning in the corridor. She also suggested that I break up the china which was chipped, and then she and her secretary left me in entire charge. Here was a portrait which was said to have cost several thousand dollars, and two others of less value, left to my care; and no thought that she could not trust me with this important duty ever entered her mind. I had the canvasses taken from their frames and, unwilling to trust any one else with them, I took them to the cellar myself and placed them in the furnace. The hands in the Chartran portrait were simply marvellous, and for a moment I was tempted to save one of these from the flames, but did not think it was the honourable thing to do. I will reserve the china for another occasion.

Secretary of State Bacon sent for me this morning and told me of the trouble in Liberia. He said to me:

"This is the only bit of country in the world where the Negro had a chance to show himself capable of government, and the situation there has reached an acute stage. We are bound to protect it if we can and hold it for this race. I am going to appoint a commission, or, rather, recommend one to the President to appoint. There is one man whom we must put on it, and that is Booker Washington. There will be two others, but he must go, and I do not see how I can help but ask for a naval vessel to send the commission in. It is necessary to have a vessel there, and the safest thing to do is to have it convey the commission. What do you think?"

I knew just why he sought my advice, so I gave it squarely from the shoulder.

"I agree with you, Mr. Secretary, that the government of Liberia should be preserved for the Negroes, and also that Booker Washington should go on any commission which is sent there. I also believe that a navy vessel should be anchored off the coast, but I do not believe that a navy vessel should be used to convey Booker Washington there. The people will understand why he ought to go, and will not hesitate to endorse it, but they will make a hue and cry against such a marked distinction in sending him on a government vessel. They will not forgive the President for doing it, either.

"There is no telling what is going to happen in the next four years, and should the cry for Roosevelt ever become a demand for his renomination he ought not to be hampered in his fight for the South by too much Booker Washington. If it cannot be held over for Mr. Taft to handle, then protect the President from the charge that he forced naval officers to sit down with him at their mess table. There will be no such difficulty arise if you send a vessel there. Any naval officer will do the proper thing. He will voluntarily entertain the commission on board, and if the commanding officer be a Southern man he will do it with a grace which a Northern man will not have, but it will be between the commanding officer and Washington, and the President will be out of it. I know that when we had a vessel at Haiti the commanding officer was Hilary Jones, a cousin of Thomas Nelson Page and a great-grandson of Chief Justice Marshall. While Jones repudiates the Negro socially, he paid the Negro consul or minister there every mark of official respect, and the same thing would happen in Liberia, but as you love the President and hope for his renomination some day don't hamper him now with another incident with Booker Washington."

The secretary told me that it was to get just this viewpoint that he wanted to talk with me, and later he saw the President. He put the case squarely and the President told him to do what he thought to be right, no matter what the consequences were. The case stands so now, and

I am anxious to see the result. The President will not give direct orders to have him sent by a naval vessel, but will permit it if the State Department so recommends it. I am in hopes that my advice will be taken—namely, to send the commission by a liner and have the naval vessel meet it there.

My postscript has run into a letter as it usually does, for I never know what I am going to write until my hands touch the keys and my thoughts get weakened from their comatose state.

I have been called to the telephone twice since I began to write this letter by persons who want me to recommend them for one thing or the other to Mrs. Taft. I find that I have the reputation of being the chief confidant of the Tafts, which is rather amusing as I am more uncertain of my attitude to them, or rather their attitude to me, than possibly any one who is near them at all. I try to adjust my position in relation to them for your interest, otherwise I would not bother to think twice about the matter. If I have any interest in remaining with them at all it comes from the fact that I should like to see from the inside just what they will do and how they will act.

I have ordered cards for dinners, luncheons, and receptions engraved for them, for I presume they will want to begin at once to issue invitations, but I am not certain whether they want the old form followed or not, or whether they will change the name from "The White House" back to the hideous name "Executive Mansion." If they do this I will leave of my own accord, for it will mean that there is something fundamentally wrong with them. Bad temper I can stand, but not bad taste. Twenty days from now this will be lese-majesty.

As ever, your affectionate brother,

ARCHIBALD.

LXXXVI

Washington, D. C.,
February 16, 1909.

DEAR CLARA:

All of my theories about Mrs. Taft vanish when I see Mr. Taft. And he has a wonderful way of dispelling all forebodings.

They arrived this morning and telephoned me before I was out of bed to call at 10 o'clock. A lot of things had to be gone over and settled about the inauguration. She greeted me so friendly, and the Secretary was so wholesome and cheerful, that I really felt remorse at what I had written last night about them. She thanked me for all that I have done, and when I asked her whom she wanted to go with her to the Capitol on the day of inauguration she said she wanted me if it were permissible. We will go alone in the motor car, one which she will pick out while she is in New York, and come back before the procession starts from the Capitol, in order to have lunch ready by the time the President arrives. She will ask about seventy-five guests and relatives, and in addition to these she will probably have the class of 'Seventy-eight from Yale. I think that is the year. But it will be his classmates.

She is going to retain all the servants in the White House and only make such changes as she sees fit from time to time. She feels that I have managed everything so far with great tact and without having any friction arise between the Roosevelts and themselves. I feel that if others had tried to be as friendly to both there would be no friction at all. But at such times people will carry tales and harp on fears until they make both parties suspicious, and once suspicion is aroused, it is so easy to misconstrue every act. She starts in with nine guests on the 5th of March, and as soon as these go there will be others to come. She naïvely remarked:

"I think it better to entertain all the relatives as soon as possible, for they will all expect to be entertained at the White House sooner or later, and it is well to have these obligations over and done with."

Mr. Taft was looking bronzed and tanned from his trip to Panama, and seemed in fine humour. As he came into the room he said:

"Hello, Archie, how is my fellow Georgian?"

I felt that Georgia was certainly gaining in distinction when I have two Presidents claiming clanship through my old state. It is one of Mr. Roosevelt's favourite forms of greetings.

He [Mr. Taft] heard me talking of the arrangements for the inauguration day and asked me what we were discussing. I told him and said that it was customary for the wife of the President-elect to take with her to the Senate Chamber the wives of the incoming Cabinet. He cut me off short and said:

"No need to consider that, then, for I will have no other Cabinet on the 4th of March but the one now in. Neither the members of the prospective Cabinet and certainly not their wives will have the slightest standing on the 4th of March. I will continue to meet with the present Cabinet until my own will have been confirmed by the Senate."

That settled that point, but he did not gratify my curiosity as to who these members of the new Cabinet would be.

The luncheon at the White House to-day was for the members of the [African] hunting party, and it was rather a dreary affair. . . .

The President said he was taking nine pairs of eyeglasses with him, for if he should lose his glasses or be without them, he would have to return at once or wait for other glasses to reach him. He says he is not a first-class shot and thinks it due to his eyes. He does not hesitate to speak of his weaknesses, and it is a matter of great mortification to him that he is not a more certain shot. However, he is far above the average from what little I have seen of his practice with the rifle.

I have no fear that he will not be able to get the lion where he needs must get him or be eaten.

The meeting between the President and Taft was most cordial to-day.

ARCHIBALD.

LXXXVII

Sunday, Washington, D. C.,
February 21, 1909.

MY DEAR CLARA:

Events are passing now with kinetoscopic rapidity. Each day is so crowded that there is no time to do anything but take part in them and drift with the rapids which lie between this time and the 4th of March.

The marvellous thing about it all to me is that the President is busier now than he has ever been before, and that he fills the public mind and eye to a greater extent at this hour, when he has less than two weeks to serve, than he did when he had four years ahead of him. I tried to find time during the last four days to record some of the interesting things which pass before me at the White House and have been unable to do so.

It is now Sunday and I have just finished breakfasting with Preston Gibson. I have taken his apartment for the next three months, as I have rented my house to the

Bennetts for that period. I get $200 a month for mine, and Winship and I get Preston's for $60, so you see it has paid me to undergo the discomfiture of moving. Last night Preston gave his farewell dinner before his marriage, which takes place on Tuesday, and there were some forty guests, all men, many coming from New York, Chicago, and Baltimore. Larz Anderson sat on the left of the host and Reggie Vanderbilt on his right. Ralph Parr of Baltimore helped to make the dinner a go, and so did one Wallie Keith, who did a good stunt. . . .

I am getting up much earlier these latter days for the reason that the President has had to forego his usual programme in the morning and come to his office an hour earlier in order to get through with the day's work. He has never allowed anything in the past to interfere with the morning hour, which he always devotes to Mrs. Roosevelt, either walking in the south grounds with her or sitting on the balcony or in front of the fire in the library when the weather is bad. But the press of engagements is such that now he is at the office before she is out of bed, and he works steadily until after midnight.

The reception to the army and navy Thursday evening was the most brilliant of the season, and he says it was the most brilliant reception ever held during his administration. Nearly two thousand persons passed in line, and the pressure for invitations was something extraordinary. There were only five women there in high neck gowns, and there was not a man who was not either in uniform or dress suit. This is really a wonderful record when you think of the freakish effects most of the receptions have been in the past.

The house has been full of guests most of the time, which always adds to the strain on Mrs. Roosevelt. Among the guests was a Miss Potter, sister of James Brown Potter, and of my old friend of Philippine days, Ashton Potter. She is no longer a girl, but she possesses such charm and beauty that it is a keen pleasure to be in her company. She is a very old friend of the Roosevelts and calls the President Theodore, and, what is more, never rises when he comes into the room. He was late for dinner the other evening and as he entered every guest arose (Mrs. Roosevelt never rises) with the exception of Miss Potter. As he took some time to sit down, as he went from one to the other speaking a word of welcome, it made her attitude all the more conspicuous. The old type of incense swingers looked aghast at the breach of etiquette and felt correspondingly shocked, but she was as unconcerned as if no one else had arisen. I don't think it ever occurred to her that he was any other than her childhood's playmate, Theodore.

The household goods are nearly all packed, and there only remain the tapestries in the state dining room to go. A lot more guests will come this week end, but most of them are Miss Ethel's friends and they remain over Sunday, and by Tuesday everyone will have left except the President and Mrs. Roosevelt. The Tafts are going to spend the night of the 3d with them, and early on the morning of the 4th Mrs. Roosevelt goes to Admiral Cowles's and later joins the President at the station.

Both the President and his wife these days are busy distributing souvenirs among their friends. He has divided his foils and hand sticks and gloves among the younger aides. He gave me a pair of spurs; evidently old Spanish silver and hand carved. The spur itself is made by the figure of a woman designed very much like the bowsprit of the old-time vessels, her head ending with a helmet in which revolves the circular saw spur. He said they are more than two hundred years old and were given him when he was in the West. He has worn them some, but not often.

He gave Sims a signed photograph, and he has presented canes to the members of his cabinet. I carried one to Secretary Wright, which had been made from wood taken from the Hermitage, and the cane he gave Secretary Newberry was made from wood from Alexander Hamilton's place. Some publication was made of it, and he was evidently very angry about it, for when he saw me at lunch yesterday he asked me if I could imagine how the facts got out, rather suspecting me of having given them out, I thought. I was very glad to be able to tell him that I could not imagine how they got out unless the newspaper men saw me go with them to the War and Navy Building, which is most probable, or else unless the Secretaries themselves gave out the news. The Washington *Post* reporter asked me about the sticks, but I refused to give him any satisfaction. I do not know why it is regarded as of such importance by him, unless he does not want those who presented him with the sticks to know that he is giving them away, or else there are some of his cabinet to whom he has not given anything.

It is a very sad time for the intimate friends of the Roosevelts, and it would be correspondingly sad for the Roosevelts if they were not kept busy every minute of their time. She gave a musicale of a very informal character Friday at noon, only inviting the Old Guard, as it were, to be present. The occasion was one of general breakdown on the part of many. I suppose the nature of the music had something to do with it. The Buffalo Quartette—violins and 'cello—played selections which were not adapted to enliven any occasion and were well fitted to bring out any temperamental qualities which might be latent in the audience. . . .

Each friend wanted to take away with her some little recollection of the hostess to feed her hungry heart in the future. One by one they came to say good-bye and each went away weeping. Dear Isabel Hagner stood in one of the windows with Mary Carlisle and wept as if her heart would break. It is the first time I have seen her break down during all these trying weeks. I left Mrs. Roosevelt and went over to see if I could cheer Belle, and I got a smile from her for a moment when I told her of one worldly old dame, the wife of an assistant secretary, who tried to sniffle but couldn't. I suggested that she could advance her fortunes by bottling a few of her tears and selling them to the hypocrites on just such occasions.

There were very few who feigned grief, however, for it was real to most of them. Mrs. Lowndes, Miss Tuckerman, Mrs. Leiter even, unbended enough to weep, and poor Mary Carlisle could hardly say good-bye at all. The only man present except the aides was Edward Everett Hale, and he made a striking figure among all those fashionably dressed women.

Mrs. Roosevelt is really greatly beloved by those who know her. She has such poise. That always strikes me as her greatest characteristic. She stood among all those weeping women Friday apparently as unmoved as if she were an iceberg, and yet I knew that her heart was being torn just the same as theirs, yet she retained her dignity and composure through all and never let down once; only later Belle Hagner told me that when she went to her room she had one good wholesome weep, and when I saw her later she was smiling through her tears and laughed at some of the little incidents which had gone on about her.

Saturday night I accompanied him [the President] to the reception at Senator Depew's, given for the incoming Vice-President and Mrs. Sherman. There were very few persons there, and most of those were either Senators or families of Senators. His reception, I thought, was somewhat chilly, for only a few of the Senators went up to speak to him. Most of those who did not acted most cowardly and slipped out of this room or that hallway so that he would not see them. I said to Senator Bacon:

"Have you spoken to the President?"

"I have not," he said. "I have been too angry with him of late to play the hypocrite now," and as he saw the President coming he slipped behind a portière so he would not have to speak.

There is no doubt that the feeling in Congress against him is very bitter, but he is not through with it yet, for driving back he told me that he had loaded his gun for the Senate again and was going after some of them on Monday. He has a perfect contempt for their methods and refuses ever to compromise with them. What makes them more enraged than anything else is that he makes them do his will in spite of the fact that they do not want to do so.

We leave this afternoon for Hampton Roads to welcome the fleet. It will be an historic occasion and one well worth witnessing. He has asked only a few friends and his party is made up purely on a personal basis. While I am very lucky in being asked, yet it does not add to my popularity with either Sims or Bromwell. The Longworths, Senator and Mrs. Lodge, and Admiral Cowles are to be among the party, and a few others whose names I have not yet learned. We start from the Navy Yard at 5 o'clock and will, I understand, steam out until we meet the fleet. The whole will pass in review of the President, and to-morrow night there is to be a great dinner at the Chamberlain. There will be two thousand craft afloat in the Hampton Roads, and every pantry in Old Point Comfort, they say, is rented as a suite of rooms.

His departure from the Presidency is certainly going to be in a blaze of glory and a flare of trumpets. Everyone has been predicting that he would do something extraordinary, but little did any one think among the last things he would do would be to call a Congress of the world to meet at The Hague on the conservation of the world's energies. Really the scope of his mind is masterful. I was talking with Alfred Henry Lewis yesterday and he made this pertinent remark:

"Of course, I don't like this African play he is making, but it may be the very thing needed to add to his fame. Taft, I believe, is going to turn the Government over to the men whom Roosevelt will regard as the enemy: I know that the old crowd is licking its chops and looking forward to seven fat years after the seven lean years which are just now drawing to a close. A reversal of policy means a return to Roosevelt when he comes out of Africa, and on concluding his tour of Europe, if he will come to the States again by the way of San Francisco, and make a zig-zag trip across the country, nothing in the world can prevent his renomination. His unpopularity in Congress is as nothing. He has not got as much respect for the Senate as a dog has for a marriage license, and every time he swats either House, it is so much popularity from the people."

This is not my prediction, but the words of Lewis, who was even more picturesque in his language than I have given it.

Most affectionately as ever,

ARCHIE.

LXXXVIII

Washington, D. C.,
February 24, 1909.

Dear Clara:

I returned yesterday from Hampton Roads, where I went with the President on Sunday. It would have been an ideal experience had not the shadow of death and tragedy been among our little party. The news of the death of young Stuart Robinson reached the White House Sunday shortly before noon. . . .

Mrs. Robinson is the favourite sister of the President, and when I saw him he showed unmistakable signs of grief over her sorrow. Mrs. Roosevelt was bowed with sorrow in her sympathy for the stricken mother, but when she came on board she assumed the rôle of First Lady of the Land and carried off the duties with great composure and dignity. . . .

From the moment the President put his foot over the gangway he was the President and not brother nor uncle to the stricken sister or affectionate nephew. Yet one who watched him narrowly could see at times the great sympathy which welled in his breast. He sat more alone than usual and sometimes at table he would appear oblivious to everything around him and sit with his eyes half closed fixed on vacancy. How well I knew the picture he was conjuring up. This lovely, graceful sister, who had left the White House only a few days before, bowed heartbroken over the casket which they dared not open for her.

These moments of absorption were reserved for below decks alone, for the moment he appeared upon the bridge he was the Commander-in-Chief of the United States Navy. I was standing by his side when he first got a glimpse of the white ships through the fog. The Captain had seen them through his glasses and had tried to point them out to the President, but he could make out nothing through the glasses. He kept his eyes strained to the point on the horizon where the Captain said they would appear, and when he first felt that he had them he gave a shout of joy:

"Here they are. That is the answer to my critics. Another chapter is complete, and I could not ask a finer concluding scene to my administrations."

Then, turning to Commander Sims, his naval aide, he said:

"Sims, not until some American fleet returns victorious from a great sea battle will there be another such home-coming."[1]

He afterward used this sentence several times in addressing the officers and men on the various ships, but it was spontaneous here and voiced his enthusiasm. He used it next to his wife, who came on the bridge a few minutes later, as if to impress it on his mind, and afterward in the saloon when he toasted the American Navy to Admiral Sperry and his officers who came aboard the *Mayflower* to pay their respects. . . .

Every craft in the waters came sooner or later near us and whistled and shrieked until the President would appear and lift his hat. When every ship opened up her twenty-one guns, the President's salute, and every steam whistle blew itself hoarse, it was perfect pandemonium. The moment we enjoyed most, I think, next to that when we first got sight of the fleet, was that when we steamed through the double line of battleships, up one side close enough to those on the port to hear the cheers, and then

---

[1]Roosevelt's comment on the voyage of the battle fleet, written in his Autobiography five years after the event, will be found appended to Letter XXV.

down the other side so close that we could recognize friends on the deck.

It is the last time the ships will be seen in white. It will not be the white squadron any more unless some other President reverses Mr. Roosevelt's order, for he has commanded that henceforth every vessel in the navy shall be painted a dull drab or gray.[1]

"They look too much like pleasure yachts as they are. They are grim engines and they should not be disguised."

We passed several which had already been painted gray, and it was easy to see that the women, and I fear some of the men, too, felt a keen disappointment at the change. We did not wait over for the dinner and ball, but left the Roads about dark and came slowly up the river. . . .

We had a nice quiet dinner in the small dining room, and it did seem so cosy after the big state dining room. He was most confidential and good humoured. He laughed when I asked him why we were dining in the breakfast room and asked me if I could not guess. I frankly said I could not, unless it was more quiet.

"No," he said, "nothing could be more quiet than the state dining room, but it is somewhat torn up just now," and when I looked puzzled he added: "I have caught you all napping, including my most wideawake wife. If you will go in there to-morrow you will see two bison heads carved in the mantelpiece in place of the lion heads which McKim[2] and Mrs. Roosevelt forced me to accept when the White House was being remodelled. You know art is about the only subject of which I feel some

---

[1]To decrease visibility. This practice, inaugurated by Roosevelt, is still followed in the navy.

[2]The well-known architects, Messrs. McKim, Mead and White, had remodelled the White House offices and had skilfully bound them as an architectural whole to the main edifice.

uncertainty, but I am getting to believe that I have some ideas of my own regarding it. When the question of the mantelpiece was under consideration, I suggested that the heads which McKim seemed determined to have carved at the top of the columns should be bison and not lion heads. He is so imbued with the classics that he would not hear of it, and I would have insisted on the bison heads had not my good wife sneered me out of the idea. When the architects were here last fall I had five of the most eminent ones here to lunch and very modestly told them of my former suggestion to McKim. They not only agreed with me, but urged me to have the change made and showed me how it could be done. You remember, Archie, I asked you if I had any money left."

"Yes, sir," I interpolated, "and I answered you had, although I was not sure if you had any left or not."

"Well, I did not care, for I was so pleased at having my judgment upheld by such eminent authorities that I gave the order that afternoon without saying anything more to any of you. If I were only going to be in authority two months longer I would have those lions on the new Connecticut Avenue Bridge thrown in the river and bisons placed there in their stead."[1]

I then told him how he had caught me napping to a greater extent than he would think.

"How's that?" he said.

"Several weeks ago you asked me how the nation would receive an order to carve back the name of Jefferson Davis on Aqueduct Bridge, and I told you that while I thought the North would have a spasm for a few minutes the South

[1]Roosevelt used to protest good-humouredly about the lions at the entrance to the Public Library in New York. He wanted bisons placed there also. The protests were a symptom of his enthusiastic Americanism. He felt that American history, scenery, flora, and fauna should minister to American art and literature and drama.

Memorial Fountain to Major Butt and Francis Davis Millet, the painter, both of whom went down on the *Titanic*. It is just south of the White House grounds in Washington

would feel it to be an act of justice and would appreciate it more than I dared to think, and added that while I would like to see it done as a Southern man, I would advise against it."

"Yes, I remember it," he said, "but I had then decided that it was the only right and just thing to do and so gave the order to Secretary Wright. It is no criticism for those who had the name erased, for at that period it was a very natural thing to do, just as it is a natural thing to restore it at this period."

I remember perfectly the casual way he mentioned it to me, and I came very near mentioning it in my letter to you the next day, and yet the suggestion appeared to me to be so absolutely preposterous that I would not even repeat it to you in confidence. That he actually contemplated it seriously never entered my mind, and here now is the order published on the same day as the homecoming of the fleet and on George Washington's birthday, and there is hardly a ripple of criticism from any part of the country. I have come to the conclusion that he better understands the American people than any one man in the past fifty years; else they believe more thoroughly in him than in any man in that period. . . .

Jimmie Williams has just been in and volunteers the information that every man who hopes to help run the next administration has a candidate for my post at the White House. I am perfectly cognizant of what wires are being pulled, and if I was especially interested in remaining I would be annoyed, but as it is, it is a matter of amusement to me. . . .

It is really comical to see the petty intrigues which are going on. No one is able to use me, and therefore I doubt if any one wants to see me remain. My only strength is that each would prefer me to remain in command, as it were, to seeing the other install his favourite. They realize that as soon as Mr. Taft is inaugurated every attitude is changed of necessity and the door to free communication is closed to everyone except to the personal inmates, so to speak, of the White House. . . .

We Americans are poor bunglers as intriguers, and the less one intrigues for place the better off he is, in my judgment. My only fear is that this is a forerunner of what may be expected later on. It looks a little like the old weak days of McKinley. The Ohio school of politics breeds a peculiar genius and corruption always flourishes under it.[1] I think I see the Government drifting into the control of those whom Mr. Roosevelt would regard as the "enemy." The old crowd, especially as typified by the rich Senators, such as Aldrich, Wetmore, Depew, are already "licking their chops and looking forward to seven fat years after the seven lean years just about to close." I have no fear of Mr. Taft, but only of Mr. Taft's amiability and doctrine of expediency.

Good-bye. As ever, your affectionate brother,

ARCHIBALD.

LXXXIX

Washington, D. C.,
Sunday [Feb.] 28, 1909.

MY DEAR CLARA:

I have only time these days to jot down from time to time incidents which I think may amuse you or to give you bits of gossip which will not be carried by the press. I am surprised to see how many interesting things do escape the press, or else the indifference to matters which I think of great special interest.

---

[1] "The Ohio school of politics!" A significant phrase when read in the light of the recent oil scandals and the unsavoury régime of ex-Attorney-General Daugherty.

For instance, I have sold both of the President's horses and yet nothing about it has as yet appeared in the papers. One went to Secretary Straus, for which he paid $600. That was some time ago, but I have been greatly worried over the sale of Roswell, the famous jumper, which the President has used for the last six years. I was very much afraid it would have to be put up at auction, for whenever I suggested to any one to purchase it, he would look dubious and I began to feel like a second-class horse trader. The reluctance to buy was due largely to the reputation which the President has of riding his animals to death. The fact is, Roswell is in perfect condition, and the only blemish on him is the small pin splint on the cannon bone, and at a point which does not detract from the value of the horse.

However, there was some lively bidding for him at the last and I sold him Friday to Mr. De Naige of New Orleans, now living in Washington, who had been at Harvard with the President. He said he was not especially anxious for the horse, but rather than see the President's horse go on the block he would buy him. I told him frankly not to buy him from any sentimental reasons, that I had several bids under consideration, and that I had refused one or more as the probable purchasers were persons whom the President did not wish to own Roswell. I got five hundred for him at last, and two hours after I sold him I was offered a hundred more by Mr. Kellogg,[1] known as the "trust buster."

The White House is entirely denuded of all the personal belongings of the Roosevelts, and it seems to have little character left. Mrs. Roosevelt has worked herself almost to death to see that every nook and corner is cleaned and garnished, and that every piece of linen is left white and

[1]Senator Frank Kellogg, now Ambassador to England.

spotless. The more I reflect on my position, the more anomalous it seems. The only thing which makes it possible is being perfectly frank with both parties and slipping in a few diplomatic compliments from one to the other.

Friday Major Sylvester sent for me to say that he had news which worried him greatly. It was to the effect that there was a well-organized plan evidently on foot to destroy one or more public buildings, and he merely wanted to warn me to use every precaution within the White House; that he himself had strengthened the guard outside the White House, and that on Inauguration Day he was going to ask for a company of soldiers to be placed in the south grounds. As a rule he is not an alarmist and is not credulous, so his attitude affected me more than the fears of most men would have done. I have asked to have the police in the house put under my control, which will be done from the 4th of March, and I hope in the future to keep it under whatever army officer may be stationed there in my place.

A number of threatening letters have been received by the Roosevelts of late, but most of them Miss Hagner and Mr. Loeb purloin before they are seen by either the President or Mrs. Roosevelt. One especially nasty came only yesterday, which Miss Hagner turned over to me to read as a sample, she said, of those which are coming in daily through the mails. It threatened to injure some one of the children as soon as the police protection of the Government ended, on account of his attitude in the Japanese matter on the Pacific coast. It went into detail as to what could be expected in the way of vitriol and poison. I am not a great believer in capital punishment, but there is one type of criminal whom I should put to death with relish, and that type is the anonymous letter writer. A person who would write an anonymous letter would commit any crime if there was no fear of detection.

Saturday we had a most enjoyable luncheon at the White House, the first one since the death of Stuart Robinson. Admiral Sperry was the guest of honour, and I had an opportunity to study him at close range. He well bears out his reputation for frigidity on close inspection. . . .

One of his eyelids droops, which gives him a rather cynical appearance, and may account for much of his reputation as a cynic. Speaking of the photographs which have appeared of him, he said that he had the melancholy comfort of confessing that they seemed to be regarded as good likenesses by his family. He is a hard disciplinarian, and I heard him say to the President regarding ——'s court martial:

"Had there been one captain in that fleet as I steamed up the Roads and formed into double column whom I knew to be a periodical drinker, I would have changed my manœuvres, for one moment's hesitation or one second's indecision might have left us bereft of reputation and millions of dollars' worth of property, and minus many valuable lives. I am severe regarding intemperance in the service, but I do not believe any one can be too severe in this matter."

Maxim, the great gun manufacturer, was there also, and after luncheon the President invited us all down to see the test of firing with his latest invention, the noiseless rifle. A rifle shot which one could hear at 500 yards cannot be heard more than seventy-five yards with this invention. The President was greatly interested, and at once ordered two rifles of different calibres to take with him for target practice while crossing the water.[1]

Mr. and Mrs. Taft came yesterday afternoon. I had not expected to see them until to-day, but the chairman of the Inaugural Committee sent for me to beg me to act as go-between; saying that all arrangements had become

[1]The much-discussed Maxim "Silencer" was not used in the World War.

tied up for the reason that the committee had been unable to get the list of guests for the inaugural ball supper, the arrangement from the White House, and what was expected regarding the programme at the White House. Fortunately, I had one of the new White House motors which I was trying, and I volunteered to beard the Tafts, tired as they might be. . . .

It was at this interview that I asked her [Mrs. Taft] how she intended to come from the Capitol, and she said in a motor, of course, and wanted to know why I asked. I then told her that the suggestion had been made for her to ride back from the Capitol with the newly inaugurated President, which idea found lodgment in her mind at once. I told her that the committee from the House and Senate had made different plans and had arranged to have the President ride with a committee, as had been the custom for the last century.

"Since Mr. Roosevelt has seen fit to change the order of things," she said, "I see no reason why the President's wife may not now come into some rights on that day also. The reason that I do not enjoy accompanying Mr. Taft on trips is just for this: He is taken in charge by committees and escorted everywhere with honour, while I am usually sent with a lot of uninteresting women through some side street to wait for him at some tea or luncheon. When you come back to-morrow we will talk it over with him and see what can be done."

Before I left I settled a lot of things with her and secured her promise to have the supper list and luncheon list ready by 10 o'clock.

To-day, beginning at 10 o'clock, has been a rushing one. I have paid her and the President-elect three visits, and between times was with the inaugural committee settling matters definitely. I telephoned to the joint committee of the House and Senate of her proposition to drive back with the President, and it was like an explosion in camp. They got her by 'phone and told her that the committees had not considered the matter at all, for they had followed the custom of a century. They rather frightened her off until I got her on the 'phone later and said that there was no reason why the custom should not be changed, and she told me to tell them that she had decided to make the change. She went to luncheon at Senator Hale's, and there she was squelched again, she said, by Senator Lodge when she broached the subject, but that other members of the committee backed her up, and so she decided to stand by her resolution and, as the President-elect stood by her, it was not a very difficult thing for her to do.

So instead of my returning to the White House with her I came back alone and prepared the White House for their reception. I propose to have the lunch on the table by the time they arrive, and I will see to it that he is on that reviewing stand within a half hour after he enters the White House. If he wants to spend the time smiling and shaking hands instead of eating, he will have to go hungry before the day is over, that is all. I have asked all the aides to meet me at 10:00 to-morrow and I will then distribute their passes and invitations and give final directions. I inclose you a copy of what I have mapped out for them to do, to show you what aides really have to do on such occasions.

I found both the President-elect and Mrs. Taft most cordial, and they seemed to look upon me as one whom they can trust to do things. For instance, Commander Sims, the President's naval aide, has been relieved from duty, and Mr. Taft said he would not name one for some time. I suggested that he should either name one at once or else appoint a temporary aide for that branch of the service, and Mrs. Taft agreed with me.

"Then let us leave it to Archie to settle and any one he names will be suitable to me, I am sure."

She took the same point of view, which I thought was leaving a good deal to me. However, I settled on two names, one being the aide of Admiral Sperry, and the other Lieutenant-Commander L. C. Palmer, a fine fellow I knew in the Philippines, and one whom I knew to be popular in the navy. I have discovered that even when they leave things to one, Presidents like to have a final say-so in matters about them, so I presented the two names, calling Mrs. Taft out from a tea at the Boardmans' to do so, and when she asked me for my choice I told her Palmer, and so Palmer it is. I know it will be pleasing to the navy, and I only hope that he will be so impressed by Palmer as to retain him as his permanent naval aide. If I remain on I would like to be associated with him.

ARCHIBALD.

XC

Washington, D. C.,
March 1, 1909.

MY DEAR CLARA:

We are certainly on the home stretch when the first of March is reached. Crowds have been gathered about the White House office all day trying to see the President. When I went over at 9:30 there were a number of Senators and Representatives and a large number of minor officials, all wanting merely to say good-bye, and incidentally to ask some favour. The few who only want to say good-bye find some other occasion usually to do it.

The President is frightfully rushed this morning, and when he came in waved his hand and said to the door-keepers who were waiting for him:

"Let no one in until I have finished with Captain Butt."

Then, turning to me, he said:

"I have thirty-one at my Cabinet luncheon, and we want to seat it irrespective of rank and mix the tennis players with the wolf hunters and the 'two-gun' men so that the various elements of what is known as my tennis cabinet will get acquainted. The papers have made a good deal of fun of my tennis cabinet, but they have never known how extensive or what a part it has played in my administrations. It will be gathered together to-day for the first time, and I regard this luncheon as my only official recognition of it."

We then seated the thirty-one guests, and there will never be such a smashing of precedence again as to rank.

I had a meeting of the aides at 10:30 and mapped out the programme for the fourth. After that I went into the basement to smash the china which had been gathering for the last seven years. I took out two plates, broken but with the pieces intact, for myself, one of the Cleveland Administration and one of the Roosevelt. I selected two small broken butter plates for Miss Hagner and several chipped pieces of the Roosevelt china for Mrs. Roosevelt. Her eyes filled with tears when I gave them to her, and she said she had not a piece of the china, and it was so thoughtful of me to save her some; that she wanted to ask me to do it but felt it was not right to do so. I saw Mrs. Taft for a minute and we had a good laugh over the fact that the papers were still ignorant about her determination to drive from the Capitol. Well, it is almost luncheon time and I am off. I will add notes from time to time and will run them under a date line.

11:30 P. M.

I went to the luncheon, and never have I been to a more interesting luncheon, not even at the White House. It was given to the tennis cabinet. The tennis cabinet is made up not only of men who play tennis, but of men who have been and still are the playmates of the President. There were men there who have caught wolves with him in the West, we who have ridden with him and played tennis, or else who have swum the Potomac, and then again, men who have done nothing more than encourage him in certain reforms and, as he says, who held the sponge and bottle while he has done the fighting. There were thirty-one present and each man has had some personal relation with him that has endeared him to the President.[1]

[1]The following is a list of the thirty-one attending this unusual luncheon:
The President
The French Ambassador, Jean J. Jusserand
The Secretary of State, Elihu Root
Mr. Justice William Henry Moody
The Postmaster-General, George von Lengerke Meyer
The Secretary of the Navy, Victor Howard Metcalf
The Secretary of the Interior, James R. Garfield
The Secretary to the President, William Loeb, Jr.
The Solicitor-General, Henry M. Hoyt
Assistant Secretary of State, John Callan O'Laughlin
Assistant Secretary of the Treasury, Beekman Winthrop
Assistant Secretary of the Navy, Herbert L. Satterlee
Assistant Secretary of State, William Phillips
Assistant Attorney-General, George W. Woodruff
Comptroller of the Currency, Lawrence O. Murray
Commissioner Francis E. Leupp, of the Indian Bureau
Commissioner Charles P. Neill, of the Labour Bureau
Commissioner Herbert Knox Smith, of the Bureau of Corporations
Civil Service Commissioner, John A. McIllhenny
Commissioner-General of Immigration, Daniel J. Keefe
Hon. John C. Rose, United States District Attorney for Maryland
Hon. Henry L. Stimson, United States District Attorney for Southern District of N. Y.
Dr. Henry S. Pritchett, President of the Carnegie Foundation
Mr. Gifford Pinchot, Chief of the Forest Service
Mr. James B. Reynclds
Mr. W. W. Heffelfinger
Capt. L. S. Kelly
Mr. W. W. Sewell
Capt. Seth Bullock
Mr. John Abernathy
Captain Butt

For instance, there was nothing in the world which could have brought him to invite me had I not played the game with him. My ride of 104 miles alone did not make me eligible for the tennis cabinet, but I have played the game as he sees the game; whether it be tennis or walking or swimming, I have done it with him and kept up to the mark he has set. In other words, he regards me as a playmate, and I could not ask higher praise in this life, for to be his playmate means to have qualities which are manly, or which pass for such, and to be honest and square.

The luncheon was as picturesque as the title might imply it to be. There were wolf catchers, fox hunters, one or two men who have been arrested some time in the past for holding up trains and killing desperadoes, and side by side with them were members of the Cabinet, a foreign ambassador, one or two lawyers who have done notable things in the prosecution of criminals. His speech told it all.

At the close of the luncheon he arose to his feet, the first time I have ever seen him do such a thing in the White House, and called the mixed assemblage to order. At the time we were eating waffles and syrup, and as toothsome as they were, we promptly stopped the clatter of knives and forks to hear what he was saying. He spoke from notes and those notes appeared in the press later, but the printed accounts did not contain the interpolations which added the ginger to his remarks and which affected those present to such an extent that there was not a dry eye in the room.

I choked up and looked about the table, and there was Abernathy, the wolf catcher, with tears streaming down his cheeks; Jusserand, the French Ambassador, could not speak for fear of disgracing his sex; Billy Phillips, who sat next to me, was almost sobbing, while Bacon, the Secretary of State, and Postmaster-General Meyer, who like myself is a holdover, were crying visibly. Heffelfinger, one of the most famous football players and towering over the rest of us like a titan, sat there trying to choke back the tears, and poor old Seth Bullock, the "desperado" of the West and now Marshal of Oklahoma, tried to drown his emotion in drink but failed piteously.

I remember what he said of Jusserand, which did not appear in print. He said that possibly there was never such a relation between an ambassador and a president or ruler of a country as there had been between Jusserand and himself; they were friends and playmates—and the help, the courage which the Ambassador had imparted to him at times, could not be estimated. He paid a glowing tribute to Garfield, the chief member of the tennis cabinet, and then sat down.

As I say, there was not a dry eye around all that table. Doctor Pritchett was visibly moved, and so was McIllhenny of New Orleans, and I thought more of Meyer than all the rest, for he has been criticized as one who was staying on in the Cabinet when the others were all leaving. He showed his grief and did not attempt to hide it as I did, and when the President sat down there was this alleged cold-blooded New Englander in tears. I shall always think more of Meyer for the emotion he showed during this speech of the President.

He had hardly been seated a minute when we began to make motions to Seth Bullock, for it was he whom we had chosen to make the speech and to present a lion in bronze by Proctor. But instead of addressing the President, as he had promised to do, he suddenly arose from the table and leaning toward the centre began to tear away the centrepiece. The President thought him drunk and was inclined to rejoice at this exhibition of his friend of olden days, when there appeared the head of a lion. The President began to take notice, and Seth, who was still unable to say a word on account of his emotion, merely pointed at the figure of the Jungle King in the centre of the table.

At last it dawned on the President what it was and his eyes filled with tears and he sat staring at it, merely laughing.

"You have taken me by surprise. You have caught me napping."

Strange as it may seem, all this feeling was brought about, as Abernathy said later, on a "cold collar," for we had nothing to drink but sherry. I am sure I have not conveyed to you the dramatic appearance of this luncheon or its solemnity. It was the last entertainment of the President, and he had chosen these men for the occasion. All precedence was smashed. Dear old Adee of the State Department would have died of mortification had he seen the table chart. Madame Jusserand said to me this afternoon when I met her at the Garfields':

"Is there any other man in the world who is at the head of a nation who could have had such a luncheon, or who, having it, could have had on one side of him the Ambassador of a great country and on the other a 'desperado' from Oklahoma?"

Stimson made the address Seth Bullock could not make, and one thing he said which struck us all as true. He told the President that Bullock's inability to express his feelings was the same as possessed us all, that no one loving a father could express that love he felt; that he, the President, had glorified each one by his friendship to that point when each man had been reborn in matters of principle, in character, and in mind.

We each felt this to be true. I feel it, and I am sure all others felt it, that none of us were what he thought us to be, but his faith in each made of each a man worthy of his confidence and trust.

When we got up from the table McIllhenny said what a pity we had not thought to have a photographer, and Pinchot said he would send for one when the President asked that we meet at some other time. I suggested that I send a motor for Clinedinst and, all agreeing, I went myself. It only took a minute to rush one to the scene, and we were photographed in front of the White House, the same disregard being paid to rank there as there had been at the luncheon.

The President has departed from his usual rule and during these last few days is accepting a few invitations from persons he likes. This afternoon at 4 o'clock he agreed to go to tea at the Garfields', and later to go to Mrs. Townsend's for a cup of tea also.

A great surprise met him at the Garfields'. He was ushered into the back room where the tennis cabinet were waiting for him. There were only eleven present, I not being among the number, but we were invited later to see the table. It was most unique. The centre of the table was made into a tennis court, with nets, sand, and players. The players were four teddy bears, each dressed in sweaters to represent the players seen most often on the White House court. The whole was most ingeniously got together. Jusserand was there, all in white; the Postmaster-General was in brown, which he always wears; Mr. Garfield in drab, and the President in a funny-looking white shirt. The tennis court was surrounded by forests, which was a take off of his forestry bureau.

Then began a panoramic review of his most notable acts during his administration. Beginning was a teddy bear and a little black Negro, sitting at a table together being a take-off of the Booker Washington incident. Then next appeared a miniature Uncle Sam interfering with a railroad. Also Uncle Sam and a teddy bear presiding over a cradle which contained twenty-five sleeping doll babies. This was called Race Suicide. A mirror running through the forests represented the Panama Canal, while small men with lighted lanterns represented the secret-service controversy. A large teddy bear holding the flags of Russia and Japan commemorated the peace at Portsmouth, while the big stick was in evidence over the prostrate forms of the House and Senate.

After the tea the tennis cabinet, as represented by the few at the Garfields', presented the President with a large silver basin and a diploma certifying to his presidency of the tennis cabinet. From here he went to Mrs. Townsend's, he and Mrs. Roosevelt, and there they met only about a half a dozen people. We spent a pleasant half hour here and to-night he dines with the Bacons.

Later, Mrs. Cowles, his sister, and I took a long motor ride, and we became very critical toward those friends of the President and Mrs. Roosevelt who are acting as if the Tafts had committed some breach of friendship by becoming occupants of the White House. . . . To hear them talk one would think that Mr. Roosevelt was being driven from the White House by Mr. Taft and that Mrs. Taft was not even civil toward his wife. Everyone forgets, seemingly, that the President chose Mr. Taft as his successor, that he refused to stand for reëlection and that he regarded the election of Mr. Taft as his greatest personal triumph.

Good-night until to-morrow.

ARCHIBALD.

Not being a big-game hunter Captain Butt did not, perhaps, quite appreciate Roosevelt's almost jealous interest in American fauna, an interest which led him to change the lion heads to bison heads on the mantelpiece in the state dining room of the White House. Some of the other members of the Tennis Cabinet, however, had hunted with Roosevelt in the mountains of the far West, and therefore it was not a bronze lion which they presented to the President at the luncheon described in the foregoing letter but a cougar or American panther. Roosevelt in his Autobiography gives the following description of the presentation:

> On March 1, 1909, three days before leaving the Presidency, various members of the Tennis Cabinet lunched with me at the White House. "Tennis Cabinet" was an elastic term, and of course many who ought to have been at the lunch were, for one reason or another, away from Washington; but, to make up for this, a goodly number of out-of-town honorary members, so to speak, were present—for instance, Seth Bullock; Luther Kelly, better known as Yellowstone Kelly in the days when he was an army scout against the Sioux; and Abernathy, the wolf-hunter. At the end of the lunch Seth Bullock suddenly reached forward, swept aside a mass of flowers which made a centrepiece on the table, and revealed a bronze cougar by Proctor, which was a parting gift for me. The lunch party and the cougar were then photographed on the lawn.[1]

When Archie refers to Seth Bullock as a "desperado" he does it, of course, jocosely. As a matter of fact, Roosevelt was very fond of Bullock, who, although a typical frontiersman, was a man of fine physical appearance and bearing, and of great dignity of character. Roosevelt speaks of him in his Autobiography in these terms:

---

[1]The illustration opposite page 148 is a reproduction of this photograph. The bronze cougar may be seen in the foreground. The tall man, with drooping black moustache and with his folded hands in front of him, is Seth Bullock.

It was while with Bill Jones [in Roosevelt's cowboy days] that I first made acquaintance with Seth Bullock. Seth was at that time sheriff in the Black Hills district, and a man he had wanted—a horse thief—I finally got, I being at the time deputy sheriff two or three hundred miles to the North. The man went by a nickname which I will call "Crazy Steve"; a year or two afterwards I received a letter asking about him from his uncle, a thoroughly respectable man in a Western state; and later this uncle and I met at Washington when I was President and he a United States Senator. It was some time after "Steve's" capture that I went down to Deadwood on business, Sylvane Ferris and I on horseback, while Bill Jones drove the wagon. At a little town, Spearfish, I think, after crossing the last eighty or ninety miles of gumbo prairie, we met Seth Bullock. We had had a rather rough trip, and had lain out for a fortnight, so I suppose we looked somewhat unkempt. Seth received us with rather distant courtesy at first, but unbent when he found out who we were, remarking, "You see, by your looks I thought you were some kind of a tin-horn gambling outfit, and that I might have to keep an eye on you!" He then inquired after the capture of "Steve"—with a little of the air of one sportsman when another has shot a quail that either might have claimed—"My bird, I believe?" Later Seth Bullock became, and has ever since remained, one of my stanchest and most valued friends. He served as Marshal for South Dakota under me as President. When, after the close of my term, I went to Africa, on getting back to Europe I cabled Seth Bullock to bring over Mrs. Bullock and meet me in London, which he did; by that time I felt that I just had to meet my own people, who spoke my neighbourhood dialect.

I remember very well seeing Seth Bullock in London with Roosevelt. Tall, sinewy, lithe, clean-shaven, but with a long flowing black moustache, wearing a black frock coat, a black string tie, and a broad-brimmed black slouch hat, he made a fine picture of an upstanding American pioneer in his hours of ease, and Roosevelt introduced him with manifest pride to many distinguished personages, including some royal ones. These two "one hundred per cent. Americans," thus in company together, reflected honour upon their country.

Although the parting gift at the Tennis Cabinet luncheon was a cougar and not a lion, it might very well have been a bronze "figure of the Jungle King," as Archie Butt thought it was, for some of Roosevelt's friends, and even some members of his family, were wont to describe certain of his characteristics in leonine terms. In a recently published book of reminiscences, entitled "In Brightest Africa," Carl Akeley, the distinguished big-game hunter, naturalist, and sculptor, tells why he thinks that the figure of a lion would be the most appropriate monumental symbol of Roosevelt:

I have done another lion—one that interests me more than all the others. And this piece of sculpture came about in this way. When I met President Roosevelt at the White House on my return from Africa in 1906, I was impressed with the power and humanity of the man as all were who knew him. One of the great experiences of my life was that quiet talk with Theodore Roosevelt in the shade of the acacia tree on the Uasin Gishu Plateau when I came to know the man and to love him. After our return from Africa, he was constantly reminding me of my unwritten African book and saying that he wanted to write a foreword and a chapter for that book. But I had no such hankering to write as I had to do sculpture, and so I put it off. At last, however, in 1919, after the war was over, I sat down one day and started to write him a letter to say that I would begin the book. I had written the two words, "Dear Colonel," when the telephone rang. It was my friend, George H. Sherwood, the executive secretary of the Museum. [The American Museum of Natural History.]

"Ake," he said, "I have bad news for you. Colonel Roosevelt died this morning."

For me the bottom dropped out of everything. From that time until I got back from the funeral I did nothing. When I returned from the funeral I was terribly depressed. I had to find expression. I found it most naturally in modelling. I set to work on a lion. I meant to make it symbolic of Roosevelt, of his strength, courage, fearlessness—of his kingly qualities in the old-fashioned sense. And this modelling afforded me great comfort and relief. I worked on it day after day. Taxidermy, groups, and bronzes, were all forgotten. While I was so engaged one day an old friend of mine, James Brite, an architect, called me up on the telephone. I asked him if he wouldn't come up and design a pedestal for the lion. He came up not only that day but many others. Neither of us knew just what we were going to do with it when it was finished. I had a vague idea of casting it, making one bronze for Mrs. Roosevelt, and destroying the model.

We were still working when one day Archie Roosevelt came in. I showed the lion to him.

"None of us want to see statues of Father," he said. "They can't make Father," and as he put his arms about the pedestal of the lion, "but this is Father. Of course, you do not know it, but among ourselves we boys always called him the 'Old Lion' and when he died I cabled the others in France, 'The Old Lion is dead.'"

XCI

Washington, D. C.,
March 2, 1909.

DEAR CLARA:

I had a small luncheon at the Metropolitan Club for Palmer at noon and immediately afterward hastened to the White House to present the new Minister from Haiti. He is a perfectly coal-black Negro, but one who speaks beautiful French and had quite an air. The President says he is sure that he learned his French cooking in some high-class French café.

"It will be interesting to know what they do with him at the next diplomatic dinner," he said. "I know what they will do with him: they will sandwich him in between two South Americans or else will place him at the corner of a table next to an aide."

As soon as he had concluded his speech, and the President had answered him, we withdrew to the East Room, where there were some forty or fifty of the First Roosevelt Club in St. Paul. He then received the choir of St. Paul's Church and shook hands with each youngster. At 3:30 the entire diplomatic corps came to say good-bye. This was of necessity formal, yet the reception of each Minister, Ambassador, or attaché whom the Roosevelts happened to know personally, made the reception of an informal nature. Some of them actually wept as they said good-bye. The poor little Baroness Takahara could not say a word, but burst out crying, and the Ambassador was not much better. They passed from the East Room to the state dining room and were presented in the Blue Room. The state dining room, as seen from the reception point, looked most attractive. It was lighted up and a large fire was burning in the open fireplace, which gave it a peculiar soft glow. The President called attention to it to most of the diplomats:

"Does the White House look lovely this afternoon? I am so glad it does," he would say.

The reception was over by 4:30, the hour set for the reception of the intimate friends of the President and Mrs. Roosevelt. There were not more than fifty or sixty, and in the list were those women in Washington society who gave the string of diamonds to Mrs. Roosevelt. It was quite as sniffly as the musicale, and there was a sincere note in it all that went to the hearts of us all. Nearly every woman wept a little and the eyes of the men were oftentimes dimmed. I have never seen so much feeling in evidence in all my life as there has been during the last few days of the Administration. The French Ambassador yesterday broke down when trying to make a speech at the Garfields' in presenting the silver bowl from the tennis cabinet, and to-day old cynical politicians apparently would be utterly unable to say more than a perfunctory good-bye. I shall be glad when it is over, for it is trying on Mrs. Roosevelt, and she is so sympathetic and kind to each that it makes it all the worse.

Even the President, who must have broken many ties

in his long and upward career, broke down yesterday afternoon when he and Mrs. Roosevelt came from the Townsends' and found lying on her bureau the diamond necklace. It is very simple but very beautiful, only one string of solitaires inlaid in platinum to fasten about the neck. It was entirely unsuspected by either of them and they had gone into her room to dress for the Bacon dinner and Miss Ethel was with them. They were talking about the kindness of everyone when Mrs. Roosevelt opened the package and saw the gift with the note from the donors. Mrs. Roosevelt said she had a good cry, and when she told Ethel that some day the necklace would be hers she began to cry, and the President when he tried to cheer them broke down himself. He has the humour to carry these little scenes off well and says he feels heartily ashamed of such apparent weakness. But the love which does manifest itself on all sides, coming just now after the bitter attacks from the political world, has gone to their hearts.

Much has happened that was pleasant, much more that was sad, and some things which were very funny. Several aides have been on duty all day, as the President would work awhile and would then rush to the house to shake hands with some delegations which had come to say good-bye. I went in and out continuously, but I had too much to do on the outside to take many of the formations, as we call these receptions, so Cheney and Lieutenant Shackford took the routine.

The Tafts came just before dinner time. The table had been laid for fourteen, but just before dinner Senator Knox telegraphed that Mr. Taft desired him to remain in the Senate Chamber in the interest of the treaty with Canada and that neither he nor Mrs. Knox would be present. That left only the President and Mrs. Roosevelt, Admiral and Mrs. Cowles, Nick Longworth and his wife, Senator-elect Root and his wife, Mr. and Mrs. Taft, and Miss Boardman and myself.

I think we all dreaded this dinner, the last one in the White House for the Roosevelts and the first one for the Tafts, but it went off without a hitch and there was none of the embarrassment which everyone seemed to predict there would be.

After the dinner was over I said to Mrs. Roosevelt that the dinner would have been hopeless had it not been for the President, for so it would have been had he not from the very start, when everyone was waiting for someone else to start topics of conversation, begun talking as naturally and entertainingly as he does usually at his luncheons. The conversation was general—made so by him—and the salad course was reached before one had time to realize it. I have often said that had he not been a great statesman he would have made his mark as a great social success. He puts most of the marcaronis about the clubs to shame in the matter of mere social chat.

I never saw Mrs. Roosevelt looking lovelier, and I have never seen Mrs. Taft more gracious than she was this evening. She had on a superb gown of white satin and filmy tulle effects about the sleeves and bodice, while Mrs. Roosevelt was gowned in black silk and lace with a dark aigrette. She was very pale, but did not look tired. I never saw Mrs. Roosevelt in the rôle of hostess to a better advantage than she was to the woman who is to take her place to-morrow. She never once referred to that fact, and the question of housekeeping or domestic affairs was never mentioned by either.

Mrs. Roosevelt had had fires lighted in every fireplace in the house, so the old place looked homey and comfortable. As we were leaving the dining room the President-elect took me aside and asked me to get Senator William

Alden Smith at the Senate and to ask him what was the result of their conversation earlier in the day. I struggled over the lines for about a half hour, and when I finally got him his reply was:

"Please tell Mr. Taft that I have not been able to hear from my people in Michigan, as the wires are working badly, but as soon as I do I will let him know."

When we went upstairs the men took their coffee in the President's study and the women in the library. I was called downstairs for a minute and received this message over the 'phone from Secretary of State Bacon:

"Tell Mr. Taft that the only way to save the treaty with Canada is for him to sit down hard on Smith."

I read the message to Mr. Taft in front of the others, and the President said:

"By George, Will, I would take their advice."

"I did sit on him, I thought, this afternoon, but William Alden is a bobbing sort of a cuss and doesn't know when he is sat upon."

"Then I would get him by telephone and threaten him," said the President.

"Not in the presence of witnesses," laughed Taft, and he added that he would take a whirl with Mr. Smith before midnight.

This started a general discussion on the cussedness of Congressmen in general, which finally ended, as usual, on the Senate. I was much surprised to hear the President tell Nick Longworth that he had not believed formerly in the contention of the insurgents in the House, but that he had come to the conclusion that either Congress itself should elect its committees or else elect its committee on rules. Mr. Taft said he had the same change of heart, and while he did not think the Speaker should be deprived of all power of appointment yet he should agree with the

President that the House should elect the steering committee.

Mr. Taft went for a while to the Willard Hotel, where the Yale men were having a smoker, and that started guests to going. Finally there were left only the President, Mrs. Taft, and Mrs. Roosevelt, and myself. Mrs. Roosevelt finally arose and said she would go to her room and advised Mrs. Taft to do the same. She took her hand kindly and expressed the earnest hope that her first night in the White House would be one of sweet sleep. . . .

Thoughtful and gentle to the last, I thought, and wondered when the White House would again have such a mistress. In all the months and as many as five, six, and seven times a day as I have seen her, I have never heard an impatient word from her or an unkind thing which I thought to be unjust about any one. Giving more always than she has received, she has stood, the embodiment of womanly dignity and social culture, before the entire nation, never unbending in the matter of official etiquette, yet always the gentle, high-bred hostess; smiling often at what went on about her, yet never critical of the ignorant and tolerant always of the little insincerities of political life. I envy Osterhouse, whom I have detailed to remain with her to-morrow until her train goes at 3:00. When I said good-night to her in the hall I felt that I had closed the book as far as she is concerned, for to-morrow she will only wear a mask to conceal the real heart pain she will feel as she passes out of the White House for the last time.

Were we living in the days of chivalry, I could easily believe myself in the rôle of knight for a mistress so gentle, so sweet, and so altogether lovely.

Good-night, Clara. It will always be a regret that my own dear mother never knew this woman and that she in turn never knew my mother. They had so much in common and yet how far apart the world had placed them.

ARCHIE.

XCII

Washington, D. C.,
March 5, 1909.

DEAR CLARA:

The inauguration of Mr. Taft has passed into history. The weather was terrible, so stormy in fact that the oath had to be administered in the Senate Chamber, which seemed to be so much more appropriate than having it taken on a cheap pine platform built of rough boards in front of the Capitol. Mr. Taft thinks, too, it is the place to hold the inaugural exercises, for, driving to the ball last night in his new motor car, he made this comment:

"I do not regret anything save the disappointment of the crowd. It is more dignified to hold the ceremonies in the Senate than in the open air, in my opinion, and if I had my way all inaugurations would take place either there or else in the House."

It changed my plans considerably, however, as I had planned to escort Mrs. Taft to the Senate and from there to the platform, where I would have turned her over to the Inaugural Committee. This would have enabled me to escort Mr. Roosevelt from the platform to his carriage. As it was, however, Mrs. Taft had to leave the Senate Chamber before the President finished his address, so as to meet him in the rotunda and there go with him to the carriage. I am glad it cleared sufficiently for the top of the carriage to be let down, as she had looked forward with such pleasure to the ride down the avenue with her husband.

I went to the President's rooms in the Senate just before he left for the chamber and told him good-bye. It was an awful wrench to part with him, and I felt choky and about as depressed as I have ever felt in parting with any one in my life, save only my own mother.

"It isn't good-bye," he said. "We will meet again, and possibly you will yet serve me in a more important capacity than the one you have now."

I enclose you a copy of the letter[1] he wrote to the Secretary of War, as I know you will be glad to see it. It is far more than I deserve, but it may inspire me to live up to it as the years go by and opportunities are afforded to achieve some fame in actual warfare. . . .

Good-night. I am too tired to go further, even to tell you how Quentin cut his school in Alexandria and saw the parade from the President's box. He and Charlie Taft sat on the same chair, and he was the only Roosevelt anywhere in evidence.

ARCHIBALD.

---

[1]This letter will be found in the Introduction.

THE END

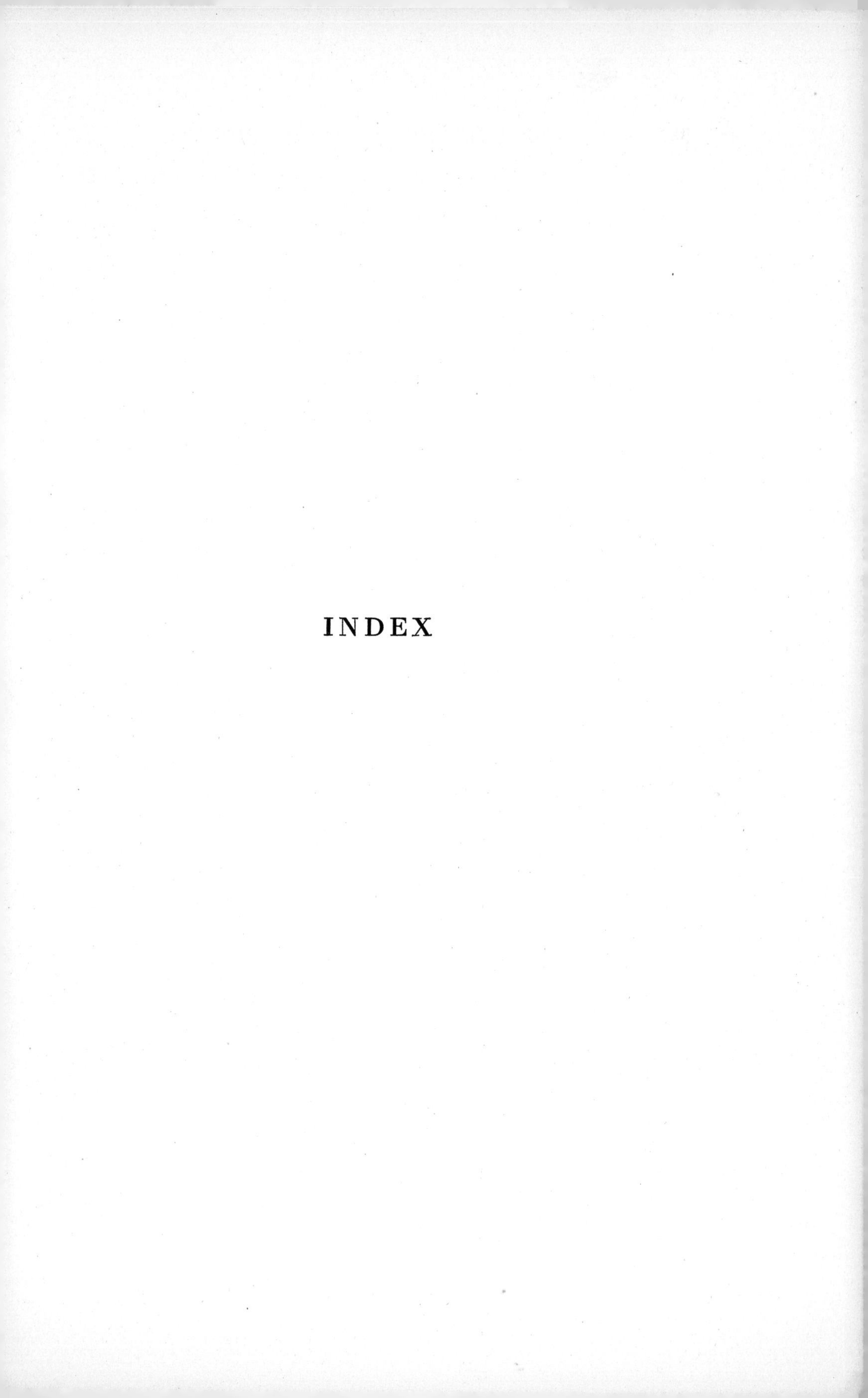

INDEX

INDEX